NORITAKE FANCYWARE

A TO Z

A PICTORIAL RECORD AND GUIDE TO VALUES

David Spain

Schiffer Publishing Ltd ®

4880 Lower Valley Road, Atglen, PA 19310 USA

This book is dedicated to
Keishi ("Casey") Suzuki
Senior Managing Director (Retired),
The Noritake Co., Ltd., Nagoya.
Casey's enormous interest in "Old Noritake"
over the years has been an inspiration to me
and to many others. He is legendary among
Noritake collectors everywhere not only for
his knowledge, but also for his enthusiasm and
personal warmth. All Noritake collectors are
greatly indebted to him.

Library of Congress Cataloging-in-Publication Data

Spain, David H.
Noritake fancyware A to Z : a pictorial record and guide to values / David
Spain.
p. cm.
ISBN 0-7643-1507-2
1. Noritake, Kabushiki Kaisha--Collectibles--Catalogs. 2. Porcelain, Japanese-
-20th century--Catalogs. I. Title.
NK4210.N56 A4 2002
738.2'0952'1674075--dc21
2001006940

Designed by Bonnie M. Hensley
Cover design by Bruce M. Waters
Type set in Parisian BT/Dutch801 Rm BT

ISBN: 0-7643-1507-2
Printed in China
1 2 3 4
Published by Schiffer Publishing Ltd.
4880 Lower Valley Road
Atglen, PA 19310
Phone: (610) 593-1777; Fax: (610) 593-2002
E-mail: Schifferbk@aol.com
Please visit our web site catalog at **www.schifferbooks.com**
We are always looking for people to write books on new and related sub-
jects. If you have an idea for a book please contact us at the above address.

This book may be purchased from the publisher.
Include $3.95 for shipping.
Please try your bookstore first.
You may write for a free catalog.

In Europe, Schiffer books are distributed by
Bushwood Books
6 Marksbury Ave.
Kew Gardens
Surrey TW9 4JF England
Phone: 44 (0) 20 8392-8585; Fax: 44 (0) 20 8392-9876
E-mail: Bushwd@aol.com
Free postage in the U.K., Europe; air mail at cost.

Contents

Acknowledgments 4

Part One

Chapter 1   Aims and Scope of This Book 6
Chapter 2   Noritake Dialogues: Views from *Noritake News* 11
Chapter 3   Noritake Backstamps: An Overview and Update 21
            Table 3.1: Noritake Backstamps Relevant to
                Fancyware Items of the Sort Shown in This Book
                (with color photos) 28

Part Two

Introduction   37
Chapter A   Ashtrays and Other Items Pertaining to Smoking 42
Chapter B   Bowls and Boxes 58
Chapter C   Condiment Sets and Related Items 143
Chapter D   Desk and Dresser Items 167
Chapter E   Ephemera Pertaining to Noritake Fancyware Designs 184
Chapter F   Figurines 193
Chapter H   Holiday and Special Occasion Items 199
Chapter L   Lamps, Night Lights and Other Related Items 203
Chapter P   Plaques, Plates, Trays and Other Basically Flat Items ... 212
Chapter T   Tea Sets and Other Items Pertaining to Beverages 243
Chapter V   Vases and Other Items Pertaining to Flowers 259
Chapter Z   Miscellaneous Items 295

Bibliography   300
Index   301

Acknowledgments

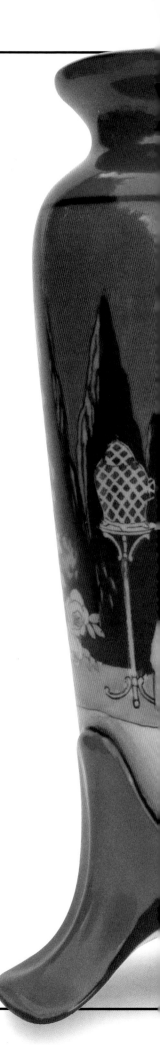

Many Noritake collectors have met and had the pleasure of chatting with Keishi "Casey" Suzuki. Those who have not yet met him, however, have a lot to look forward to because Casey is truly a gem. Casey probably knows more about the history of the Noritake Company than any living person. He led and was centrally involved in the effort that culminated in the publishing of a record of the basic Noritake backstamps. The Noritake Company will soon be celebrating the centennial of its founding in 1904. Casey was selected to head the committee that will coordinate events associated with that celebration. In view of his lifelong association with the Noritake Company, in both Japan and the United States (and other places as well), and his longstanding interest in Old Noritake, this was the perfect choice.

Many of my friends and fellow Noritake collectors have contributed enormously to the creation of this book. Since the photographs in this book will be of greatest interest to most users of it, it is appropriate to begin by thanking those who contributed photographs that appear in it. Of the many collectors who made such contributions, I want particularly to thank Judi Camero, Margaret Hetzler, Gary Kaufman, Diane Kovarik and Jerry and Sally Stefferud for their amazing photographic efforts. Diane Kovarik also generously agreed to let me use, in Chapter E of this book, a version of her essay, printed originally in *Noritake News*, on Noritake-related ephemera as well as some of the photographs which went with it. I am *very* grateful to her for this.

Others also made very important photographic contributions including John and Pauline Bennett, Jean Dillard, Wayne Forsyth, Sheldon Harmeling, Mike Kocor, Tom Mathis, Shinsuke Nomura and Bob Trennert. Each went way above and beyond the call of duty so that the rest of us can see how incredibly beautiful Noritake fancyware collectibles really are. For fine photographs provided by others, I also wish to thank Melissa Arenson, Michael Conrad, Eileen and Wilkie Decker, Christina Dunnell, Brian Hurst, Dick Nelson, Bill and Christopher Phillipson and Bob Suslowicz.

I am especially pleased and honored to acknowledge an unusual and extremely generous gesture of good will and comradeship by Kazuhiko Kimura, Kohtaro Aoi, and Takahiro Morikawa. They kindly loaned to me about twenty wonderful photographs of Noritake items shown in Kimura, Kazuhiko and Kohtaro Aoi's 1999 book *Noritake China 1891-1945: Collector's Guide,* published in Osaka, Japan. Of these, I used fifteen, as follows: B.335, B.476, B.503, B.555, B.559; P.224, P.245; T.117, T.121, T.136-139, T.145; and V.299. Their willingness to let me include their photographs of these items greatly improved not only the chapters mentioned but also the entire book. My debt to Kazuhiko and Takahiro is enormous, obviously. I am also most grateful to Kazuhiko's publisher, S. Umeda, for allowing me to do this. I humbly thank him as well.

Although it may not seem like it, given all those named above who have supplied photographs at one point or another, I actually did take a good portion of the photos that appear in this book (and my previous ones). Taking these photos has been an interesting experience. It involves both great pleasure on the one hand and considerable tension and sheer hard work on the other. The pleasure, of course, comes from being able to look *closely* at beautiful Noritake. But that is not the half of it. I love to look at Noritake through a camera lens because I am absolutely convinced it is one of the very best ways to really *see* it (or anything). Done right, photography requires one to focus (no pun

intended) and concentrate in a manner unlike typical ways of seeing. The tension, as ought to be evident with just a moment's reflection, comes from the fact that in order to take many pictures, I need to handle many pieces of Noritake that belong to other people.

More frequently than you would imagine, the items I handle in this way are either unique, very valuable, or have special sentimental value; sometimes all three. For good reason, therefore, collectors of fragile and valuable items like Noritake porcelain tend to be very protective of them. Even so, many Noritake collectors happily invited me into their homes to handle and photograph their beautiful and precious pieces. I am *very* grateful for their willingness to allow me to do this. It says a great deal, I think, about their enthusiasm for their hobby, an enthusiasm I *fully* share. I can only hope this book will make them glad they agreed to let me disrupt their lives in this way. For help of this kind on this book specifically, I thank Christel A. Bachert, Donna and Doug Bingaman, Dr. Dennis and Susan Buonafede, Gary and Joanna Goodman, Deirdre Cimiano, Claire and Michael Conrad, Marilyn Derrin, Norm and Lida Derrin, Patricia Engel, Rosemary Farrell, Lisa and Gary Gibson, Dewaine and Bonnie Glyda, Gerald Iaquinta, Leslie and Mike Iarusso, Sheldon and Sayo Harmeling, Bob and Bernadette Jackson, Lois and Howard Joseph, Jackie and Dave Kopp, Laurie Larson, Arlene Markey, Jim Martin, Tom and Cille Mathis, Katsu and Emiko Moriguchi, Dick and Sally Nelson, Dale and Sandy Payne, Rhonda and the late John Perroncino, Robert and Rita Rosso, Tom and Gerri Seitz, Steve and Lydia Shaw, Earl and Roberta Sloboda, Earl Smith and Mark Griffin, Bob Suslowicz, Tim and Janet Trapani, Bob and Linda Trennert, Dennis and Lori Trishman, Rhoda and Joe Westler, Nancy and Charlie Wilson (sadly, both now gone), Barbara Winfree and Don and Nancy Wright. In an act of trust and daring that I appreciate deeply, some collectors and dealers have actually brought or sent pieces to me to photograph. For such efforts for this book, I am grateful to Deanna Kantor, Dick Nelson and Elizabeth Rouse.

I am happy to note that I have received permission and authorization from The Noritake Company to publish my photographs of various Noritake backstamps. This permission and authorization was facilitated by the good offices of Mr. Tadashi Kawamura, Senior Managing Director, Noritake and Mr. Yoshimi Fukuoka, General Manager, Tabletop Group, Noritake. I of course appreciate very much receiving this authorization from them. I was particularly impressed, however, both by their courtesy and thoughtfulness and by their obvious desire to support this effort to show others the beautiful porcelains produced over the years by the Noritake Company.

Over the years, I have received considerable moral support and encouragement from many good friends and neighbors who are not Noritake collectors (and, indeed, in some cases, who are frankly puzzled that anyone should be so enthusiastic about a "bunch of old dishes"). Because I did so in my previous books, I will not name them again here. They should know, however, that I deeply appreciate their tolerance of my crazy passion or, more precisely, for my tendency to talk about it at length with the least provocation (and sometimes with none at all). For their able assistance in helping me record vital information about the pieces as I was photographing them, I happily thank, in addition to virtually every collector named above, Carly Derrin, Grant Gibson and my daughter Rachel. For support and encouragement of other kinds, I gratefully thank my adult sons Andrew and Ryan, and particularly my daughter-in-law Margaret Doherty Spain who inspired me by painting a large and much admired mural on my office wall based on the motif in P.139 of *Collecting Noritake A to Z*. I also am pleased to thank Ginny Apicella, Judy Boyd, Robin Brewer, Marshall Brown, Dennis and Diane Burnickas, Christina Dunnell, Joane McCaslin Ferguson, Diane and Bill Ginsberg, Nat Goldstein, Truman and Brenda Hawes, Stewart Hopewell, Nancy Hunn, Yoshie Itani, Lita Kaufman, Isamu Kuroda, Alex Leininger, Neil Mitchell and Greg Slater, Brandy Moore, Pat Murphy, Yumiko Oga, Mike and Connie Owen, Bill Strohl, Keishi ("Casey") Suzuki, Tim and Janet Trapani, Tomoaki Takeuchi, Dennis and Lori Todd Trishman and Charlotte Wilcoxen for their help and encouragement.

Finally, I am pleased—indeed, I am honored—to thank my wife Jannie and daughter Rachel for their love, understanding, and, most of all, for putting up with me during several intense periods of work on this book. Truly, anyone who finds this book of value should thank them, for their burden was greater than mine.

Part One

Chapter 1
Aims and Scope of This Book

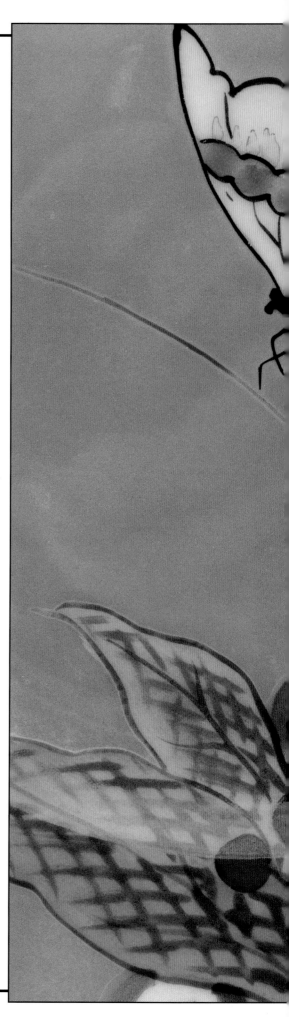

This book follows up on themes and materials presented in my two previous books on Noritake collectibles. The first book, *Noritake Collectibles A to Z* (1997), was then and still is the largest and most comprehensive book in the field, with color photos of more than 1000 different items. The second book, *Collecting Noritake A to Z* (1999), had more of an Art Deco focus. Although smaller than the first book, it still added photographs of over 550 items to the record. As I noted in that book, using a terrible metaphor for a collector of porcelain, the 1600 items I had presented in those two books only scratched the surface of what is "out there." This third book, *Noritake Fancyware A to Z*, has photographs of more than 750 pieces not shown in the first two books, bringing the total for the three books to over 2300 different items. The basic aim has been the same in all three books: to present a large number of high quality photos that well-represent the range of fancyware produced by the Noritake Company and to arrange them in a manner that would enable users to locate *rapidly and easily* any item of interest.

That the Noritake Company could produce such a huge and diverse array of high quality porcelains in so short a time (primarily from 1921 to about 1931) continues to amaze and impress all Noritake collectors and many non-collectors as well. It is a fact that becomes all the more noteworthy when one realizes that these gift ware porcelains were not even the bulk or mainstay of the Company's output during this time. The Company's "bread and butter," so to speak, was dinnerware. From about 1914 to the present day, the Noritake Company has been famous for producing and effectively marketing high quality complete porcelain dinnerware sets that could be purchased for modest prices. Because these products were such an excellent value and because much of the porcelain dinnerware production in Europe ceased during World War I, the Noritake Company was hugely successful. Indeed, to most people not only in the United States and Canada but also throughout much of the Western world, the name "Noritake" has meant and still means "dinnerware" (Robin Brewer has published an excellent guide to these products, see *Bibliography* for details).

Although the successful launching of their dinnerware line makes 1914 an incredibly important date for the Noritake Company, this was not the year the company was founded. This occurred in 1904. Because it took a decade to overcome various technical difficulties associated with the mass production

of Western style dinnerware, one may wonder what sorts of products the Company made that enabled them to stay in business during that early, pre-dinnerware period. Although the answer is fairly simple, the key products were not. The Company thrived in those days by producing relatively large, often lavish (*lots* of gilding over and around extensive, painstakingly detailed surface decorations), expensive Belle Epoch and Art Nouveau porcelains. Often, the particulars of these items were inspired by works produced by extremely fashionable European decorative porcelain makers (Limoges, Sevres, etc.). A good portion of these items—decorative pieces such as large urns and ornate vases, for example—were meant mostly for display or for use on special occasions (for a truly awesome example, see V.299 in this book). The Noritake Company produced a *very* wide array of such items, as can be sensed in part by the fact that, so far, six large books showing these materials have been published and, as of this writing, a seventh is planned (for details, see the Van Patten entries in the *Bibliography*).

By the end of World War I (or shortly thereafter), however, Noritake dinnerware was rapidly becoming a very important part of the Company's export business. Indeed, one suspects that, by roughly the late teens, the Company could have prospered on their dinnerware products alone. Even so, the Noritake Company did not stop producing non-dinnerware products. The decorative items they were producing by this time, however, tended to be smaller and often less elaborately decorated than those seen earlier—changes that may have been dictated as much by increases in labor costs and the use of modern kilns and machines as by shifting artistic sensibilities. Indeed, changes in aesthetics do not appear to influence Noritake fancyware designs significantly until after the Paris Exposition of 1925. Even so, the Noritake decorative giftware items made after World War I continued to be successful, in part because changes in production details made them even more affordable just when customers were enjoying the post-war economic boom that became the "Roaring Twenties."

Most of the materials presented in this book are from this inter-war period. Indeed, for at least two decades, Noritake collectors (myself included) have routinely said that the items they were interested in had been made between 1921 and 1941. The first date was never in dispute because it was the year that Noritake fancyware exported to North America began to have backstamps with the words "Japan" and "Noritake" in them. The latter date seemed equally solid because it was the year that the New York office of Morimura Brothers closed. In a recent essay, however, the Noritake Company's Keishi Suzuki provides grounds for emphasizing another date: 1931. He offers four points that bear on the matter. First, he states (p.7 of "About Old Noritake"; see *Bibliography* for details), that Art Deco works were produced "for ten years from Taishou 9 (1920) to Shouwa 5 (1930)." Second, Suzuki notes (p.8), that Cyril Leigh, the chief of the design staff in New York, held this position only until 1931. Third, that was also the year, according to Suzuki (p.10), that the sales manager for Morimura Brothers in New York, Charles Kaiser, traveled to Japan for the last time. Finally, Suzuki states (p.10) that the production of Noritake fancyware "ceased" in 1931. If we recall that the Paris Exposition, the event that led to the popularization of Art Deco, did not end until late 1925, then Suzuki's comments mean that *nearly all **Art Deco** Noritake fancyware was made in just 5 glorious, astoundingly productive years: 1926-1931.*

One of the first and undoubtedly most expert collectors of these porcelains, and especially those from the 1921-1931 period, was the late Howard Kottler. An outstanding ceramist and Professor at the University of Washington who traveled and lectured widely, Dr. Kottler was, and still is, well-known although he died in January of 1989, when he was only 59. By that time, I too had discovered these wonderful Noritake porcelains. This occurred quite by chance in early December of 1979, while I was visiting a colleague in Illinois. What I did not know, then, was that in September of that same year, Dr. Kottler had exhibited 36 pieces from his by then massive collection in Seattle, the very town where I lived. The exhibit, which featured items from several other collections and included Noritake-made works from as far back as 1904, was held in a large downtown department store (where I seldom shopped, apparently). In 1981, Kottler gave an illustrated lecture in New York City at the International Ceramics Symposium. His presentation, entitled "Popular Culture and Ceramics," led directly to two other important developments. The first of these occurred in April 1982, at the Triton Museum of Art in Santa Clara, California. For the first time, Noritake works from the 1920s (mostly items from Kottler's collection) were displayed in an American art museum. The second development was the formation of a Smithsonian-sponsored traveling exhibit of the Kottler collection. The organizing museum was the Museum of Art at Washington State University (not to be confused with the University of Washington, especially in Washington where the schools are arch rivals). Importantly, a small catalog was published in conjunction with that exhibition. An essential resource for collectors and dealers, it has excellent color photographs and several informative essays, including two by Kottler (see *Bibliography* for publication details).

In an interesting Foreword, Jo Farb Hernandez, the organizer of the Triton Museum Noritake exhibit, discusses briefly the role of ceramic and other aesthetically interesting "throw away items" on then new and important artistic trends in the work of certain leading West Coast ceramists, Kottler among them. "Other artists," she says (p.8), "have synthesized their use of these materials with an overt expression of their indebtedness to the aesthetic of ceramic knickknacks or 'fancy wares' such as those produced by Noritake." I do not know whether she created the term "fancy wares" (one that I prefer to write as one word in the singular, just like another very common term among Noritake collectors: "lusterware"). What I do know is that Kottler used the word "fancyware" fairly often during conversations I began having with him in the mid 1980s, after I finally found out about the catalog and, thereby, discovered that I shared an interest with a colleague just a few buildings away on the same campus. A similar term, "fancy line," shows up in the Noritake Company's marvelous book on *Early Noritake* (see *Bibliography*) published in 1997 by the Noritake Museum in Nagoya and because of this, I used it now and then in my second Noritake book. As I see it, however, all these words (fancy ware, fancyware, gift ware and fancy line) are essentially equivalent. They all designate non-dinnerware Noritake porcelain products now thought of by most people, quite simply, as highly desirable "Noritake collectibles."

This book, then, is about *part* of the porcelain fancyware produced by the Noritake Company. Excluded are Noritake-made fancyware items with a backstamp with the word "Nippon" in it (except for the phrase "Nippon Toki Kaisha" which means Japanese Ceramics Company). These materials are shown in the Van Patten books. Included is Noritake-made fancyware with the words "Noritake" and "Japan" in the backstamp or with other backstamps lacking these words that are known to be Noritake Company backstamps. Dinnerware porcelains (except for the Azalea, Roseara, Tree-in-the-Meadow and "Howo" patterns) are excluded, for reasons spelled out in detail in my first book. Most of the items shown in this book were designed in America and made in Nagoya for export to North America and Great Britain as well as

other countries of the Commonwealth (Australia, India and New Zealand, are represented in this book). The exceptions are a few items with backstamps indicating they were intended for the domestic (i.e., Japanese) market.

This book has two parts. If you are typical, you have already looked at Part Two because that is where one can find the vast majority of what is most wanted in a book like this: good color photographs. As you have probably discovered, they are grouped into 12 chapters with names and alphabetic designations designed to make it easy to find particular items. Some important details about this part of the book are discussed in the Introduction to Part Two. Now that you have begun looking into Part One, I will note that it has three chapters. You are reading the first one, in which I discuss the scope and organization of the book. In Chapter 2, I present a diverse array of topics from *Noritake News* that are of general interest to both Noritake collectors and dealers. In Chapter 3, I *briefly* review, in a *non-technical* manner, some of the available information about backstamps and other "marks" that are usually, but not always, on the bottom of Noritake fancyware porcelains. In that chapter, there is a table (Table 3.1) which summarizes this material, including important updated information from the Noritake Company regarding backstamp *registration* dates.

The scope of this book is the same as both of my previous books on Noritake fancyware collectibles. This scope, I feel it is important to emphasize, was set largely *for*, rather than *by*, me. In other words, it mostly reflects matters over which I had little or no control. One such factor, and in many ways the most important one, has to do with the interests of people who call themselves "Noritake collectors." The other two factors are what are sometimes referred to as "accidents" of history—i.e., events (whether planned or not) which shape the future (or the course of history) even if there is no particular rational reason that this should have been the case.

The first "accident of history" grew out of American and British laws regulating the importing of goods from foreign countries. These laws established how the country of origin was to be indicated on imported items. Prior to 1921, the word "Nippon" had been used by virtually all Japanese companies to label their exports to the United States. "Nippon" is the English rendering of the Japanese name for the country we know as "Japan." In the United States, *after* 1921, the country of origin had to be the English version of the country's name. This meant that, after 1921, imported goods could no longer bear the word "Nippon." Instead, the word "Japan" or the words "Made in Japan" were to be used. At about the same time, the word "Noritake" also began to be incorporated into the identifying backstamps for Noritake Company goods exported to the United States.

As it happens, however, the Noritake Company treated differently the porcelains destined for Great Britain even though its laws regarding the name of the country of origin were similar to those in the United States. Specifically, on products exported to Great Britain as early as 1908, there were backstamps with the words "Noritake" (rather than no explicit company name as was the case for goods exported to the United States) and "Japan" or "Made in Japan" (rather than "Nippon"). This was more than ten years earlier than was the case for similar goods destined for the United States. We will return to this point shortly. First, however, we need to consider the second historical accident.

This "accident" has to do with largely unplanned differences in the history of "Nippon" and "Noritake" collecting in North America. By the early 1970s, porcelains marked with the word "Nippon" (meaning, in effect, "Made in Japan") were being collected seriously by a fairly sizable number of people.

Newsletters for Nippon collectors were published and, by the last years of that decade, interest was sufficient to warrant the publishing of the first high quality book on the subject: Van Patten's *Collector's Encyclopedia of Nippon* (1979). Two years later, Nippon collectors, by this time organized as the International Nippon Collectors Club (INCC), began to hold an annual convention. Van Patten has continued to publish books on Nippon collectibles throughout the 1980s and up to the present (see *Bibliography* for details). In 1992, Kathy Wojciechkowski, published *The Wonderful World of Nippon Porcelain: 1891-1921.*

The history of Noritake collecting in North America is rather different. For one thing, three Noritake books were published long before there was a Noritake newsletter or club. The story begins in 1979, when Lou Ann Donahue published her small but important book entitled *Noritake Collectibles* (see *Bibliography*). Although the title refers only to Noritake, it is significant that she included *both* "Nippon" and "Noritake" collectibles in it. So far, it is the only American book covering both of these collecting areas equally, although several books of similar size and scope have been published in Japan. Howard Kottler was the second Noritake-collecting pioneer to bring widespread public attention to Noritake fancyware porcelains by means of a publication, although as noted above, he accomplished this in various other ways as well. This was the booklet published in 1982 in connection with the traveling exhibition of his collection. In contrast to Donahue, however, this booklet focused exclusively on Art Deco Noritake, which Kottler had begun to collect seriously in 1970. Neither Donahue nor Kottler was involved in any significant way with a Noritake or Nippon collector group when they published their books. The third book, by Joan Van Patten, one of the founders of the INCC, was published in 1984 (see *Bibliography* for details). It was not until the very late 1980s, after Kottler's death, that it started to become clear that the collecting of porcelains marked with the words "Japan" and "Noritake" might see growth comparable to what had occurred in the "Nippon" field fifteen years before. One harbinger was the launching, in 1989, of *Noritake News*, a quarterly newsletter for collectors of and dealers in Noritake as well as other Japanese porcelain collectibles. This was followed, in 1994, by Van Patten's second Noritake book and by the formation of the Noritake Collectors' Society (for information about *Noritake News* or the Society, write to the author, c/o Schiffer Publishing). My Noritake books followed in 1997 and 1999. There is evidence that interest in Noritake fancyware collectibles is still growing. In January 2000, for example, Pat Murphy started a newsletter for Noritake collectors in England and founded, there, what has become a rapidly growing Noritake Collectors Club (UK) Ltd. Moreover, in 2001, his book *Noritake for Europe* was published (see *Bibliography*).

It was in light of this history, one shaped in part by certain "historical accidents," that I expanded the scope of my books on Noritake fancyware beyond the traditional (in North America) 1921-1931 definition of the Noritake range. In doing this, I also and at once achieved another of my goals: to include materials pertaining to the *full* range of Noritake collecting interests to which those in all parts of the world who called themselves "Noritake collectors" were committed. All of this also explains, at least partly, why I went into so much detail in my first book about who Noritake collectors were, what they collected and how these facts were linked to the scope of that book. All of that applies to the aim and scope of this book as well.

Introduction

Letters from readers with questions and commentaries on various issues of the day are a vital part of *Noritake News*, the newsletter for collectors of and dealers in Noritake fancyware collectibles as well as other related Japanese porcelains. Indeed, it is not only one of the very best parts of the newsletter, but also the single most important reason for having it. Being actively involved in the free exchange of ideas with other open-minded, inquisitive people who share an interest is one of the most enjoyable things a human being can do. As editor, I thrive on the challenge of trying to respond, thoughtfully and clearly, to the authors of the letters I receive. Often, and even when the questions are fairly simple, this effort can lead (and has led) me to fairly lengthy meditations on the matters raised. In the best of circumstances, my reply will provoke others into raising still more questions and making other comments. I *thoroughly* enjoy such dialogues—a fact that surely is linked to having taught at the University of Washington for more than 30 years.

All the materials in this chapter, and portions of several others in this book (e.g., Chapter 3 and the Introduction to Part II as well as Chapters E and F), are *based on* these dialogues. I emphasize the words "based on" for two reasons. First, in *Noritake News*, the letters are printed more-or-less as received. In addition to the author's name, this tends to mean that the letters contain comments on a variety of current newsletter issues. Here, I do not include the name of the person who raised the subject. Indeed, in some cases, when the topics in several letters were the same, I have combined the letters and, accordingly, have merged several of my responses. Moreover, I have re-written the original questions and comments so they are more focused, less context-dependent and, thus, of more general interest. Second, I have heavily edited my original responses, sometimes in order to remove errors of fact but mostly in order to make the responses clearer. Four topics are considered in this chapter. In order, these pertain to "fake" Noritake, whether all Noritake from the 1921-1931 period were *really* painted by hand, the impact on value of repairs and lack of backstamps and, finally, the impact on desirability when a factory decorated Noritake item is signed by the artist who painted it. To make it easier for users of this book to find these topics (letters), they are printed in Italics.

I was at an antique show recently and spoke with a dealer who said that lusterware is now being produced in Brazil. Then, on eBay the other day, I unknowingly bought my first Nippon reproduction. With the seller's description of the backstamp on it and the shape of the piece, I thought I had a rare one but, alas, when it came and I could touch it, I could tell right away that it was just an imitation. Do you have any information about Noritake fakes? Are such items on the collectibles market? What backstamps do they have?

Noritake collectors have worried for some years now about reproductions and fakes. This is *not* because they are often seen. Indeed, I have never seen one. Rather, it is primarily because our Nippon-collecting cousins (alas) see them so often—a fact masterfully documented in Joan Van Patten's Nippon books and elsewhere. The words "fake," "imitation," and "reproduction" do not, however, designate the same thing, at least not in my usage. A "reproduction" is usually identified as such by the manufacturer, sometimes right on the piece or, at other times, more indirectly but generally adequately, at least for the careful and informed collector. The term "fake," on the other hand, is reserved, with suitable scorn, for items made today with the intent to benefit by a specific deception—that of making it appear that a new piece is old (e.g., by the inappropriate use of certain marks or backstamps that can be dated to a period in the relatively distant past). Fortunately, there is no evidence, so far, that anyone is producing Noritake "fakes."

The term "imitation" is somewhat more complex. To begin our consideration of it, recall the familiar saying: "Imitation is the sincerest form of flattery." Accordingly, I tend to use the word "imitation" to refer to items with design elements, both shape and motif, that make the piece very much like other works from the same period. A slang term for this that one sometimes hears is "knock off" as in the statement "That piece is just a knock off of a Noritake (or Royal Doulton or Limoges) piece." A more-or-less tacit assumption in this view (and one that should sometimes be questioned) is that the imitation is of lesser quality than the original that inspired it. Noritake collectors are (or should be) familiar with ceramic items made by Goldcastle, Meito, and other makers of "Made in Japan" works from the 1920s and 1930s that, in many cases, almost certainly were imitations of (no doubt popular) Noritake originals. Indeed, most of us would probably not even think of them as imitations in the negative sense that this term often has (recall, here, the common phrase "cheap imitation"). They are, we would tend to say instead, merely items "inspired by" Noritake designs and, not trivially, by the success of those Noritake Company wares. Of course, even the Noritake "originals" were often not totally "original"—a fact consistent with a centuries-old tradition among ceramics manufacturers to rather freely "borrow" design ideas originated by others. (In this context, it will be of interest to know that, when a designer friend of mine saw my first book, her first and *immediate* response was, "Oh, a book like this will be of great interest to all of my colleagues. They are always on the lookout for sources of inspiration.")

As of July 1, 2001, when the manuscript version of this book was complete, I knew of no confirmed reports showing that anyone had produced lusterware porcelains that, shall we say (to use a different word), fraudulently "emulated" Noritake from the 1921-1931 period. Indeed, in recent months I have seldom even heard the rumor, for that is what it is, although when I have, the country involved tends to be different. It may be, however, that a reasonable person can be somewhat more optimistic about this entire issue. For two reasons, making fraudulent copies of items marked "Noritake" may be far less likely than the making of items with "Nippon" in the backstamp. In the

first place, the technical difficulties of working with luster glazes will be a significant impediment. Second, making Noritake marked items is probably much more risky than the making of items with the word "Nippon" in the backstamp. The word "Noritake" is associated with a large and active corporation—one that almost certainly would vigorously protect its right to use the word "Noritake" on porcelains and similar products. The same cannot be said of the word "Nippon" which, as an old version of the name of a country, may not enjoy the same protections as a word like "Noritake."

Finally, I offer a few thoughts on the "when I could touch it" comment in the letter. This is indeed a key part of the process of identifying not only "fakes" in the sinister sense used here but also imitations and reproductions. The only trouble with this fact is that just about the only way to know, by feel, the difference between Noritake originals and reproductions and fakes is by extensive experience. Some guidelines can be given, of course, and they can be very helpful to the novice. Thus, it often is the case that imitations—i.e., porcelains from Japan from the time period in question—are both heavier and less perfectly shaped than Noritake pieces. Bumps, lumps, bends, bulges, thorns, splits and other surface imperfections are very rare on Noritake and, when found, tend to have a very minor impact on the appearance of the piece. The same cannot be said of non-Noritake works from the period. This is all the more true for many (but alas, not all) of the recently made Nippon fakes. Indeed, many Nippon fakes are, frankly, quite crudely done, with the most carefully executed and thus most misleading feature being the backstamp. Ironically, many reproductions (e.g., Museum Collection items made by the Noritake Company) can be detected by feel because they are as nearly flawless as such porcelain items can be.

In Noritake Collectibles A to Z, *I noticed two examples of Noritake pieces decorated with a lithograph used in about 1925 by Wilkinson's, the English company that produced Clarice Cliff wares. The illustrations are L.2 (p.194) and V.41 (p.262). On the candlesticks, the frieze of roses below the main design is a separate lithograph and was used by Wilkinson's as a separate design on other pieces. It would seem that Noritake purchased the lithographs from the manufacturer, as did Wilkinson's because this would be more economically rational than copying. Is this the case?*

The short answer to each part of the above is the same: "yes." It does indeed appear that some of the decorative details on some Noritake items from the 1921-1931 period, including the examples mentioned, are not entirely handpainted. Some lithographs (or decals and transfers as they are also termed) were used by the Noritake Company in the decoration process. In addition to the examples mentioned, we should recall that Howard Kottler, who surely was as knowledgeable on the subject as anyone could be, indicates that many of the items in the exhibition of his collection (a small portion of it, actually) were at least partly decorated with decals (lithographs or transfers). Given all this, it could be argued that the matter is settled. Even so, there is (as usual) more that can and should be said about this important matter, in part because Noritake fancyware collectibles are famous and eminently collectable *because* they are hand painted, as the backstamps indicate.

For one thing, it is interesting to consider why the question keeps coming up. One of the reasons, ironically, derives from one of the appeals of lithographs from the manufacturer's perspective: it usually is very difficult to tell just by looking with the unaided eye, if a decoration is a lithograph. Since it is difficult to determine if the decoration is a lithograph, the matter tends to remain essentially unsettled with regard to many motifs and so the question keeps on being asked. A key step in deciding whether a decoration incorporates a lithograph is to use a powerful magnifying glass to examine the surface of a piece. If, on doing so, one can see very evenly distributed, telltale "microdots" that are a product of the "screening" process used in printing the typical lithograph, then one can more reasonably conclude that what one is looking at is *not* handpainted. Rather, the design, or at least portions of it, has been "transferred" (hence the word "transfer" as another name for the lithographic decals used in the decoration of ceramics) from the lithograph to the porcelain during the firing process. Unfortunately, this is not an entirely foolproof method since the dots are not always visible. Below, I present an alternate method which, while not foolproof either, is worthwhile.

Another reason that people continue to wonder whether Noritake fancyware was truly handpainted is that it just boggles the mind that so much handwork could have been done within the economic constraints that any business like the Noritake Company would have faced (and still does face). Moreover, even if one leaves economic constraints aside, it still boggles the mind to contemplate the organizational effort and talent pool that would have been required to hand-decorate at a high level of quality literally thousands upon thousands of rather different items totally by hand in a short time. As a result, some version of the basic question gets asked repeatedly.

2.1 Noritake plate. 1.13"h x 8.63"w. Backstamp: 27.1.

In light of what we take as the rather clear evidence provided in the letter above, we can shift the question from its "all or none, did they or didn't they" form to one which asks about extent, especially for items made in the all-important 1921-1931 period. In this context, two things may be noted. First, transfers *seem to be* found more often on "Nippon" era fancyware than on later Noritake (1925-1931) items. I emphasize "seem to be," here, because an empirical study of the sort necessary to warrant deleting those words simply has not yet been carried out. I use the phrase in the next sentence for the same reason. Nippon era transfers *seem to be* used most often when the motif includes elaborate and/or relatively small images such as portraits and other portions of European (or European style) paintings. Three examples of such a motif, albeit on Noritake-marked items, are shown below in Chapter B (see B.349, B.541 and B.541A-B). Although it is only a surmise on my part, this pattern of use can perhaps be accounted for by two factors. First, if porcelain production in England and Europe dropped during the years of World War I, which seems quite likely, then the European makers of lithographs for such porcelains might have found it in their interests to make them available to potteries elsewhere. Second, lithographs would be, by far, a more economical way to produce decorative porcelains with such motifs in quantity.

While acknowledging the reminder, in the letter above, that these transfers almost certainly were used in the decoration of Noritake-era fancyware, it is likely that most such uses involved finely detailed and repetitive patterns placed around the rims or bases of pieces where precision in placement and spacing was vital. The central elements of most

2.3 Detail of Noritake plate shown in 2.1.

2.2 Noritake plate. 1.13"h x 8.63"w. Backstamp: 27.1.

of the motifs seen in the 1921-1931 era, I believe, were not transfers. Although again a surmise on my part, we can once more invoke economics to account for this. In Chapter 1 of *Collecting Noritake A to Z*, I discussed in some detail the differences in the fancyware porcelains from the pre-1921 Nippon era and the 1921-1941 era. Among other things, I noted that the later items tended to be far less elaborate or detailed than many of the designs from the earlier period. Also, the motifs on the later, decidedly non-traditional items appear to have changed constantly and rapidly in response to rapidly changing fashions and styles in the areas where these items were to be marketed. Because of such production and marketing trends, we may question whether it would have been feasible, economically or otherwise, for makers of lithographs to manufacture the necessary products and supply them in a timely enough manner. Because of issues such as these, it may well have been more economical to decorate by hand most of the motifs on Noritake-era fancyware.

Having offered, with some trepidation, these admittedly speculative observations, we may turn now to something that is far clearer—the alternative method, alluded to above, for deciding whether a motif is a transfer or, alternatively, the product of an original decorative effort. Although this method is simple and does not require the use of a powerful magnifying glass, it does require something that is frequently difficult and that, in some instances, may be impossible: comparing very closely two examples of the same motif on the same type of item. With this in mind, I presented photographs of several different pairs of items in both of my previous Noritake books (see, for example, the images on pp.24-25 and 269 of *Noritake Collectibles A to Z* and on p. 11 of *Collecting Noritake A to Z*). Although these certainly were useful, I provide four additional and, I think, more helpful photos (2.1-2.4) here.

These photos should be more instructive for three reasons. First, the motif is a very well-known, Art Deco era image found on many different kinds of items. Second, several areas of the motif have relatively complex, detailed patterns (in the woman's dress, especially). That the motif was used extensively and is so complex would seem to make it an excellent candidate for lithographic decoration. Third, rather large photos of small portions of some of the more detailed areas of the motif (2.3 and 2.4) are available for inspection. If a decal was used, these small areas should be the same; if they were handpainted, they should differ. As should be obvious from even a cursory inspection of the photos in 2.3 and 2.4, however, the dresses and other details differ considerably, thus indicating almost certainly that each and every square inch of both plates was painted by hand. In my opinion, similar results using this method will be seen with an overwhelming majority of Noritake fancyware from the 1921-1931 period.

I have seen pieces of Deco Noritake with chips or other flaws and, for several reasons, have not bought them. For example, I doubt there would be a way to cover the luster area (when the problem is there) and that, even if there were a way to do this, that a repaired item might still be almost worthless. Lately, however, I have seen some repaired items

2.4 Detail of Noritake plate shown in 2.2.

that look quite good on display as "cabinet pieces." As a result, I am sorry now that I passed on a lady plate with a chip out of it that was priced at only $25 since I think it could have been made presentable. What do you think about this and, specifically, what do you think is the impact of a repair on the value of a piece? And, while I am on the subject, what is the impact on value of a lack of backstamp?

Although both of the subjects raised in this letter (the impact on value of repair or lack of backstamp) are complex and, frankly, emotionally charged issues for many Noritake collectors and dealers, I begin with a few comments on porcelain repair. I address the matter of a missing backstamp later in this response. Bottom line: I am in favor of repair. Moreover, collectors owe it to themselves to become more informed about where and how to get items repaired and what it does to the value of pieces. Also, in my opinion, we ought to be more accepting of repaired pieces. By the same token (and this is *vital*), dealers have an obligation to inform potential buyers of any repairs that an item may have. These are, however, broad and rapidly stated views. In the paragraphs that follow, I attempt to justify and clarify them.

I begin by noting what it appears that you (the letter writer) are *not* saying. Given your reference to "cabinet pieces" (a term used by collectors and dealers to refer to pieces with imperfections that cannot be seen when displayed in a normal manner), you do not seem to be saying that the repair is invisible. For now, I will speak to these sorts of (usually amateur) inadequate repairs. In general, collectors should limit rather strictly the number of imperfect un- or inadequately repaired pieces in their collections, even if these items are "bargain-priced." Poorly or unrepaired pieces have *significantly* lower values than well-repaired counterparts. Even so, I am also inclined to the view that we ought to be more accepting of what are commonly known as "cabinet pieces." I have three in my collection, all purchased knowingly (though not therefore unwisely according to some or perhaps many of you who are reading this). In all cases, they are rare items and the problems cannot be seen from any angle when displayed. If I can find perfect ones (always a possibility), then I will upgrade (i.e., buy the perfect one and sell the one with the imperfection) *if* the price of the perfect piece is tolerable (less and less likely these days).

It is the last factor (the likelihood of the price of the perfect item being reasonable) that makes the situation complex and difficult, at least for me *as a collector*. It would be difficult because I would be reluctant to pay a high premium (e.g., the sorts of prices seen on eBay for major pieces) if I already own an imperfect and relatively inexpensive version of the piece that displays well (a cabinet piece). This is not simply because I am a tightwad. It is because, as a collector, my primary goal is to acquire pieces so I can *look* at them. If, in the cabinet, a piece looks great (i.e., if the imperfection does not show), it seems to me that I can legitimately question why I should pay a *lot* of money for a perfect piece. As an *investor*, however, the choice is duck soup easy: *go with perfection every time*.

Here is another point to ponder. We've all heard the old saying about the cure being worse than the ailment. Well, although it may not be common, it is worth remembering that some repair efforts can end up being worse than the problem they were designed to solve. It is essential, therefore, that one learn all one can about how much experience a potential restorer has with the particular type of repair you need. Luster glazes, as you note, are *extremely* difficult to repair well. Anyone contemplating having damaged luster repaired needs to determine that the restorer really is capable of doing an adequate job. There is more to consider than this, however, before deciding whether to

repair and who should do it. An analogy may help, here. In medicine, some repairs of our bodies are fairly simple and yet, from time to time, do not go well. Many factors can influence the outcome. In medicine, one of them is getting the right person to do the procedure. Obviously, you need to do more than go to the same hospital that your friend did who successfully underwent a procedure. At the very least, you need to get the same physician. The same is true with the repair of porcelain bodies. Find out if the repair shop has a staff of people doing repairs. Will a trainee do the work? Find out if the person who actually will do the repair really knows how to do it. Also, you need to establish what the repairer's policies are regarding satisfaction. If you are unsatisfied for legitimate reasons, can you refuse to pay *and* get your piece back? Who is to be the judge of the adequacy of the repair? These and *many* other issues need to be dealt with before deciding whether it is wise to send your damaged porcelain to the "bowl and vase hospital."

As noted at the outset, another vital issue is how repaired pieces are represented when they are sold. On eBay, for example, there seems to be a stock phrase about the condition of a piece: "no chips, cracks or repairs." Well, the "no chips, cracks" part I can accept. These can be seen and so they either are there or they are not there (with the difficulty of seeing some hairline cracks being duly noted, though I do not propose to digress and discuss this here). *But, by definition, a good repair should be virtually impossible to see,* at least by the unaided eye. Given this, some rather interesting questions arise. For example, if an item is well-repaired by a previous collector, a dealer may not know this just by looking at the piece with the unaided eye. If repairs have been made but are detectable only with special lights or chemicals or microscopes, has the dealer who has sold it as "not repaired" been unethical? Or, to put it another way, is every seller obligated to use such technical procedures in an attempt to find non-obvious repairs before selling a piece? Even if I thought the answer is "yes" (which I do not), is it reasonable to expect that this will actually be done by most dealers?

Now, to the really tough part of your question: estimating the impact of repairs on value? If this question is put as it usually is, it is a simple matter. If it is assumed that one should always prefer a perfect piece to one that is merely well-repaired, then (other things equal) the well-repaired piece should cost less (or, put another way, it would be worth less—but *not* worthless). But, as with so many issues, the next question is the hard one: *how much less?* Is it 10%? 20%? 50%? 80%? or...? One way to dodge this question is to say, "let the market dictate. Let's see what people do."

Although a desirable approach, I do not happen to have enough records (e.g., from eBay) of relevant cases to say what people will do. There is, however, a way to *estimate* what people will do. We can ask them. Although an imperfect method, it at least is feasible and, in general, has been shown to be worth doing. With that in mind, I asked certain tell-tale questions of a convenience (non-random) sample of Noritake collectors and dealers. In the paragraphs below, I describe the study, indicating who responded and to what questions and summarize the responses. I think you will find the results of interest.

Two hypothetical questions were posed in a mailed survey. In the first one, recipients were asked to suggest a price for a Noritake dresser doll that, except for an almost invisible professional repair, was identical to another one priced at $1000. In the second question, which was similar in structure to the first one, recipients were asked to suggest a price for a dresser doll that, except for the lack of a backstamp, was identical to another piece with a backstamp that a dealer had priced at $1000. Before continuing, you might wish to participate in the following way: record your answers to these questions on the spaces provided at the end of this paragraph. On the first line, indicate (in dollars) what you think would be a fair price for a $1000 Noritake dresser doll that has been professionally repaired so well that you probably would not be able to see the repair without the help of somebody who knows where it is. On the second line, indicate (in dollars) what you think would be a fair price for a $1000 piece that looks for all the world like a well-known Noritake piece but that does not have a backstamp. (Although this request that you write your thoughts on the matter in the spaces below is, I admit, a bit unconventional, I am certain you will get more out of the remainder of this discussion if you do it. So come on, give it a try!)

repaired $ _____   *no backstamp* $ _____

In response to the two questions posed, there were 135 opinions that could be used in the analysis. These came from about 70 people ("about" because in some instances it appeared the responses were from couples in a single household). In addition, 20 surveys were returned with both answer lines blank; there were 5 others with responses indicating, in one way or another, that they had no idea how to answer. In the remainder of this report, all the figures given will reflect the views of only those who made a clear numerical response. The main, general outcome of this inquiry is clear: those responding said that a Noritake piece with repairs (even nearly invisible, professional ones) or that lacks a backstamp should definitely be priced lower than an equivalent unrepaired or marked piece should be priced. Another very clear general finding is that the negative impact of a repair is greater than the lack of a backstamp. A third finding is that experienced dealers and non-dealers expressed similar yet distinctive views.

Of the 70 who responded, a clear majority (45 or 64%) said that the price for the repaired piece should be lower than the unmarked piece. Only 10 (14%) said that the prices should be the same. Of these, 1 said they both should be $1000 and 2 said they both should be zero. There were 15 (21%) who said the repaired piece should be more than the piece lacking a backstamp. If we consider separately the views of the dealers who responded, the results are similar but even more forcefully expressed. An overwhelming majority of the 19 dealers (16 or 84%) said the repaired piece should be priced less than the piece that lacked a backstamp. Only 1 said they should be priced the same. The remainder (2 or 10%) said the piece lacking the backstamp should be priced lower than the repaired piece.

These results can be examined more closely, however, by looking at the actual dollar amounts suggested. In doing such an analysis, one standard question is about the *average* figure given. In due course, that will be reported. First, though, it needs to be noted that there are several ways to describe an array of figures given in response to questions of the sort being discussed here. So, in addition to the "average" or "mean" scores, we provide several other equally interesting ones. There were 66 people who gave clear numerical figures for the question about the repaired piece. The amounts suggested ranged from zero to $1000. The average amount was $535. The *median* figure (the one in the middle of the entire distribution) was $500; this also was the most frequently given amount (i.e., the mode); it was suggested by 12 people (18%). There were 69 people who gave clear numerical figures for the question about the piece with no backstamp. Again, the amounts suggested ranged from zero to $1000. The average amount, however, was much higher: $668. The *median* figure was $725 and, quite significantly in my opinion, the most frequently given amount (i.e., the mode) was $1000—a figure suggested by 13 people (19%).

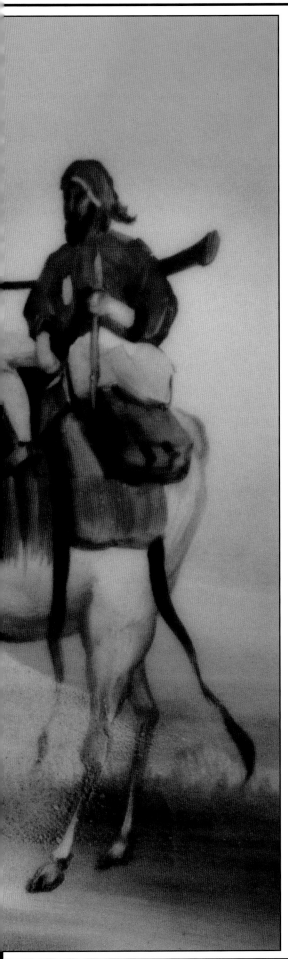

The figures in the previous paragraph combine the views of dealers and non-dealers. When their views are considered separately, the results are interesting. As noted at the outset of this story, their basic views are the same. That is, both dealers and non-dealers (collectors) think the repaired piece should be priced lower than the piece without a backstamp. The groups differ, however, regarding what may be called the "price spread"—i.e., the difference between the *average* prices suggested for the two pieces. Using the average figures proposed by the dealers, the spread between the repaired and unmarked piece is $265. That is, the dealers said, on average, that the unmarked piece should sell for $265 more than the repaired piece. For the non-dealers, on the other hand, this same gap (calculated in the same way) was only $81. These data are presented in Table 2.1.

Table 2.1: The *average* dollar amounts suggested by dealers and non-dealers for the prices of certain kinds of Noritake pieces.

Circumstance	Non-dealers	Dealers	Total sample
Repaired $1000 piece	$563 (N = 49)	$454 (N = 17)	$535 (N = 66)
Unmarked $1000 piece	$644 (N = 51)	$719 (N = 18)	$668 (N = 69)

Finally, we must take note of the views of those who responded with words rather than or in addition to numbers and, as is often the case, those comments were almost as interesting as the numerical trends. Several noted that the figure they gave would shift as a function of how much they had wanted the piece. Some said that the type of repair would have an impact on their suggested amounts. One said that they would never buy a repaired piece because the different materials (the original porcelain and the repair material) would age at different rates so that, eventually, the repair would show. Regarding his/her $1000 suggested price for the unmarked piece, one dealer noted that in other high quality porcelain and glass collectibles the lack of a backstamp is not of much concern. Finally, one person said, "This is so difficult to answer. For me, it would have to be on a piece to piece basis. … I wish you could come up with some rule of thumb that everyone would agree upon. Wouldn't life be wonderful then!!!" To this, I would say, "But of course, but then what would survey takers do for a living!?" More seriously, though, I would add that it is because there are so few such universally accepted "rules of thumb" that survey results like these are so important. They help each one of us put our own (often strongly held) views into perspective. That, I believe, is *very* important.

Recently we bought a beautiful Noritake bowl on a pedestal. The painted design was signed by B. Fushimi. Does the Noritake Collectors Society have a list of the various artists who have worked for Noritake? Does the Society have any information on these artists? If so, are they ranked by skill or by their status? Could the artist's reputation have reached such proportions that the Noritake Company thought the signed product might bring a bigger return? Could the artist have insisted that he sign the piece? Would the artist, as an artist, have enjoyed a higher status in Japanese culture? Where would artists have been placed in the Japanese cultural hierarchy? Where did the decorators of Noritake china do their work? In a factory? At home? Were the signatures we see their usual way of signing things or were they asked to do western style signatures in view of the fact that Japanese style signatures would have no significance or meaning for most Ameri-

can or European buyers? Are there many bowls, of the kind we bought, that have the signature B. Fushimi? Are signed pieces of greater value than unsigned pieces?

I hope the reader will be assured, rather than worried, if I begin by saying that I cannot answer all these questions. And the worn out "lack of space" excuse will not be invoked here. I simply do not know the answer to some of these questions. Even so, I present them because, taken together, they so beautifully show how much there is to learn about Noritake fancyware collectibles. Perhaps someone reading this book will have answers to some of the questions I will neglect and they will send them to me (in care of Schiffer Publishing). In the meantime, let me respond briefly to those questions that I do have an opinion about or an answer to. Before doing so, however, it should be noted that several items are shown, in this book, that are artist-signed (e.g., see Chapter P, items P.242, P.246—also signed by S. Fushimi—and P.247).

Having said this, I now turn to *some* of the questions you raise. The Noritake Collectors Society does not have a list of the artists who have signed their work. We also do not have any information about them as individuals. In a book on Old Noritake by Kazuhiko Kimura (see *Bibliography* for details) published in Japan, recently, there is a short list (in Japanese on p.32) of artist names (signatures) seen on known Noritake items. There is some indication that one or two of these artists may have been of higher rank than others but at this point I know very little about this. I do not know whether the signature B. Fushimi is particularly rare. It may not be common on the sort of piece you have though. In my experience, most signed pieces are either plates (or plaques) and simple bowls.

As for the signatures themselves, it would be interesting indeed to know when it became common for Japanese to sign their names in the manner familiar to us, using a Western-style script. Clearly it would not be too informative for goods exported to the West to be signed with Japanese characters. I doubt that artists insisted that they sign items. Although it is entirely a guess, I suspect it was something of an honor to be permitted to sign a piece. I believe that much, but by no means all, decorating was done at the Noritake factory or at the work place of a subcontractor, not in homes, in part because of the need for dust-free conditions.

For many collectors, as indicated by the questions above, the big issue is whether the signature has any impact on the value of a piece. The answer, I think, can be had by conducting a simple thought experiment. Imagine two plates that are *identical* in every way except that one is signed by the artist and the other is not signed. Do you think there would be exactly the same level of interest in each piece? If not, then the basic answer is at hand: the piece that generates more interest among potential buyers would have the higher value. There is, however, another question that follows immediately on the heels of the answer just given—namely, *how much more value?* My *guess* is that in today's market and for the sorts of plates I have seen that are artist-signed, the impact of the artist signature is not more than 10%. This is, I must emphasize, a rough estimate and may well be wrong. To suggest why, consider one more thought experiment. What do you think would happen if an artist-signed Art Deco lady plate were to be offered at auction? Personally, I think such an item would generate *considerable* interest among collectors. There are at least two reasons for this. First, the motif is of more interest to more collectors (apparently). Second, no such piece is known, as of this writing and so, if one emerged, I think it would generate considerable excitement. In short, as with most such matters, it is not as simple as it might seem at first. This, however, is part of the fun of a hobby like ours.

Chapter 3

Noritake Backstamps: An Overview and Update

At the start of this chapter in my second book, I attempted to lure readers into it with wry humor. I have no idea whether that tactic worked. My hunch is that it takes more than a bit of humor to get people to read about the "tiny and arcane" details of Noritake backstamps. With this in mind, let me assure you of something right away. Although you may find some "tiny and arcane" details in this chapter, they are few in number and you do not have to wade through them in order to enjoy your hobby or be successful at your antique business. Put more positively, there are only a few truly basic facts about Noritake backstamps that one really needs to know and they are not likely to be confused with the so-called "tiny and arcane" details. Moreover, there is a very brief "summary" of the main points of this chapter immediately after this paragraph and I guarantee that there are no "tiny and arcane" details in it.

Summary

There are four points in this summary. Although these four topics are not presented in the order given here, certain layout features of the chapter will make it easy for users to find the sections of this chapter that are of interest. First, four Chikaramachi backstamps are shown in this book. They are part of well over a dozen "new" backstamps shown at the end of this chapter. Second, a spokesman for the Noritake Company has noted that the name of a most important symbol found in many backstamps has been changed. Consequently, I no longer use the word "Komaru" (the out-of-date name for the round symbol at the center of #16 type backstamps as well as many others). Instead, I use the new name: "Maruki." Third, there is an expanded discussion of the various forms of true Noritake "Japan" and "Made in Japan" backstamps. More of them are shown at the end of the chapter using much better photographs. Fourth, I provide a succinct overview of how the backstamp numbering system used in this book works. I also discuss, just as briefly, a few other matters raised in previous versions of this chapter that bear repeating. I do that right after this paragraph.

Review

In this section, I review only those topics that, to me, seem absolutely essential if one is to be reasonably well-informed about Noritake backstamps.

Those interested in more details should consult the third chapters of *Noritake Collectibles A to Z* and *Collecting Noritake A to Z*. In this review, there are 4 topics.

The scope of the backstamp list

Users of this book should know that the list of backstamps in Table 3.1 and the 80 or so color photographs that are shown at the end of this chapter do not include all of the backstamps known to occur on Noritake fancyware collectibles. There are line drawings of several hundred non-dinnerware backstamps in a booklet on the subject published by the Noritake Company (see *Bibliography* for details). One of the main reasons certain backstamps are not shown in this book is quite simple: I do not have photos of them. In virtually every case, they are seldom seen on Noritake fancyware collectibles of the sort emphasized in this book. Moreover, only a few of these missing backstamps lack the word "Noritake" and so, if encountered, there should be little doubt on anyone's part that they are true Noritake backstamps. Even so, some backstamps not shown in this chapter do not have the company name and so uncertainty about the provenance of some items of interest to users will remain. Readers with questions about such backstamps are invited to contact me via Schiffer Publishing.

Defining a backstamp

Most everything printed on the bottom of Noritake fancyware collectibles is considered to be part of the backstamp, at least for purposes of distinguishing, classifying, or assigning backstamp numbers. On some Noritake pieces, there are words near a generally recognized backstamp, put there by the Noritake Company, which give information such as the number of pieces made, the occasions for which the pieces were made or for whom they were made. In this book, such words and marks usually are not part of the "backstamp" in the narrow or "proper" sense.

The backstamp numbering system

The backstamp numbering system used in these books (and elsewhere) is explained in considerable detail in *Noritake Collectibles A to Z*, my first book on Noritake fancyware. Although it pains me a bit to say so, users of this book can treat the backstamp numbers as though they were mostly arbitrary. They are not at all arbitrary but, for the most part, this will not matter to typical users of this book. There are three aspects of the backstamp numbering system that most users will want to understand, however. First, these backstamp numbers typically take this form (expressed abstractly, here): ##.# or, sometimes, ##.###. Second, as the numbers to the left of the decimal get larger it generally is true that the items they are on were made closer to the present. Third, the numerals to the *right* of the decimal indicate the *color* of the backstamp.

The colors most often seen on Noritake fancyware of the sort shown in this book are green and red. If there are two or more colors in a single backstamp, there will be a numeral for each color to the right of the decimal. The *order* of the numerals to the right of the decimal has no meaning. A sequence like 15 would convey the same information as 51. For the sake of simplicity and standardization, however, the numerals are in order from lowest to highest moving from left to right. Information about the color of the backstamp is encoded in the backstamp number. This information is provided because,

for reasons that need not be addressed here, it has been of interest to collectors of Noritake fancyware for many years. In my opinion, however, the color of Noritake backstamps is far less significant than many other people seem to think it is. The list below shows what colors are designated by the numerals to the right of the decimal in a backstamp number.

.0 = green
.1 = red (or maroon)
.2 = blue
.3 = magenta (similar to but not the same as red or maroon)
.4 = teal (similar to but not the same as blue)
.5 = black
.6 = yellow (including mustard and similar shades but not gold)
.7 = gold
.8 = silver (including metallic—e.g., backstamps embossed in metal)
.9 = tan, brown, beige and other similar shades.

Cherry Blossom backstamps

Although there may be lingering uncertainty here and there, there really can be no doubt about it: the "Cherry Blossom" backstamp (backstamp # 19) *is* a genuine Noritake backstamp. According to a Noritake Company publication on backstamps (see *Bibliography* for details) the Cherry Blossom backstamp was first registered in 1924. By now this is probably old news to most of those reading this book and so I will not rehearse other details of this matter here. It should be noted, however, that there are non-Noritake backstamps that, in overall appearance, are rather similar to true Noritake Cherry Blossom backstamps. Consequently, both collectors and dealers need to compare potential Cherry Blossom-marked pieces with the backstamps shown at the end of this chapter.

One other point about this backstamp deserves careful consideration. There are suggestions here and there that Noritake fancyware items with a Cherry Blossom backstamp tend to be of lower quality than similar items with other Noritake backstamps. According to the Noritake Company publication just mentioned, for example, it says (p.12) that this backstamp was used on pieces "which failed to reach the quality level of Noritake in terms of body and painting." The fact that it is the Noritake Company itself making this statement tends to give it considerable authority. As a result, many collectors and dealers seem to presume almost automatically that any piece with a Cherry Blossom backstamp must be inferior to Noritake marked pieces. Since quality is closely linked to value (and price), many presume just as automatically that an item with a Cherry Blossom backstamp should be lower in price or value than other similar pieces with another "regular" Noritake backstamp. It is my considered opinion that, in many cases, such a conclusion is simply incorrect. Some pieces with a Cherry Blossom backstamp are *completely indistinguishable* from pieces bearing standard "Noritake" backstamps and, from time to time, they are superior in certain respects. Therefore, collectors and dealers should *not* use this important comment by the Noritake Company mindlessly. There are no shortcuts to judging the quality of the artwork on or the workmanship of *any* Noritake fancyware item. *When making such evaluations, collectors and dealers should always look at the artwork and workmanship, <u>not</u> the backstamp.*

Chikaramachi backstamps

For the first time, I have included items with Chikaramachi backstamps in this series of books on Noritake fancyware collectibles. Much as was the case for items with a Cherry Blossom backstamp, there has long been uncertainty as to the provenance of items with these marks. With the publication of the Noritake Company booklet on their backstamps, the matter can no longer be considered in doubt, although some interesting questions about the history and use of this backstamp remain. The earliest Chikaramachi backstamp is dated as 1912 (I do not have a photograph of that backstamp and no piece shown in this book has it). The Noritake Company dates all the others as 1928. Although the available information is unclear on this point, this date, like the others in their book, can only be used to estimate the maximum *possible* age of an item bearing such a backstamp. Because the information I have does not indicate when the company ceased using the backstamp, it is difficult to put a time range on pieces with it. On stylistic and other grounds, however, it seems very safe to say that Chikaramachi backstamps were not used after 1941.

3.1 A Chikaramachi backstamp (this one is number C20.1).

The Company booklet tells us that these backstamps were first used when certain painting factories in Tokyo and Kyoto (and unnamed other places) that did work exclusively for Noritake "were integrated at Chikaramachi and Shumoku-cho in Nagoya." One Chikaramachi backstamp features a generalized rendering of a Samurai battle helmet at the center (C23 in the list of backstamps in Table 3.1 and in the backstamp photographs). This backstamp may have been used primarily or perhaps exclusively on items exported to Great Britain. This suggestion is supported both by certain comments in the Company backstamp booklet and by information available from collectors as to the places where items with this backstamp have been found.

The rationale behind the numbers assigned to these backstamps is quite simple. The backstamp numbers have two digits to the left of the decimal just as the other Noritake backstamps do. All the numbers are in the twenties (20-29) because the Chikaramachi backstamps shown in this book began to be used in the 1920s. Unlike most of the other backstamps, however, a letter precedes the two-digit Chikaramachi numbers. This is done to distinguish them from other Noritake backstamps that have the same numbers. The letter chosen, C, was picked for its mnemonic value (the word Chikaramachi begins with the letter C). (Letters have been added to several other backstamp numbers and these too have been chosen for their mnemonic value.) When and if a piece with the 1912 backstamp shows up, I will give it a two-digit number in the teens preceded by the letter C. Since we know it to be a backstamp registered in 1912, the most appropriate number would be C12.

Maruki backstamps

A prominent, centrally located symbol in many Noritake backstamps is a circle that encloses a six-armed element. For years, various publications (including mine) referred to this symbol as a "Komaru" and, accordingly, most backstamps with this symbol were thought of as Komaru backstamps (e.g., backstamp #16 and its variants in this book). Recently, however, a spokesman for the Noritake Company has indicated that, from now on, this symbol and associated backstamps should be known as Maruki, not Komaru. Until further notice, therefore, the word Maruki will be used in my publications to designate or refer to such backstamps or backstamp symbols.

MIJ and J backstamps

In keeping with a theme introduced in Chapter 2, various matters pertaining to MIJ (Made in Japan) or J (Japan) backstamps are presented here in the form of a "Noritake Dialogue." Thus, the discussion begins with an edited version of a letter that I received about a year ago. As in Chapter 2, this letter is shown in Italics for ease of identification. My reply, which is a heavily edited version of material presented in *Noritake News*, follows. The central issue raised pertains to details ("tiny and arcane"?) pertinent to the description and identification of confirmed Noritake variants of the MIJ and J backstamps.

I want to know how one can be sure that the various "Made in Japan" and "Japan" backstamps we see are really on pieces made by the Noritake Company. I sometimes see pieces that, in quality and style, seem almost certainly to be Noritake but then, when I pick them up and look at the bottom, I find an MIJ or J backstamp in black rather than red or green. What are your thoughts about such a black MIJ or J mark? Can you refer me to one of your red or green MIJ marks that you absolutely know to be Noritake?

3.2 A "Japan" (J.0) backstamp from an item in a Chikaramachi-marked set.

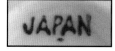

3.3 A "Japan" (J.5) backstamp from an item in a Chikaramachi-marked set.

For many years and like most experienced Noritake collectors, I was convinced that there was no such thing as a black J or MIJ Noritake backstamp. Then I found one. It was a very tiny black MIJ backstamp on what could *only* be a Noritake piece: a porcelain display sign. It was on a post-1960 piece and the base was too small for a full backstamp; indeed, it was so small, even the typical pre-war MIJ backstamps would not have fit. After that discovery, I took refuge in this thought: even though they do exist, they are not found on items prior to World War II. Well, that turns out to be incorrect as well. Chikaramachi Noritake sets with small items can have these marks. An example is shown to the left (3.3). Obviously this is a black "Japan" backstamp. So far, I have not seen a *known* (more on what this means in a moment) Noritake MIJ.5 (Made in Japan, in black) backstamp.

Because it was common knowledge, if not a rule, that pre-war Noritake J and MIJ backstamps were either red or green, most would have seen the gren Chikaramachi backstamp in 3.2 (left) as a Noritake backstamp. It is this "rule" that made a J.5 backstamp problematical. Well, it is not just the black backstamp in 3.3 that proves this rule incorrect. There are, in fact, *blue* J and MIJ Noritake backstamps as well (they are shown in the backstamp photo section at the end of this chapter).

One of the most basic issues, of course, is how one decides whether a J or MIJ backstamp is on a genuine Noritake-made and decorated pre-war piece. There are several ways, a conservative one that I will discuss in a moment and a common one that is, in a sense, mentioned in the letter (above). Experienced collectors are convinced, with good reason, that they can tell genuine pre-war Noritake items from non-Noritake made in Japan items simply by *feel*. It is not necessary here to review what one has to know and what one looks for in order to be able to do this. All I need to do is acknowledge that it is a relevant method for making such a judgment. There are some obvious problems with this approach, however, and the main one is not what most people think. The main problem is not whether it is really possible for people to distinguish, by touch, differences in the quality of various porcelains. The main problem is that the Noritake Company was not the only maker of pre-war Japanese porcelains of high quality. Without a doubt, they had a much more impressive record in this regard, but there were items made in and around Nagoya in the 1920s and 1930s with porcelain and decorations that *sometimes* virtually matched those produced by the Noritake Company.

Given this, and I think it indeed must be considered a given, we should consider another way to identify with confidence the provenance of items with an MIJ or J backstamp. The method I have adopted is to examine MIJ and J backstamps on items in *sets* where (a) all the pieces *clearly* match in porcelain quality and design and (b) at least one of the pieces has a full Noritake backstamp. ***All of the MIJ and J backstamps shown at the end of this chapter (or anywhere else in it) are from such sets.*** As it turns out, there are not only quite a few such backstamps, but they differ somewhat in *size*. With one *possible* exception to be noted shortly, they do not differ (so far anyway) in the *basic* characteristics of the letters. In particular, the letter J in "Japan," so far as I know, never has a crossbar when it is on an item that truly is part of a Noritake set. The one possible exception, one that I am still investigating, is a *script* "Japan" in a green color that is the same as that seen in Noritake backstamps from the 1920s. Stay tuned.

Using this method for identifying true Noritake MIJ and J backstamps, I obtained a sample of them and measured their *widths* carefully. I did this because, as just noted, these backstamps do vary, but mostly in size. Here is what I have found, *so far*. True Noritake "Japan" backstamps, whether green, red, *or blue*, range in width from 5/16 to 6/16 of an inch (measurements were made using a ruler marked in 1/32" increments). True Noritake "Made in Japan" backstamps in green or blue (I had only one blue example) range in width from 4/16 to 7/16 of an inch. True Noritake "Made in Japan" backstamps in red exhibit a slightly narrower range: from 4/16 to 6/16 of an inch. The one shown in the backstamp section in my first two books was 5/16 of an inch wide. Interestingly enough, the full backstamp on the set with an item with a blue MIJ backstamp was number 26 in *green*, but the decoration and quality of all the items matched completely.

There are two other interesting details pertaining to J and MIJ backstamps that need to be noted, briefly, before concluding. First, I show (3.4, right, and at the end of the chapter) an interesting MIJ backstamp that, in addition to the basic words, has others in Chinese/Japanese characters. These items clearly were part of sets with a 29.1 backstamp (a stamp that also has these characters). Several options were considered when deciding what number to give this backstamp. Ultimately, I opted for adding the letter "w" (in lower case) to the right of the numeral to the right of the decimal designating the color of the backstamp. I picked that letter for is mnemonic value ("w" for "writing"). Second, there is an interesting *double* backstamped piece shown in Chapter C (see C.235 and C.235A). The two backstamps are J.1 and MIJ.1. The size of the letters in the J.1 backstamp *seem* fairly large but, unfortunately, that photo was taken at a dealer's shop *long* before I thought it would be useful to know how wide the word was. And, because of its location at the time, I now have no idea where these items are. Although a "tiny and arcane" detail to some, perhaps, it is one that will be of considerable interest to others.

In summary, those with items having an MIJ or J backstamp (including *black* or *blue* ones!) on items that are not part of a set with a full backstamp will want to use these data and the photos in this book as they work *carefully* toward deciding whether they truly were made in the 1920s and 1930s by the Noritake Company. I would note, with emphasis, that I do not claim that the examples in my sample (about two dozen items) represent the full range. Anyone with examples that fall outside the ranges given that are parts of sets

3.4 A "Made in Japan" backstamp (MIJ.1w) with Chinese/Japanese characters, indicating that originally the item with this backstamp was part of a Noritake set with backstamp 29.1.

with a full Noritake backstamp is encouraged to contact me via Schiffer Publishing.

Regarding Table 3.1

This table displays important information, in summary form, about the backstamps commonly seen on the porcelains that are the subject of this book. This table is *not,* nor was it ever intended to be, a complete compendium of Noritake Company backstamps. Neither is it a record of all backstamps of possible interest to Noritake collectors. With one or two exceptions, the backstamps described in this table appear on an item shown in this or my previous Noritake books. The backstamp numbers used in this book are in the column headed "DHS #s."

Table 3.1 has eight columns. Column 1, on the far left (DHS #s), shows, with three exceptions, the numerals to the left of the decimal which designate the "specific kinds" of Noritake backstamp relevant to this book. The exceptions are backstamps designated entirely by letters. Usually, these backstamps occur on pieces, particularly from the 1920s, which were parts of larger sets or which were too small to permit the application of the full backstamp (or both). In such cases, the Noritake Company simply marked a piece with the words "Japan" or "Made in Japan." Because those words are also found on many non-Noritake Company porcelains, collectors and dealers should make sure that the words in these two backstamps match, in color and other characteristics, these same words as found on full Noritake backstamps (and especially backstamp # 27.). Sometimes, in column #1, the numerals to the right of the decimal also will be given.

Column 2 (Description) states, as briefly as possible using words, what the defining features of the backstamps are. This is a simplified guide only. All the backstamps described here are shown in photos that follow this table. Users should certainly consult those photos. Also in this column, when appropriate, certain features which one may notice but which are *not* "defining features" will be mentioned. Unless stated otherwise, all of these backstamps contain the word "Noritake" and none have the word "Nippon" except when it is part of the phrase "Nippon Toki Kaisha" which means, in essence, "Japanese Ceramics Company." Column 3 (Year) gives, *according to Noritake Company information* (see *Bibliography* for further information about their backstamp pamphlet), the year of *registration* of the backstamp *or* the year when *production* of pieces bearing the backstamp *started.* These years, therefore, give only a very *rough* estimate of the age of a piece with a given backstamp. Column 4 (D or E) indicates, again using information from the Noritake Company, whether a backstamp was used for goods *exported* (E) from Japan or sold *domestically* (D)—i.e., within Japan. Columns 5-8 (A&R #s, LAD #s, NC #s, JVP #s) provide a cross-reference to the numbers used for these backstamps (or their nearest equivalents) by, respectively, Alden and Richardson, Lou Ann Donahue, the Noritake Company and Joan Van Patten (see *Bibliography*).

Table 3.1: Noritake Backstamps Relevant to Fancyware Items of the Sort Shown in This Book (Permission and authorization of the Noritake Company to publish these photographs of Noritake backstamps is herewith gratefully acknowledged.)

DHS #s	DEFINING FEATURES OF SPECIFIC KINDS OF NORITAKE BACKSTAMPS	YEAR	D/ E	A&R #s	LAD #s	NC #s	JVP #s
J.	the word "Japan," in colors and general appearance as found on backstamp 27.	1918?	E	none	none	none	none
J.1w	the word "Japan" in red *plus* Chinese/ Japanese characters (indicates item was originally part of a set with backstamp 29.1)	1918?	E	none	none	none	none
MIJ.	the words "Made in Japan," like those found on backstamp 27	1918?	E	none	none	none	none
07.0	RC + Balance symbol + Nippon Toki Kaisha + Chinese/Japanese characters in green; sometimes with a design number)	1912	D	none	none	20	7
07.3	same as 07.0 but in magenta (found on especially fine, highly decorated sets, often with extensive gold)	1912	D	none	none	20	7
07.7	same as 07.0 but in gold	1912	D	none	none	20	7
13.	Cherry Blossom symbol but *without* leaves and with a letter M in the center	1916	E	MM-17	none	28	none
14.	Maruki symbol + Made in Japan +Design Patent Applied For	?	E?	none	none	10? 120?	17
15.01	Maruki symbol + Made in Japan (in green) + Chinese/Japanese characters (in red) (whether or not there is a design number which, in captions, is given within parentheses with backstamp #)	?	E?	MM-9A	none	10? 120?	none
16.0	Maruki symbol + Made in Japan in green (but no Chinese/Japanese characters)	1908 and 1949	E	none	11	10 and 120	16
16.1	Maruki symbol + Made in Japan in red (but no Chinese/Japanese characters)	1908 and 1949	E	none	11	10 and 120	16
16.4	Maruki symbol + Made in Japan in teal (but no Chinese/Japanese characters); has an accent on the "e" in Noritake, a flat-topped letter "r" & thick central element	1908	E	MM-9	11	9	16
16.7	Maruki symbol + Made in Japan in gold (but no Chinese/Japanese characters)	?	E	none		10 and 120	16
18.	large letter M inside a thin 5-lobed "cherry blossom" + Made in Japan + the word "Noritake"	1925	E	MM-20	none	34	none
19.0	5-lobed "cherry blossom" with a center of radiating lines + Made in Japan or just Japan but without the word "Noritake"; in green; decorated by subcontractors	1924	E	MM-23 (but no pattern name)	none	33	none
19.1	same as 19.0 but in red; decorated by subcontractors	1924	E	as above	none	33	none
19.2	same as 19.0 but in blue; decorated by subcontractors	1924	E	as above	none	33	none
21.	large letter M inside an abstract wreath + Japan	1935	E	MM-15	none	87	none
C20.1	the words "Chikaramachi" and "Handpainted" in curved lines above and "Made in Japan" in a curved line below a wreath with a small crown inside, in red	1928	E	none	none	37	none

DHS #s	DEFINING FEATURES OF SPECIFIC KINDS OF NORITAKE BACKSTAMPS	YEAR	D/E	A&R #s	LAD #s	NC #s	JVP #s
C21.0	the words "Chikaramachi" (but *not* "Handpainted") in a curved line above and "Made in Japan" in a straight line below a wreath with a large crown inside, in green	1928	E	none	none	38	none
C21.5	same as C21.0 but in black	1928	E	none	none	38	none
C22.0 (30040)	same as C21.0 *plus* Chinese/Japanese characters and a design number, in green (particulars of design numbers will be shown after the backstamp number as in this example)	1928?	E	none	none	none	none
C23.1	the word "Chikaramachi" in script above and "Made in Japan" (not script) below a samurai helmet, in red; may have been for items exported to Great Britain	1928	E	none	none	39	none
C23.5	same as C23.1 but in black	1928	E	none	none	39	none
RC26.0	the letters "RC" and the words "Made in Japan" under a single feathery laurel branch; for items exported to India	1926		none	none	35	26
RC26.2	same as RC26, except in blue						
24.1	M-in-Wreath + Japan (no "Handpainted" or "Made in"); although both are known, red color is more common than green	1918	E	MM-18	none	29	52
25.1	M-in-Wreath + Handpainted + Japan 1918 (no "Made in"); although both are known, red color is more common than green		E	MM-26	none	29	50
26.0	M-in-Wreath + Made in Japan (no "Handpainted") in green	1918	E	none	10	29	38
26.1	same as 26.0 but in red	1918	E	MM-22	10	29	38
26.8	same as 26.0 but silver (embossed metal)	1918	E	none	none	none	none
27.0	M-in-Wreath + Handpainted + Made in Japan in green	1918	E	MM-19	9	29	27
27.1	same as 27.0 but in red (decorated by Noritake Company subcontractors)	1918	E	MM-19A	9	29	27
27.2	same as 27.0 but in blue (mostly on some items for children)	1918	E	none	none	29	none
27.3	same as 27.0 but in magenta (on extra fine items, often with extensive gold)	1918	E	MM-19A	none	29	none
28.	M-in-Wreath + Made in Japan + Design Patent Applied For [ignores variations due to abbreviations or whether it has the words "Handpainted" and "Made in" and/or to presence the of various pattern names, which, in captions, are added in parentheses after the backstamp number — e.g., 28.1 (Roseara)]	1918	E	MM	none -22B & C, plus MM-19B & G-L plus others	29	28 plus 36, 39, 41-48 and 98
29.	M-in-Wreath + Made in Japan + any Chinese /Japanese characters [ignores variations due to whether it says "Handpainted" or "Made in" or to the particulars of pattern numbers which, in captions, are added in parentheses after the backstamp number—e.g., 29.1 (29812)]	1918	E	MM-19C	none	29	29 plus 30-35, 37, 49 & 99

DHS #s	DEFINING FEATURES OF SPECIFIC KINDS OF NORITAKE BACKSTAMPS	YEAR	D/ E	A&R #s	LAD #s	NC #s	JVP #s
31.7	floral wreath (in "vases?") with the letter "M" at the top and the words "Noritake China Japan" in the center; often on acid etched, Pickard-like items	1931	E	MM-31	13	45	59
33.056	Shield-and-Wreath-under-Crown; in this example, the backstamp has 3 colors	1935	E	none	none	86	none
34.1	the word "Noritake" above Azalea blossoms + the words "AzaleaPatt." and "Handpainted Japan" plus a design number or numbers (whether 1 or 2, the backstamp number is the same)	1934	E	none	17	67	75 and 76
35.1	"Noritake China" + "Handpainted" above the Maruki symbol; "Nippontokikaisha Ltd" (printed as just 2 words) + "Nagoya, Japan" below it	1935	D	none	none	none	none
38.1	M-with-Banner-and-Crown + Handpainted + Japan in maroon	1940	E	like MM-42	none	107	79
38.016	same as 38.1 but in three colors	1940	E	same as above	none	107	79
39.	M-with-Banner-and-Crown +Japan but no "Handpainted"	1940?	E	MM-43	24?	107?	none
43.056	lacey double laurel with "Noritake China" above + "Hand Painted Japan" in 2 lines below + letter "M" in center	1933	E	MM-35	15	56	63
44.0156	same as 43.056 + the words "Japanese Design Pattern Applied For" in red, usually located some distance from the rest of the backstamp	1933	E	none	none	none	none
50.3	"Noritake" above the Maruki symbol plus "Nippon Toki Kaisha" below	1949	D	MM-50	27	119	90
52.7	"Noritake" above the Maruki symbol plus "Foreign" below; used for items sent to Great Britain	1954	E	none	none	133	none
54.0	Maruki-in-Wreath + Made in Japan; often seen on items from Australia and New Zealand	1933	E	none	none	61	none
55.	Maruki-in-Wreath + Bone China + Nippon Toki Kaisha (does not have the word "Noritake")	1940	D	none	21	105	80
56.15	Maruki-in-Wreath + Bone China + Nippon Toki Kaisha(in black) + Made in Japan (in red) (does not have the word "Noritake")	1940?	E?	none	none	none	none
64.019	Bowl-in-Wreath + Bone China + Nippon Toki (no "Kaisha"; green, red & brown)	1946?	D	none	none	109?	none

DHS #s	DEFINING FEATURES OF SPECIFIC KINDS OF NORITAKE BACKSTAMPS	YEAR	D/E	A&R #s	LAD #s	NC #s	JVP #s
65.019	Bowl-in-Wreath + Bone China + Nippon Toki Kaisha + Japan (green, red & brown)	1946?	D?	none	29	109?	85?
65.5	Bowl-in-Wreath + Bone China + Nippon Toki Kaisha + Japan (in black)	1946?	D?	none	none	109?	85
66.57	Bowl-in-Wreath + Bone China + +Japan (in black and gold)	1980	E + D	none	57	231	86
67.019	Bowl-in-Wreath + Bone China + Nippon Toki Kaisha (no Japan or Made in Japan) (in green, red and brown)	1946	D	none	none	109	none
68.7	"Noritake" above + "Japan" below the Okura symbol	1968	E	none	37	152	none
70.7	Noritake Bone China Japan (in gold script; ignores edition numbers and similar details; if information is available will be noted in caption in parentheses after the backstamp number)	1950?	E	none	none	123?	none
71.7	Noritake (in script) + (in block letters; in gold) Bone China A Limited Edition (of some number) + Japan	1950?	E	none	none	123?	none
72.7	N-in-Wreath-with-Bow + Bone China + ® + Japan (example shown is in gold)	1986	D	none	none	261	none
74.5	N-in-Wreath-with-Bow + ® +Japan (ignores variations due to two tiny dots in the wreath of some versions)	1968	E + D	none	none	154	94
AP75.5	Special backstamp used only for merchandise that used Arnold Palmer's name	1975	E	none	none	200	none
76.3	N-in-Wreath (no bow) + Nippon Toki Kaisha + Japan (example is magenta)	1955	D	none	none	135	96
77.3	N-in-Wreath (no bow) + Nippon Toki Kaisha (but no Japan)	1955?	D?	none	none	135?	none
78.9	N-in-Wreath (no bow) + Studio Collection + Bone China + Japan	1976	D	none	none	207	none
86.5	Noritake Legacy Philippines, in black	1977	E	none	none	218	none

Backstamp J.0

Backstamp J.0 (Chikaramachi)

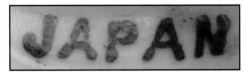

Backstamp J.1

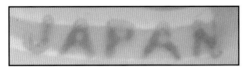

Backstamp J.2

Backstamp J.5(Chikaramachi)

Backstamp MIJ.0

Backstamp MIJ.1

Backstamp MIJ.1w

Backstamp MIJ.2

Backstamp 07.0

Backstamp 07.0 (46755)

Backstamp 07.3

Backstamp 07.7

Backstamp 13.0

Backstamp 13.1

Backstamp 14.0

Backstamp 14.0 (39539)

Backstamp 15.01

Backstamp 16.0

Backstamp 16.1

Backstamp 16.4

Backstamp 16.7

Backstamp 18.0

Backstamp 19.0

Backstamp 19.1

Backstamp 19.2

Backstamp 21.0

Backstamp C20.1

Backstamp C21.0

Backstamp C21.5

Backstamp C22.0

Backstamp C23.1

Backstamp C23.5

Backstamp RC26.0

Backstamp RC26.2

Backstamp 24.1

Backstamp 25.0

Backstamp 25.1

Backstamp 26.0

Backstamp 26.1

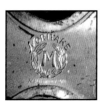

Backstamp 26.8

Backstamp 27.0

Backstamp 27.1

Backstamp 27.2

Backstamp 27.3

Backstamp 28.1

Backstamp 28.1 (Roseara)

Backstamp 29.0 (16034)

Backstamp 29.1

Backstamp 29.1 (19322)

Backstamp 29.1 (29812)

Backstamp 29.7 (20056)

Backstamp 31.7

Backstamp 33.056

Backstamp 34.1

Backstamp 35.1

Backstamp 38.1

Backstamp 38.016

Backstamp 39.019

Backstamp 43.056

Backstamp 43.0156

Backstamp 50.3

Backstamp 52.7

Backstamp 54.0

Backstamp 55.5

Backstamp 56.15

Backstamp 64.019

Backstamp 65.019

Backstamp 65.5

Backstamp 71.7

Backstamp 77.3

Backstamp 66.57

Backstamp 72.7

Backstamp 78.9

Backstamp 67.019

Backstamp 74.5

Backstamp 86.5

Backstamp 68.7

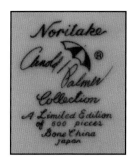

Backstamp AP75.5

Backstamp 70.7 (Fifth Edition)

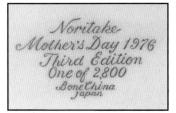

Backstamp 70.7 (Mother's Day 1976 Third
Edition One of 2,800)

Backstamp 76.3

Part Two
Introduction

Part Two is the heart and soul of this book. It is where most users of the book will spend most of their time. Because of the way Part Two is organized, you should be able to find your way around in it easily and effectively even if you do not read beyond this sentence. If you do read on, you will learn how and why the photographic materials were clustered into letter-designated chapters and how the photograph captions are structured. Also and perhaps most importantly, you will find some thought-provoking ideas to mull over pertaining to Internet auction sales events and their effect on making value range estimates of the sort provided at the end of the captions in Part Two.

Chapter organization

The chapters in Part Two are designated by letters and are sequenced alphabetically. Doing this makes the book easier to use as a reference. The chapter-designating letters have mnemonic value. Consequently, the letters will mean that users can quickly figure out and then easily remember where things of interest to them are likely to be in this book. For example, if you happened to be interested in seeing photographs of Noritake **a**shtrays, you would turn to Chapter A. If **b**owls were your interest, then the relevant chapter would be B but if it were **v**ases that you wanted to look at, then you would flip to Chapter V. Because the chapter letter designations as well as chapter names are shown as a running head on every page of Part Two, you generally will be able to locate the chapter you want within seconds just by flipping pages.

This is only part of the story, however. This book is not organized like a dictionary with each piece located in a sequence determined by the first letter of the term used to identify, name or describe it. Rather, the pieces shown in this book have been grouped into a small number of fairly broad *functional* categories, one to each chapter of Part Two. For example, the photographs in Chapter A are not just ashtrays. Included in it are photographs of all items with a close functional link to smoking. This fact is signaled by the full title of the chapter which is "Ashtrays and Other Items Related to Smoking." Accordingly, in addition to ashtrays, Chapter A has photographs of cigarette boxes, holders and jars, humidors, match holders, smoke sets and tobacco jars.

The story is much the same for all the other chapters although, in a few instances, the functional basis of a chapter's coherence may not be obvious immediately. Therefore, at the start of some chapters, comments may be made regarding the rationale for including or excluding certain items in that chapter. In addition, at the beginning of each chapter there is an alphabetic list of all the kinds of items that will be found in it, as well as the page numbers on which photographs of those pieces are located. Experience shows that, within just a few minutes, most users of the book can learn those few particulars of this organizational approach that need to be mastered. If all else fails, however, there is an index that pinpoints the location of desired material of all kinds.

Page organization

When reading English, our eyes move from left to right across the page. All the pages in this book, however, are divided into two broad columns. Because of this and the size of photographs compared to words of text, your eyes need to move *down* the page in order to view the photographs sequentially. Users of Part Two of this book should begin in the upper left corner of a page of photographs and scan *down* not across. Then, when you get to the bottom of the page, go back to the top right of the page and continue down again.

Caption organization

All full captions have five elements sequenced as follows:

PHOTOGRAPH NUMBER
DESCRIPTION
DIMENSIONS
BACKSTAMP NUMBER
APPROXIMATE RETAIL VALUE RANGE

These caption elements are largely self-explanatory. As an aid to the reader, however, certain matters are reviewed briefly here.

Photograph Numbers

Each photograph or picture "number" is actually a combination of letters and numerals. First is a letter—the same letter used to designate the chapter in which the photograph appears. Next are numerals that designate the sequential position of the photograph in that chapter. Thus, a number such as "A.193" would designate the one hundred ninety-third photograph in the "A" or "Ashtrays and Other Items Pertaining to Smoking" chapters. The letter "s" in the last word of the previous sentence is emphasized because the photograph numbers for each chapter begin with the number after the last one in the same chapter of my most recent previous book on Noritake collectibles. Thus, because there were 95 photographs in Chapter A in the first book and 57 in the second book (for a total of 152), the first photograph of Chapter A in this book is A.153.

Sometimes there is more than one photograph of a piece, usually to show the back side or to show certain details more clearly. The photograph number of these pictures has a letter that follows the sequence numerals. Thus, a photograph number like "A.193A" indicates a photograph that is, in a sense, a variant of photograph "A.193." In this instance, as the full caption in Chapter A indicates, A.193A provides additional details of one of the two cigarette jars shown in A.193. In a few instances, there may be two alternate photographs. This happens to be the case for A.193 and, accordingly, the second alternate A.193 photograph is A.193B.

Description

Any words immediately following the photograph number will indicate what an item is. Often, these words will be the same as one of the subgroup categories given in the list at the start of each chapter. If there are additional comments about the items shown, they normally are inserted at this point in the caption.

Dimensions

Inevitably, data about dimensions are approximate. It should not be assumed that other pieces like the ones shown in this book will have exactly the same dimensions. There are at least three reasons for this. For one thing, variations in size can be expected when items are made of porcelain, both because of the character of porcelain and because of the mass-production techniques used to create these particular porcelains. For another, some Noritake fancyware items were made in several distinct sizes but in some photographs these differences are not at all obvious. Finally, measurement errors are unavoidable even though, in creating this book, every reasonable effort has been made to be as precise as possible about dimensions.

Dimensions are given in decimal form to the nearest eighth inch (0.13"). Normally, the first dimension given is overall, or greatest, height (indicated by the letter "h"). This is followed by overall or greatest width ("w") and, if available or useful, *front-to-back* depth ("d"). *Diameter* is given only for basically flat and *truly* round items such as certain plates without handles, powder puff boxes and the like. Height often is not given for basically flat items such as these. For basically flat objects that are *nearly* round, such as cake plates with small handles, the dimensions given are "width" (at the widest point) *and* "depth" or, if one prefers to think of it this way, as the "other width" across the plate at the widest point *without* the handles. Finally, I have attempted to include the dimensions of all items in multi-item sets. Where certain dimensions are not provided, however, the user may presume that they simply were not available.

Backstamp

The identity of most of the backstamps on pieces shown in this book is indicated by the word "Backstamp:" followed by a number with 2 digits to the left of the decimal and from 1 to 3 to the right of it. By far the vast majority of the pieces in this book will have one of three kinds of backstamp. The most common backstamp, by far, is an "M in Wreath" type. These are all designated by a number beginning with 2; indeed, about 90% of these will be 27.0 or 27.1. The other two very common backstamps are the "Maruki" type (usually designated by the number 16.0, 16.1, etc.) and the "Cherry Blossom" type (designated by the number 19.0, 19.1, etc.).

The number to the right of the decimal indicates the color of the backstamp. By far the most commonly seen colors are green (.0) and red or maroon (.1). Blue (.2), magenta (.3), and teal (.4) are also seen regularly, but not frequently. Thus, a backstamp number such as 27.1 would be read as indicating that the item shown has a red or maroon "M in Wreath" backstamp. Other colors found on other backstamps are designated by other numerals to the right of the decimal. A complete list of the color codes used in the backstamps is given above in Chapter 3.

Value

The last numbers in the caption indicate the *approximate retail value range* in current U.S. dollars of the items shown in the photograph. For example, numbers such as $120-150 would indicate an *approximate retail value range* of U.S. $120.00-$150.00. Sellers should not presume that the top end of the range is usually the best asking price nor should buyers assume they can usually expect to purchase items at the bottom end of the range. Sometimes, both ends of the range are *not* indicated numerically. Instead, just the lower end of the range is given. For the humidor in A.197, for example, the "$900+" at the end of the caption indicates that one could expect to see a retail price of *at least* $900.00 on such a piece. This method of indicating value is reserved for rather unusual and highly desirable items which, so far, have been seen only rarely in the Noritake collectibles market.

It is impossible for the value designations to be any more than a *rough guide* to the current retail value of any of the pieces in this book. Many factors, such as the condition of the piece (presumed to be near-mint in this book; there is no such thing as a truly "mint" piece of pre-War Noritake porcelain), individual preferences and changing fashions among collectors, can have a significant impact on the utility of this information. Neither the publisher nor author is responsible for gains or losses that may occur when using or quoting the opinions expressed on these matters in this book.

These caveats are more than a formality. Some of the reasons for this being so are discussed in the remaining paragraphs of this Introduction to Part Two. I urge you strongly to read it. In keeping with a theme introduced in Chapter 2, these matters are presented as a "Noritake Dialogue." Thus, it begins with a letter that, in actuality, is an amalgam of two letters I received a year or so ago. As in Chapter 2, this letter is shown in Italics for ease of identification. My reply follows. It is a heavily edited, updated version of my responses in two separate issues of *Noritake News*. So that you will know at the outset what you are getting into, I will note that the central issues pertain to how auction sales data should be treated when determining the *approximate retail value range* of the items shown in this (or any similar) book. As I hope will be obvious, the issues raised in the paragraphs below are *vitally* important for all who plan to make any use at all of the values estimates provided at the end of each of the main captions in this part of the book.

I recently received your very nice, thick book full of beautiful color photographs [the writer is referring to my 1997 book—a fact of significance given what he/she says shortly]. There are so many patterns and designs that I have not seen in other books. I have a

question, however, on the values shown in it. Are they still at least in the "ball park," or does the fact that the figures were established several years ago make them out of date? I ask in part because the prices I am seeing now seem to be at least a little and often much higher than the ones that are given in the book. For example, on eBay recently, a super Deco item [the letter mentions a specific item but for privacy reasons it is not spelled out here and, in any case, most of the points to be made do not change vis a vis these particulars] closed at what I thought was a very high price. That item is certainly a striking piece and the person who eventually got it must be very pleased. But who could have imagined that it would go that high?! It is living proof that "price guides" in collector books are just that: GUIDES!

The questions raised and comments made in the above letter are important and quite a few people have asked and/or said to me one or another version of them. The best I can do in the way of short answers is to note the following. *Although many of the values given in my previous books are still probably "in the ball park," there certainly are exceptions— lots of them. You are correct, therefore, to note that the utility and accuracy of ANY value guide does diminish with time, but (and here is the important part) **in an uneven way**.* (This leaves unconsidered, of course, the question of how much value the price guide had to begin with—a separate and rather problematic issue all by itself.) Thus, the values given for *some* of the items in my 1997 book (and my 1999 book, too) still seem to me to be quite correct today, almost 6 years later. That is because, like it or not, the values of some items, often the more modest or downright humble ones, have not increased at all; not even a penny. Indeed, the values for some of these items have declined. Although there are various reasons for this, I will mention only one here. As knowledge increases and is disseminated, collectors tend to become more discerning in their collecting interests and tastes.

My general sense is that the values of solid but still moderately priced items—i.e., items that were pegged at about $200-$400 in 1997 terms—would, by today, have increased by *about 30% on average*. Do not overlook the Italicized words in the previous sentence. Not all $200-$400 items have increased 30% in value. Some have stayed about the same and, I think we may be sure, some have declined. Some, of course, have shot up much more than this. The overall trend, however, *seems* clear. When one considers items with the highest 1997 values (about $500 to $2000), this trend is a bit more dramatic. In 1997, items with values in that range were both rare and in *great* demand. This demand, as great as it was then, has apparently increased considerably since 1997. If forced to put a number or per cent on it, I would say that many of these items have at least doubled and some have nearly tripled in value since then.

Having made these general points, I want now to shift to some other issues. I will do so by discussing the sale of the specific item you mention. You note that it was a particularly unusual and special Art Deco item. Given what was just said in the previous paragraph, your reference to the character of the item definitely does matter. What is even more vital, however (at least from my perspective in suggesting values for the items in this book), is not so much the particulars of the item but *where and how it was sold*. This is true because of a surprising and, in a sense, quite counter-intuitive (on first glance; this changes upon reflection) fact regarding auction sales. According to the best information available from economists who specialize in the study of auctions, the top bid for any item sold at auction is *always too high* from the perspective of the others involved in the auction. Sales at an auction, therefore, are rather different events than posted-price sales at, say, an antique show.

Rather than delve, at this point, into the often arcane and technical language of economics (Thaler offers several less technical discussions; see *Bibliography* for details), I will explore these matters with you in another way. Let's consider something that is neither technical nor obscure: buyer's remorse. Economists who specialize in auction behavior discuss this frequently (they often refer to it as the "winner's curse"). Indeed, economists probably could measure its severity in dollars and cents if they wanted to. As you probably know, however, this phenomenon can easily be defined from a more informal and personal perspective. Buyer's remorse is that sinking feeling one gets when one has "won" an item at an auction—a feeling that comes *directly* from recognizing that, although you have "won" the auction, you also have paid too much for the item. This feeling is *very* common. It is not, however, inevitable. Sometimes, you may feel that you got an incredible bargain at an auction. Indeed, the lure of a hoped-for bargain is one of the more basic incentives that brings people to an auction.

At this point, you may be thinking that the three things said so far seem profoundly contradictory. As is often the case in such situations, the contradiction is only apparent and can be removed by taking note of a vital but overlooked phrase or point in the argument. This is one of those cases and I will point it out in a moment. First, though, let's review the three points that seem to have been made. (1) All winning bids at auction are too high. (2) Buyer's remorse is that sinking feel which comes when winning bidders realize they have paid too much. (3) Sometimes buyers will not feel buyer's remorse but, instead, will be elated by the bargain purchase they have made.

What is missing from this summary are 10 fairly little but very important words that were part of the original statement of principle (1): "from the perspective of the others involved in the auction." To see why these are important words, let us take an extreme but by no means unimaginable case. Suppose you are at an auction with 50 other Noritake collectors and dealers. A Noritake item is offered and bidding begins. In this case, however, you are the only bidder and "win" the piece for the $10 minimum bid. Suppose further that you are convinced that the piece is rare (perhaps because of a backstamp or some other detail). Suppose further still that you expected to have to pay $100 for it (perhaps a knowledgeable collector friend of yours recently paid that much for another edition of that piece). Since you paid "only" $10, it may seem that you have "scored" (made a bargain purchase). This is not so, however (and here we come to those 10 vital words), "from the perspective of the others involved in that auction." The 49 others at the auction sat on their hands. They all thought $10 was too much. Why? Well there are many possible reasons. Maybe they all have that piece and don't want another one. Maybe none of them knew it was a rare piece. There could even be 49 different reasons that account for the lack of bids (other than yours). None of this matters for the point being made—namely, that *from the perspective of the others involved in the auction*, that piece was not worth a $10 bid and so, *by definition*, you have overpaid even at $10! Annoyingly, we can take this a step further (though it is only a restatement of a remark that opened this part of the discussion). If the winner of an auction is defined as the person who bids the highest amount, then *by definition*, the amount the winning bidder offers in order to win is too much "from the perspective of the others involved in that auction." So, at an auction, you in essence have two bad choices: you can bid a reasonable amount and lose *or* you can bid an unreasonable amount and win.

I have gone into this point at such length for one reason: *to show why it almost certainly would be foolish to use winning bid figures from auctions to set values for a book like this*. And, as a matter of fact, I have not done so. This is not to say that I have ignored such information entirely. On the contrary, I pay *very* close attention to Noritake sales on Internet auction sites such as eBay. I also pay close attention to (but do not slavishly use) information from other auctions of Noritake items that I am able to attend.

Finally, although your question does not directly raise the subject, there is one more topic that bears on the setting of values in books like this one that needs to be raised. I call it the "eBay effect." Closely bound up with the eBay effect is another one that needs to be mentioned first. This is the well-known tendency of people to remember surprising events more vividly than mundane ones. Thank goodness this is true because were it not, we all would be almost paralyzed into inaction by an overwhelmingly large store of memories (A. R. Luria, way back in the 1960s, provided perhaps the most chilling and compelling account; see *Bibliography* for details). This said, I can now note two of the main components of the "eBay effect." First, informed sellers and buyers who pay attention to a particular sector of eBay (e.g., the auction of Noritake items) will tend to remember preferentially those events with very surprising outcomes. Potentially, of course, there are many kinds of surprising outcomes. Of these, the events most often preferentially remembered, I believe, are sales that end in what seem to be (and probably are) very high amounts. This leads to a *common* belief (I have heard it expressed *many* times): "Noritake prices are going through the roof." For some items (usually a very small subset of the total) this *may* be true but, overall, this certainly is false. That it seems true but actually is false is because it is based on a sample of remembered events that almost inevitably is very unrepresentative of the total.

Another strand of the "eBay effect" derives from the fact that bidders on some Internet auction sites tend to become saturated with buying opportunities. What this means will vary somewhat from collector to collector. Overall, however, I would hypothesize that this saturation tends to *dampen overall demand and prices*. Think about it this way. B.e., before eBay, only the most eager Noritake collector could expect to see—just *see*—as many as 1000 fancyware (non-dinnerware) pieces in a year. A.e., after eBay, even a moderately dedicated user of the various Internet auction sites and the virtual antique stores of other Internet sellers can expect to see nearly that many Noritake fancyware items in a month. B.e., many collectors, over the course of a year, can be expected to have made quite a few impulsive purchases (especially when they think about them retrospectively). After all, so the scenario goes, "after driving 200 miles and walking for 5 more over bumpy fields in the hot sun, we don't want to go home empty-handed, do we?" And so *something* is purchased.

Because viewing items on the Internet is *very* easy compared to the scenario sketched above and because there are so *many* items to chose from (the saturation I mentioned previously), I see two implications that have a bearing on values. First, we can expect that traditional high-end items will tend to sell at even higher prices. There are at least two reasons for this. For one thing, many more collectors see and are in a position to bid on these items compared with the days when people primarily obtained such pieces by tromping through relatively infrequent semi-local antique shows. For another, people can (and do) wait patiently for these items to appear. They know that, in probably far less time and certainly with far less effort than had been the case in the past, they *will* see those items. The second general implication of ease of access and saturation is that prices for non-high end items will tend to go down. With the comparatively huge volumes that are so easily seen, buyers are not as hungry. They will pass on minor items because they know they can wait for another more interesting, exciting, rare item or for a particular item they have always wanted.

As a result of all these considerations and, I am sure, other ones not considered here, the estimated retail value ranges given in this book are sometimes not going to accord with your experience. *This is especially likely to be the case if you only have in mind your experiences on such Internet sites as eBay*. Also, these value estimates are not always going to be higher than comparable items were in my previous books. Indeed, in some cases, they will be lower. Moreover, because the available data are often conflicting (a very high price this time and a very low one the next), I sometimes greatly increased the *size* of the value range. Thus, although the values estimates may appear to be the product of sloppiness or forgetfulness on my part (and I do admit to both sins), they in fact represent an honest effort to consider an incredibly large amount of information that, in my view, can be used simply and easily only with great risk of error. Finally, users of this book should know that the values given in this book are not intended as predictors of what the top price will be in one auction on an Internet auction site. Rather, and far more conservatively, they are an estimate of the *retail* price *range* that one can *generally* expect to see on a particular item that has been priced to sell in a reasonable period of time at a show or in a store. Providing such estimates is difficult enough to do well (and who knows whether I have). For reasons sketched above, estimating the likely outcome of an Internet (or any other) *auction* is a far riskier endeavor.

Chapter A

Ashtrays and Other Items Pertaining to Smoking

In this chapter are photographs of items directly related in one way or another to smoking. The following specific kinds of items are arranged in the order shown:

Ashtrays with figural elements (pp. 42-44)
Ashtrays without figural elements (pp. 45-48)
Ashtrays with match holders (pp. 48-49)
Cigarette boxes (pp. 49-50)
Cigarette holders (pp. 50-52)
Cigarette jars (pp. 52-53)
Humidors (pp. 53-56)
Match holders (p. 56)
Smoke sets (pp. 56-57)
Tobacco jar (p. 57)

Collector preferences do sometimes seem to shift like the wind but, like the wind, some steady, directional trends can be detected, too. In smoking items, figurals of almost any kind are hot. This has been true for years and almost certainly will continue to be so. At or near the top of the figurals list for most collectors are lady cigarette jars, such as the elegant one shown in A.206. It is rare to find one of these in a set. More often, but still not commonly, these are found alone, as were the two beauties shown in A.193. Of nearly equal interest to collectors are figural lady ashtrays like the one shown in A.154. The strong Deco qualities of all these items, their great facial expressions and their relative scarcity on the collector market easily make these among the most sought after items in the chapter. Indeed, smoking items with almost any "lady" motif (e.g., A.166, A.167, A.176, A.189), figural or not, continue to be very desirable.

Other figurals are definitely important to many collectors and they work hard to find them. They appeal because they are, by turns, whimsical (A.204, A.209 and A.210), colorful (A.185), impressively large (A.155 and A.160), or wonderfully wacky (A.156 and A.159). Shape in general is an important feature to collectors. If the shape is rare or offbeat in some way, it probably will have greater appeal to many even if the motif is rather ordinary. An excellent example is the ashtray shown in A.181. Although the use of yellow adds some boldness to an otherwise rather understated motif, it is the shape that makes this item special. Sometimes, both the blank and motif are unusual. Two examples are shown, one in A.165 and the other in A.173. The strength of the motif on the latter item can be appreciated easily when viewed from above (see A.173A). As for the item in A.165, the Deco colors are a definite plus as is the air-brushed geometric motif, but I still think these features pale next to the shape which is both dramatic and *very* unusual.

Geometric motifs are uncommon and rather desirable. In this chapter, several striking examples are shown (A.178, A.182, A.194 and A.207). Closely

A.154 Ashtray with figural element. 3.75"h x 5.13"w x 4.25"d. Backstamp: 27.1. $800-1000.

A.154A Detail of A.154.

A.155 Ashtray with figural element. 3.75"h x 6.25"w x 6.0"d. Backstamp: 27.0. $500-700.

A.156 Ashtray with figural element. 3.25"h x 4.5"w. Backstamp: 27.0. $290-390.

related to these pure geometric motifs are the ultra-bold, Deco geometric-florals such as the design on the fabulous cigarette holder in A.188. Although only one piece is shown, it gives one reason to expect that there is an entire set out there somewhere. Another item that may be part of what would be a stunning set is the very Deco ashtray shown in A.175. As with so many other Noritake items with great Deco motifs, this piece has a Maruki backstamp, thus indicating that it originally was exported to Great Britain (where the piece shown still resides). Another unusual Maruki marked item is the matchholder/ashtray in A.177 with rare deep blue coloring and a striking motif that is a Blue Willow variant.

Sometimes the function of a piece is ambiguous. A well-known instance is an item referred to in this book (and my previous ones) as a cigarette holder (e.g., A.186, A.189, A.191 and A.192). Many collectors refer to them as cardholders—a claim made all the more plausible by the fact that packs of playing cards from the 1920s will fit into these pieces very nicely. The motif on the holder shown in A.190, however, seems to tip the balance in the direction of those who believe these were cigarette holders. Playing card motifs of one sort or another are, however, common on smoking items (e.g., A.173, A.174 and A.211 in this chapter). In fact, an abbreviated form of this motif is found on a "cigarette" holder (A.53 in *Noritake Collectibles A to Z*). Consequently, I think we may expect this "argument" will continue. Another item whose function becomes a little clearer because of the motif on it is the small ashtray shown in A.171. One sees this type of "dish" quite often but usually presented as anything but a smoking item. I am sure I have seen these described variously as a nut dish, a trinket dish, a pin tray and as a mint dish. Even with the emergence of the ashtray shown in A.171, however, it still may be premature to conclude that all such items were ashtrays.

Another functional mystery of longstanding is apparently solved by an item shown in this chapter—namely, the very rare cigar set shown in A.205. For years, figural owls like the one shown in the center were known (although they were anything but common!) but there were questions as to their function. They were too deep to be cigarette jars, they could not have been inkwells (because there was no cavity for ink as is found in the well-known owl inkwells) and it did not seem they could have been humidors because they did not have a place in the lid for a sponge. The large rests on the ashtrays, which are just right for cigars or cigarillos, are consistent with the previously expressed belief that the figural owl was too deep to make it useful for storing and serving cigarettes. Apparently these owls were designed to store these larger items. Case closed? I think so.

But why the close association of owls and smoking items? At this point, there is no answer to that question, at least not that I know of. What we do know is that, for Noritake fancyware at least, owls and humidors went together. Many collectors, myself included, particularly enjoy seeing the many ways that the Noritake Company decorated the same blank. This becomes all the more interesting when the variety is constrained by the use of a molded blank. The three cylindrical owl humidors shown in A.194, A.195 and A.196 are a great illustration of this, especially when one adds the one shown in A.66 in *Noritake Collectibles A to Z*. Do these four pieces represent the full range produced? Time will tell but, as collectors, we hope the answer is a resounding "no."

Finally, although only one figural owl humidor is shown in this chapter (A.197, below; three others were shown in A.63 and A.64 in *Noritake Collectibles A to Z*), it is perhaps the most unusual and dramatic one discovered to date. But every item in this chapter is interesting, dramatic and, even, spectacular in its own way. See for yourself!

A.160 Ashtray with figural element. 2.5"h x 4.5"w x 4.13"d. Backstamp: MIJ.1 $300-400.

A.157 Ashtray with figural element. 2.75"h x 4.5"w x 3.63"d. Backstamp: 27.1. $250-300.

A.161 Ashtray. 3.13"h x 5.0"w. Backstamp: 27.0. $90-120.s

A.158 Ashtray with figural element. 2.75"h x 3.88"w. Backstamp: 27.0. $120-160.

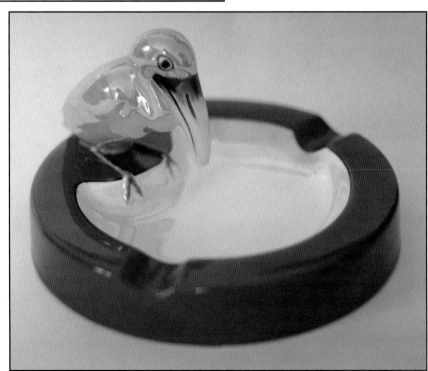

A.159 Ashtray with figural element. 2.75"h x 4.75"w. Backstamp: 27.1. $250-300.

A.165 Ashtray. 1.63"h x 5.0"w x 2.13"d. Backstamp: 27.1.$90-130.

A.162 Ashtray. 2.25"h x 5.75"w. Backstamp: 27.0. $180-230.

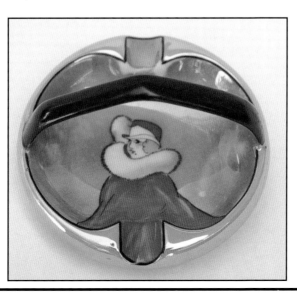

A.166 Ashtray. 1.25"h x 5.25"dia.
Backstamp: 27.1. $280-350.

A.163 Ashtray. 2.0"h x 4.5"w. Backstamp: 27.0. $90-130.

A.164 Ashtray. 2.25"h x 3.38"w.
Backstamp: 27.1. $190-280.

A.167 Ashtray. 1.25"h x 5.25" dia. Backstamp: 27.1. $280-350.

A.168 Ashtray. 1.25"h x 4.25"w x 3.88"d. Backstamp: 27.0. $100-150.

A.169 Ashtray. 1.25"h x 4.25"w x 3.88"d. Backstamp: 27.0. $70-100.

A.167A Detail of A.167.

A.170 Ashtray. 1.25"h x 5.0"w x 5.0"d. Backstamp: 27.0. $30-70.

A.172 Ashtray. 1.13"h x 6.25"w. Backstamp: 27.0. $110-160.

A.171 Ashtray. 1.25"h x 2.88"w. Backstamp: 27.1. $30-50.

A.173 Ashtray. 1.0"h x 4.13"w. Backstamp: 27.1. $190-270.

A.173A Top view of A.173.

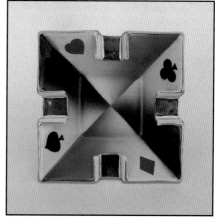

A.171A Top view of A/171.

A.174 Ashtrays. *Stack height,* 2.0"h x 3.25"w x 2.88"d. Backstamp: 27.1. Set, $100-180.

A.174A Top view of an ashtray in A.174. .75"h x 3.25"w x 2.88"d. Backstamp: 27.1 $20-40.

A.175 Ashtray. .75"h x 4.0"w x 4.0"d. Backstamp: 16.0. $150-190.

A.174B. Top view of an ashtray in A.174. .75"h x 3.25"w x 2.88"d. Backstamp: 27.1. $20-40.

A.174C. Top view of an ashtray in A.174. .75"h x 3.25"w x 2.88"d. Backstamp: 27.1. $20-40.

A.176 Ashtray. .63"h x 4.5"w. Backstamp: 27.0. $300-400.

A.174D. Top view of an ashtray in A.174. .75"h x 3.25"w x 2.88"d. Backstamp: 27.1. $20-40.

A.177 Ashtray with match holder. 3.5"h x 4.0"w x 4.0"d. Backstamp: 16.0. $70-120.

A.178 Ashtray with match holder. 2.5"h x 3.75"w. Backstamp: 27.1. $150-200.

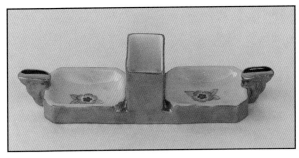

A.181 Ashtray with match holder. 1.75"h x 7.0"w x 1.75"d. Backstamp: 27.1. $40-80.

A.179 Ashtray with match holder. 2.0"h x 4.38"w x 3.75"d. Backstamp: 25.1. $70-120.

A.182 Cigarette box. 1.5"h x 3.63"w x 2.75"d. Backstamp: 27.1. $280-340.

A.180 Ashtray with match holder. 2.0"h x 4.38"w x 3.75"d. Backstamp:21.0. $50-90.

A.182A Alternate view of A.182.

A.183 Cigarette box. 1.5"h x 3.75"w x 3.0"d.
Backstamp: 27.1. $470-590.

A. 184 Cigarette box. 1.5"h x 3.5"w x
2.75"d. Backstamp: 27.0. $140-190.

A.185 Figural cigarette holder. 4.5"h x 3.0"w.
Backstamp: 19.1. $250-300.

A.184A Top view of
A.184.

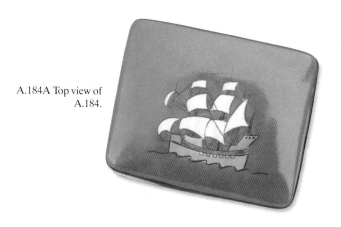

A.186 Cigarette holder. 4.25"h x 3.75"w. Backstamp: 27.1.
$280-380.

A.188 Cigarette holder. 3.75"h x
3.25"w. Backstamp: 27.1. $290-340.

A.187 Cigarette holder. 4.0"h x 3.0"w.
Backstamp: 27.1. $280-380.

A.189 Cigarette holder. 3.88"h x 2.5"w x
2.38"d. Backstamp: 27.1. $330-400.

A.187A Detail of A.187.

A.189A Detail of another example of A.189.

A.190 Cigarette holder. 3.75"h x 2.5"w x
2.38"d. Backstamp: 27.1. $90-120.

A.191 Cigarette holder. 3.75"h x 2.5"w x
2.38"d. Backstamp: 27.0. $110-160.

A.193 Cigarette jars. 5.75"h x 2.75"w. Backstamp: *Left,* 29.1 (29618). *Right,* 29.0 (25920). Each, $800-1000.

A.192 Cigarette holders. 3.75"h x 2.5"w x
2.38"d. Backstamp: 27.1. each, $40-90.

A.193A Detail of A.189, *left*.

A. 193B Detail of A.193, *right*.

A.194 Humidor. 6.75"h x 4.25"w.
Backstamp: 27.0. $500-700.

A.197 Humidor. 6.75"h x 5.0"w.
Backstamp: 27.1. $900+

A.195 Humidor. 6.75"h x 4.25"w. Backstamp:
27.0. $500-700.

A.196 Humidor. 6.75"h x 4.25"w.
Backstamp:27.0. $500-700.

A.197A Side view of A.197.

A.198 Humidor. 5.75"h x 5.5"w. Backstamp: 27.0.
$500-700.

A.199 Humidor. 5.13"h x 4.0"w. Backstamp: 27.1.
$600-700.

A.200 Humidor. 4.75"h x 4.0"w.
Backstamp: 27.0. $150-250.

A.200A. Back view of A.200.

A.201 Humidor. 4.5"h x 5.5"w x 3.5"d. Backstamp: 27.1.
$190-240.

A.204 Match holder with figural element. 3.13"h x 2.5"w x 2.0"d. Backstamp: 27.1. $200-300.

A.202 Humidor. 4.5"h x 4.38"w x 3.25"d. Backstamp: 18.0. $190-240.

A.202A Side view of A.202.

A.205 Smoke set. Tray, .5"h x 7.75"dia. Owl, 4.75"h x 3.0"w. Ashtrays, 4.63"w x 2.5"d. Backstamp: 27.1. $800+

A.203 Match holder. 3.5"h x 3.75"w. Backstamp: 19.0. $50-70.

A.205A Alternate view of A.205.

A.209 Tobacco jar. 5.5"h x 3.63"w. Backstamp: 27.1. $300-400.

A.206 Smoke set. Tray, .5"h x 6.88"dia. Cigarette jar, 5.75"h x 2.75"w. Match holder, 2.88"h x 2.25"w x 1.5"d. Ashtray, 1.13"h x 4.25"w x 3.5"d. Backstamp:27.0 (25920). Set, as shown $1000-1400.

A.210 Tobacco jar. 5.5 "h x 3.63"w. Backstamp: 27.1. $300-400.

A.207 Smoke set. Tray, .88"h x 7.25"w x 5.0"d. Cigarette box, 1.5"h x 3.5"w x 2.75"d. Match holder, 2.13"h x 2.38"w x 1.0"d. Backstamp: Match holder, MIJ.1, tray unmarked; other items, 27.1. Set, as shown, $600-800.

A.211 Tobacco jar. 3.75"h x 3.75"w. Backstamp: 27.1. $150-250.

A.208 Smoke set. Tray, .75"h x 7.0"w x 3.38"d. Cup, 2.38"h x 2.13"w. Ashtray, 1.63"h x 2.63"w. Backstamp: All items, 27.0. $120-180.

Chapter B
Bowls and Boxes

In this chapter, there are photos of over 250 Noritake bowls and boxes. If this seems like a lot, consider that these amazingly diverse and interesting materials represent less than a third of the 800-900 photos of bowls and boxes that were in my files at the time the photos for this chapter were selected. The chapter that resulted is by far the largest and most complex one in this book. Even so, the photos in it are arranged so that users of this book can *easily* become proficient at locating quickly any particular kind of bowl or box of interest.

This is possible because the materials in my files, as well as this chapter, have been organized using the classification system displayed in the list on page 61. It is a simpler list than previous ones and, with the use of numbers and other format changes, it is much clearer. It is a more comprehensive and, in certain ways, more rational list too, in part because it was created using information about far more bowls and boxes than were available to me when the two previous lists were developed. As a result of these improvements, it should be far easier to use. Even so, the organizational system recorded in this new list is still more complex than the lists at the start of the other chapters of this book. That is why the item list for this chapter, unlike any of the other chapters of this book, appears after a discussion of how it is structured.

As in my two previous books on Noritake collectibles, the materials in this chapter, as the title indicates, are clustered into two main groups: *Bowls* and *Boxes*. It is worth noting, with some emphasis, that this sequence is not haphazard. Rather, the words are in alphabetical order, a principle used extensively for sequencing decisions not only in the list below but also throughout the book. Each of these groups is divided into two subgroups. The Boxes subgroups are **Figural Boxes** and **Other Boxes**.

B.319 Pointed bowls. *Left,* 2.38"h x 8.5"w x 4.25"d. *Right,* 2.0"h x 6.5"w. Backstamp: 25.1. Each, $150-250.

B.320 Pointed bowl. 2.38"h x 8.5"w x 4.25"d. Backstamp: 27.1. $100-200.

Because there are so few items in these subgroups (alas), there was no need to divide them further. (Some Noritake boxes, however, can be found in other chapters—especially, Chapter A.) The Bowls subgroups are **General Purpose Bowls** and **Special Purpose Bowls**. Because there are so many bowls, each subgroup is divided further into various *numbered* bowl "types." All these types, as well as various subtypes ("kinds") and sub-subtypes ("varieties") to be mentioned shortly, are created and named with reference to a *few* distinctive features of bowls (e.g., the number of handles or the basic shape). These features were picked for two reasons. First, they made it possible to sort the hundreds of available photos into meaningful categories. Second, they are common, familiar and usually very easy to see (with a few exceptions; more is said about this below).

By looking at the list, one can gain a basic sense of how these features are used to subdivide bowl types. There are 4 named *types* of General Purpose Bowls and 9 named *types* of Special Purpose Bowls. These *types* of bowls have descriptive names that, in the list below, are numbered and appear in Italics to make them easier to see. Because the 4 types of General Purpose Bowls come in *many* different shapes and sizes, they were divided into subtypes (or "kinds") of bowls. There are 12 named kinds (or subtypes) of General Purpose Bowls. Because one of these subtypes ("sided bowls with two handles and no feet") is very large, it (and it alone) is divided into named sub-subtypes (or "varieties"). As can be seen in the list, there are 4 named sub-subtypes (or "varieties") of sided bowls with two handles and no feet. Their names show that they are defined with reference to the number of "sides" on the bowl or, more precisely in many cases, the number of apparent "sides" suggested by the shape of the *rim* of the bowl.

Although it may come close, I am not concerned to demonstrate (nor do I claim) that the list below records all of the known types, kinds and varieties of Noritake bowls. Producing such an inventory *might* be a worthwhile goal but it is not an essential one given the purpose of this book. I merely needed a list that is logical and conceptually simple, with components that could be alphabetically sequenced so it would be easy to use and, as a result, would enable users to determine fairly rapidly whether or not a particular bowl of interest to them is shown in this book. With boxes, as we have already seen, those goals were easily achieved with just two named groups. No types or subtypes were needed because there are so few items in either group.

Here is how to locate, quickly and easily, any *bowl* in this book. First, consider whether the bowl of interest has some specific or special purpose, function or name (e.g., is it a nut or punch bowl, or a covered bowl or compote). If you think it has, check to see if the name for it is among the 9 types of Special Purpose Bowls (including "various other") listed below. If the bowl of interest is one of these *types* (their names are in Italics in the list below), simply turn to the pages indicated. Within a minute or two, you should know whether there is a photo in this book of a Special Purpose Bowl like the one of interest.

If the bowl of interest is *not* a Special Purpose Bowl (or is not in the list of Special Purpose Bowl types), then turn to the list of General Purpose Bowls. To find a particular General Purpose Bowl in this book, first determine what *type* it is. *All of the General Purpose Bowl types in this book are based on one*

simple, easy-to-see feature: the number of handles. Once the type has been identified, there are two options. Either turn directly to the pages that show that
type of bowl or see if the piece of interest falls within one of the bowl sub-types
listed. Because there are so many bowls in virtually all of the basic General
Purpose Bowl *types*, it usually will be worthwhile to identify the subtype of the
bowl.

Bowl *subtypes* are defined with from one to three features. One of these
features is the *character of the handles.* Some bowl subtypes are defined with
reference to two specific kinds of handles: (1) loop (basket) handles and (2)
handles in a figural form. A second feature that is sometimes used to designate a bowl subtype is whether the bowl has *feet (or legs).* Because these two
features (handles and feet) are very obvious, it usually is *very* easy to place any
Noritake bowl in a subtype that is defined with reference to them. The third
feature that is used to define bowl subtypes is the basic *shape* of the bowl or,
or, more precisely in many cases, the shape suggested by the *rim* of the bowl.

This third feature, unlike the first two, is more difficult to identify in some
bowls. Some bowl shapes are simple and obvious—e.g., round bowls or square
(four-sided) ones—and fortunately, many if not most Noritake bowls have
such easily recognized, nameable shapes. Some Noritake bowls, however, have
shapes that are neither easily defined nor readily named. In light of this and in
an effort to keep things as simple as possible, the list below utilizes only 4
named bowl (or bowl rim) shapes: (1) oval (or ovoid), (2) pointed, (3) round
and (4) sided. Almost all of the bowl examples in the first three of these four
bowl shapes can usually be recognized easily and reliably. Typical users of this
book, therefore, are likely to feel that nearly all of the bowls shown in the
sections featuring these three shapes were classified correctly. With regard to
sided bowls (i.e., bowls with sides, or with rims that give the bowl the appearance of having sides), however, we may sometimes expect less agreement. For
the most part, this will occur when one needs to know the *number* of sides in
order to locate a bowl. Fortunately, this potential difficulty will arise within
only one bowl subtype: sided bowls with two handles and no feet. Unfortunately, there are many Noritake bowls in this subtype. With a little experience, however, you will see how and why these and other location decisions
were made in this chapter.

In summary, *all the types, kinds and varieties of General Purpose Bowls
listed below are designated with reference to some combination of
these features: type and/or number of handles, the presence or
absence of feet or legs, and basic shape.* Once you have identified the sub-type (or in some cases, the sub-subtype) of a bowl
of interest, simply turn to the pages indicated. Within a minute
or two, you should know if this book shows a photo of the kind
of bowl you are interested in. Nevertheless, if a bowl of interest
is not shown in the first section of the chapter you think it will
be in, consider other possible locations within the chapter. If,
after following these steps, a photo of the bowl of interest is
not found, it probably is safe to conclude that one like it is not
shown in this book. With these introductory remarks in mind
(or at least at hand), the reader is now well-positioned to make
good use of the complete list, which follows, of all the groups,
types, kinds and varieties of items in this chapter.

B.321 Round bowl. 6.38"h x 9.63"w. Backstamp: 27.1. $120-220.

Bowls

General Purpose Bowls
1. *Bowls with no handles* (pp. 58-75)
   pointed bowls with or without feet (pp. 58-59)
   round bowls with no handles and no feet (pp. 60-65)
   round bowls with no handles but with feet (pp. 66-68)
   sided bowls with no handles and no feet (pp. 69-73)
   sided bowls with no handles but with feet (pp. 74-75)

2. *Bowls with one handle* (pp. 76-90)
   basket bowls with one loop handle (pp. 76-83)
   bowls with a figural handle (pp. 83-87)
   other bowls with one handle (pp. 87-90)

3. *Bowls with two handles* (pp. 91-121)
   oval and ovoid two-handled bowls with no feet (pp. 91-94)
   round two-handled bowls with no feet (pp. 95-103)
   sided bowls with two handles and no feet (pp. 103-117)
      four-sided bowls with two handles and no feet (pp. 103-110)
      six-sided bowls with two handles and no feet (pp. 110-112)
      eight-sided bowls with two handles and no feet (pp. 112-116)
      multi (9+) sided bowls with two handles and no feet (p. 117)
   two-handled bowls (any shape) *with feet* (p. 117)

4. *Bowls with three or more handles* (pp. 118-121)

Special Purpose Bowls
1. *Celery/relish bowls* (pp. 122-125)
2. *Centerpiece/console bowls* (pp. 125-126)
3. *Compotes with handles* (pp. 127-130)
4. *Compotes without handles* (pp. 130-133)
5. *Covered bowls* (pp. 134-136)
6. *Nut bowls* (pp. 136-138)
7. *Punch bowls* (p. 138)
8. *Salad/seafood bowls* (pp. 138-140)
9. *Various other special purpose bowls* (p. 140)

Boxes

Figural Boxes (pp. 140-141)
Other Boxes (pp. 141-142)

B.322 Round bowl. 4.0"h x 9.63"w. Backstamp: 27.1. $60-80.

There are many wonderful Noritake bowls shown in this chapter; indeed, in certain ways, all of them are at least interesting and most are terrific. Even so, it also is true that bowls are not very popular among collectors. On eBay and the other Internet auction sites, bowls—rather nice ones, at least as I see things—frequently end without meeting the sellers' reserves and often with only one or two bids or, in more cases than you would think, no bids at all. I am not sure why this is the case. Some have suggested it is because Noritake bowls are so common. Noritake collectors, rightly, admire and seek the rare as much as, if not far more often than, the beautiful. From an investment standpoint, this approach to collecting may well end up being quite reasonable. Other things equal then, one can expect collectors to show less interest in bowls because they are seldom rare. From an artistic standpoint, however, this view can be questioned. Most of the collectors I know (and I know quite a few), assert that they continue with their hobby because they admire and enjoy the artistic qualities of the pieces in their collection, not because it is a good investment (although they do acknowledge that it would be fine if their aesthetic interests turned out to be a good investment too). In this respect, Noritake collectors are like those who collect any form of art. In some cases, of course, the artistic component of interest to a Noritake collector is the shape of a piece. We may discover, for example, that we have a special desire for figural lady inkwells or cylindrical humidors. If so, the decoration on such an item may not matter too much. In far more cases, however, Noritake collectors are attracted by the painted decoration on a piece. If this is so (and I think it is), then the relative lack of collector interest in Noritake bowls (and plates also, but these are discussed in Chapter P) becomes all the more puzzling because they are a terrific surface on which to place a painting.

B.323 Round bowl. 2.75"h x 8.63"w. Backstamp: 27.3. $100-180.

B.323A Top view of B.323.

To those who doubt this and/or who think all the super-duper items shown in this book will be almost anywhere but Chapter B, I say, "think again!" In this Chapter B, as was true for these chapters in *Noritake Collectibles A to Z* and *Collecting Noritake A to Z*, quite a few astounding items are shown. Some examples that can be expected to leap out at almost every reader are two bowls with the now famous "Jewels" motif (B.373 and B.486), a superb "Seated Lady" covered box (B.561), an elegant elephant box (B.562), and a fantastic figural clown box (B.563). There also are two gorgeous Gemini bowls (B.356), a truly powerful punchbowl set, complete with pedestal cups (B.555) and three large and truly marvelous molded-in-relief covered bowls (B.543-B.545). There are workaday salad bowl sets that will (or should!) almost knock your socks off. For example, the very colorful set in B.556 is unusual in having the individual salad plates as well. Although the blank of the salad bowl shown in B.557 is not really rare, this particular set is unusual for at least two reasons. First, it comes complete with its serving spoon and fork (most of the bowls like this one that I have seen do not have them, although maybe they once did). Second, the gold stripes on the exterior give this bowl extraordinary design strength. And while you are there, take an extra minute to truly savor the creative, crazy crustacean motifs on the sets in B.558-B.559.

There also are lots of bowls that may seem quite common on first glance, but that are, in fact, seldom seen. For example, the bowl shown in B.434 may *look* common but those who paused to examine the dimensional details given in the caption will have noticed that this particular bowl is much larger than are the vast majority of the others with this basic shape. The same may be said for the two bowls shown in B.439. They are bigger than the ones shown in B.440-B.441. The bowl blank shown in B.454 may seem to be a fairly common one, but look again. It has just two rolled handles whereas the vast majority of such bowls have four. And how often do you see a bowl like the one shown in B.380 with its metal handle still attached to those small knobs? The shape of those knobs is important, I think, because it suggests that a handle like the one shown almost certainly was an original component of the piece. The last item in the chapter, B.567, is equally unusual with its metalwork finial and footed frame. Or, consider the seemingly humble bowl with one handle shown in B.403. To many collectors of Art Deco Noritake, the blank will seem quite old-fashioned—a view reinforced in part by the likes of B.401-B.402, which are far more common. The piece shown in B.403, on the other hand, with its very bold floral motif that is made all the more effective by the use of gold luster, is an impressive transitional piece. The scenic motif on the bowl shown in B.445 is not unusual in itself. When, however, it is noted that the piece has a Cherry Blossom backstamp, it takes on additional interest because pieces with this mark typically have unusually bold floral motifs (e.g., B.389), not scenics.

Some collectors think that Special Purpose Bowls are prosaic and, consequently, they show little interest in them. As can be seen in this book, however, this can be a big mistake. The punch bowl in B.555 has already been mentioned. But consider, too, the centerpiece bowls shown in B.523 and B.524. They are utterly different in shape and style. Although there is no backstamp on the item shown in B.523, there are two basic clues to warrant considering it a Noritake-made item. First, the blank is precisely the same size and shape as Noritake backstamped items. Second, the quality of the decoration, including the luster, is far beyond that seen on any of the items one sees that, from the backstamp, are clearly decorated by hobbyists in the United States. The other centerpiece bowl (B.524) is noteworthy because of its very unusual shape and because it sits on a very small unmarked base (shown in B.524A). Consider also the compotes (with or without handles) shown in this book. They are all wonderful, but those shown in B.534-B.541 are particularly fine pieces, with the compote with the stunning geometric motif in B.538 being particularly noteworthy. Recalling the cigarette jar with this motif shown in A.135 (in my second Noritake book), one cannot help but wonder whether that the motif will turn up on other kinds of items. Other compotes raise some interesting questions, too. On seeing the stone-like treatment on the items in B.535-B.536, one wants to ask: how many colors are known for this stone-like motif? And, when I notice that there is a Maruki backstamp on the exquisite covered bowl in B.546, a mark registered in Great Britain, I feel compelled to ask (yet again), how did it happen that some of the most incredible Noritake designs were sent there but not to the United States? When I see a nut bowl like the amazing one shown in B.551, however, I mostly want to ask what in the world led the artists to develop *that*!? The superb molded-in-relief, basket-weave nut bowl shown in B.553 is quite reminiscent of a jam set shown in the next chapter (see C.200). Are we correct in believing that these items were inspired by Majolica ware? I think so, but regardless of the answer, we also cannot help but wonder how many basket forms will be found in Noritake fancyware and in what other colors besides the yellow and green ones shown in this book. And while we are on the subject of molded-in-relief bowls, be sure and take note of the extremely unusual one shown in B.329 (the next one, B.330, is hardly common either).

What can be more prosaic than a celery (or relish) bowl? Not much, I suppose, and yet in this book, as in previous ones, some of these items are really quite amazing, and in very diverse ways. For example, the celery/relish set shown in B.509 is a very unusual blank. The motif on the relish bowl in B.519, which probably was exported to Australia originally, is unusual in that it is a decidedly non-Deco version of a motif seen on several bowls meant for the North American market (an example is shown in B.243, in my second Noritake book). The celery bowl shown in B.511, on the other hand, is unusual in having a figural handle. Certain relish bowls often have a figural handle (e.g., B.520 is a typical one), but sometimes it is an

B.324. Round bowl. 3.0"h x 9.13"w. Backstamp: 27.0. $30-80.

unusual one (e.g., the butterfly in B.521 is relatively rare).

Cracker serving bowls like the one shown in B.560 are anything but common. With the outstanding Deco geometric motif on the one shown, however, such a piece becomes particularly desirable. That motif, by the way, appears on other food serving items (cream and sugar and muffineer sets, for example) as well as a vase and, no doubt on various other items I am overlooking. Speaking of common motifs, the lady motif on the piece shown in B.443 seems to appear on items that vary considerably in shape, size and function. The vast majority of the items seen with the motif have backstamps that indicate the piece originally was exported to Australia or New Zealand. I particularly enjoy Noritake Deco florals, in part because they are so diverse, bold and sometimes downright wacky. Many of the best of these are to be found on bowls. In this chapter, some very fine examples are shown in B.328, B.335, B.358, B.407, B.417, B.449, B.460, B.463 and B.472. There are other floral motifs that also are spectacular although they are not Deco. A great nearby example is the bowl shown in B.478, which, quite simply, is an amazingly fine work of Noritake art.

As noted, above, fine art work is indeed what draws collectors to Noritake wares from this period, and from the "Nippon" era as well. All of the items shown in this chapter illustrate this to some extent, but some are particularly compelling. For example, consider two bowls shown early in the chapter, B.323 and B.326. The floral motif on B.323 is particularly well-executed; the bowl fairly *glows* with warmth and beauty. The shape of some bowls, however, can only have made the decorative task a formidable one for the Noritake artists. For example, consider the skills that would be required to successfully paint the interior of the bowl shown in B.326; it almost boggles the mind. That piece is noteworthy also because, while the interior is traditional and quite calm in character, the exterior is modern and energetic by comparison.

Modern, traditional, Deco, Nouveau, floral, geometric, ladies, figural animals, round, square, baskets, compotes—this chapter has them all, and a *lot* more. To so many collectors, bowls are merely bargains; to me, they are, or at least can be, the heart and soul of any fine Noritake collection.

B.325 Round bowl. 1.5"h x 8.13"w. Backstamp: 27.1. $50-100.

B.326 Round bowl. 2. 5"h x 7.5"w.
Backstamp: 27.0. $90-140.

B.326A Interior detail of
B.326.

B.327 Round bowl. 2.0"h x 6.0"w.
Backstamp: 27.0. $30-60.

B.328 Round bowl with three legs. 3.0"h x 7.5"w. Backstamp:
16.0. $80-120.

B.328A Top view of B.328.

B.329 Round bowl with three legs. 3.0"h x 7.38"w. Backstamp:
27.0. $70-110.

B.329A Top view of B.329.

B.333 Round bowl with three legs. 2.75"h x 6.75"w. Backstamp: 27.0. $40-80.

B.330 Round bowl with three feet. 3.5"h x 7.25"w. Backstamp: 27.1. $60-100.

B.333A Top view of B.333.

B.331 Round bowl with three feet. 2.88"h x 5.88"w. Backstamp: 27.0. $70-120.

B.332 Round bowl with three feet. 2.63"h x 8.0"w. Backstamp: 27.0. $40-90.

B.332A Top view of B.330.

B.334 Round bowl with three feet. 2.75"h x 6.75"w. Backstamp: 27.1. $40-80.

B.336 Round bowl with three feet. 2.75"h x 6.75"w. Backstamp: 19.2. $80-140.

B.335 Round bowl with three feet. 2.75"h x 6.75"w. Backstamp: 27.1. $90-150.

B.336A Detail of B.336.

B.337 Sided bowl. 1.75"h x 7.5"w. Backstamp: 27.0. $80-100.

B.337A Detail of B.337.

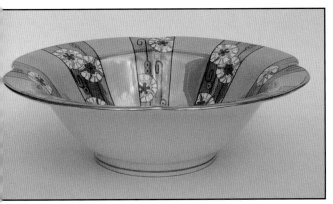

B.338 Sided bowl. 2.88"h x 9.63"w. Backstamp: 27.1. $80-160.

B.338A Interior detail of B.338.

B.339 Sided bowl. 4.0"h x 10.38"w x 9.25"d. Backstamp: 27.0. $70-120.

B.341 Sided bowl. 1.75"h x 7.88"w x 7.25"d. Backstamp: 27.0.
$50-90.

B.339A Interior detail of B.339.

B.340 Sided bowl. 1.75"h x
8.25"w x 8.25"d.
Backstamp: 27.0. $30-60.

B.342 Sided bowl. 1.75"h x 7.88"w x 7.25"d. Backstamp: 27.0. $30-70.

B.343 Sided bowl. 2.25"h x 7.25"w.
Backstamp: 27.0. $30-80.

B.344 Sided bowl. 2.5"h x 8.25"w.
Backstamp: 27.0. $40-90.

B.345 Sided bowl. 2.25"h x 7.38"w.
Backstamp: 27.0. $30-50.

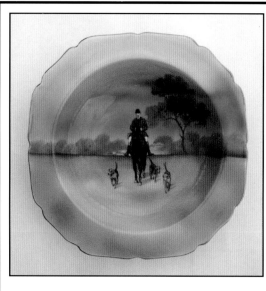

B.346 Sided bowl. 1.75"h x 8.0"w x
8.0"d. Backstamp: 14.0. $40-70.

B.347 Sided bowl. 1.75"h x 8.0"w x 8.0"d. Backstamp:
25.1. $40-70.

B.347A Detail of B.347.

B.346A Detail of B.346.

B.348 Sided bowl. 2.0"h x 7.5"w.
Backstamp: 27.0. $70-130.

B.349 Sided bowl. 2.25"h x 6.75"w.
Backstamp: 25.1. $80-120.

B.350 Sided bowl. 2.0"h x 9.63"w.
Backstamp: 43.056. $80-120.S

B.351 Sided bowl with four feet. 2.0"h x 5.75"w x 5.75"d. Backstamp: 25.1. $60-90.

B.351A Top view of B.351.

B.352 Sided bowl with four feet. 2.38"h x 9.38"w. Backstamp: 27.0. $60-90.

B.352A Top view of B.352.

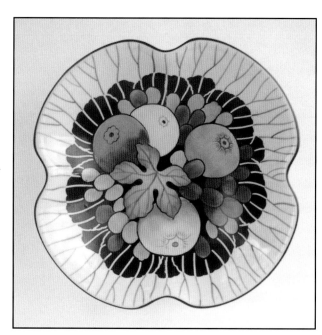

B.353 Sided bowl with three feet. 1.75"h x
5.5"w. Backstamp: 27.1. $70-110.

B.354 Sided bowls with three feet. 1.75"h
x 5.5"w. Backstamp: *Top row,* 27.0.
Bottom row, 27.1. Each, $20-40.

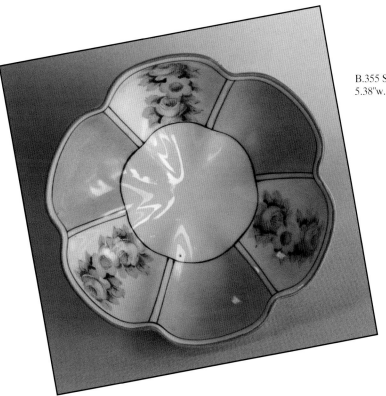

B.355 Sided bowl with three feet. 1.63"h x
5.38"w. Backstamp: 27.0. $20-40.

B.356 Gemini bowls. 6.13"h x 6.63"w x 5.0"d. Backstamp: 27.1. Each, $3500+

B.356A Top view of B.356.

B.359 Basket bowl. 5.5"h x 6.63"w x 4.5"d. Backstamp: 27.1. $60-100.

B.357 Bowl with loop handle and four feet. 6.0"h x 6.63"w. Backstamp: 27.1. $60-90.

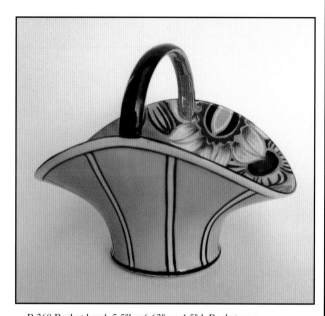

B.360 Basket bowl. 5.5"h x 6.63"w x 4.5"d. Backstamp: 27.1. $60-100.

B.358 Basket bowl. 5.5"h x 6.63""w x 4.5"d. Backstamp: 27.0. $80-130.

B.358A Back of B.358.

B.361 Basket bowl. 5.5"h x 6.63"w x 4.5"d. Backstamp: 27.1. $50-80.

B.363 Basket bowl. 5.5"h x 8.13"w x 7.13"d. Backstamp: 27.1. $50-80.

B.362 Basket bowl. 5.5"h x 6.63"w x 4.5"d. Backstamp: 27.1. $20-50.

B.363A Top view of B.363.

B.364 Basket bowl. 5.13"h x 6.75"w x 5.0"d. Backstamp: 27.1. $60-100.

B.365 Basket bowl. 4.0"h x 7.5"w. Backstamp: 16.0. $100-200.

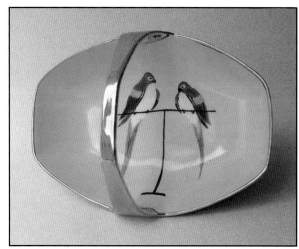

B.366 Basket bowl. 4.25"h x 5.5"w x 4.5"d. Backstamp: 27.1. $60-100.

B.367 Basket bowl. 3.75"h x 7.13"w x 4.75"d. Backstamp: 27.0. $50-90.

B.366A Top view of B.366.

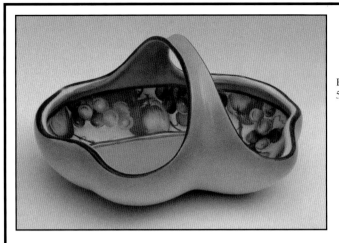

B.368 Basket bowl. 3.63"h x 7.38"w x 5.5"d. Backstamp: 27.1. $100-180.

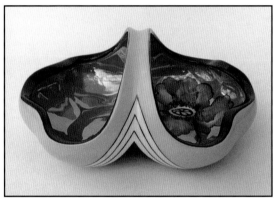

B.369 Basket bowl. 3.63"h x 7.38"w x 5.5"d. Backstamp: 27.1. $100-180.

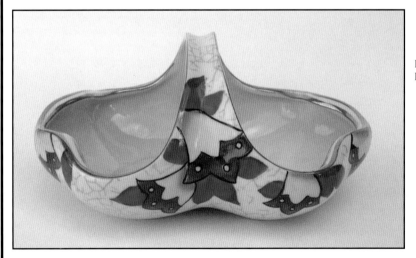

B.370 Basket bowl. 3.63"h x 7.38"w x 5. 5"d. Backstamp: 27.1. $100-180.

B.371 Basket bowl. 3.38"h x 7.0"w x 4.38"d. Backstamp: 27.3. $70-100.

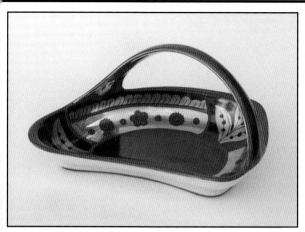

B.372 Basket bowl. 3.38"h x 7.0"w x
4.38"d. Backstamp: 27.1. $80-130.

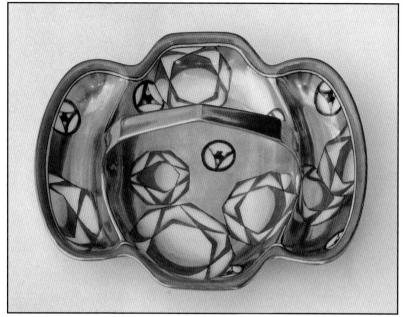

B.373 Basket bowl. 3.0"h x 7.88"w x 6.75"d.
Backstamp: 16.0. $900+

B.374 Basket bowl. 4.0"h x 11.75"w x
4.88"d. Backstamp: 27.1. $100-140.

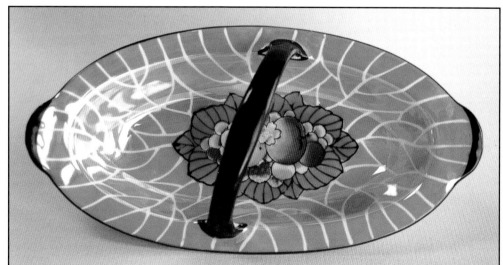

B.375 Basket bowl. 2.5"h x 8.75"w x
4.5"d. Backstamp: 19.0. $30-60.

B.376 Basket bowl. 3.63"h x 7.88"w x 5.0"d. Backstamp: 25.1 $80-130.

B.377 Basket bowl. 3.75"h x 6.75"w x 4.25"d. Backstamp: 27.1. $80-130.

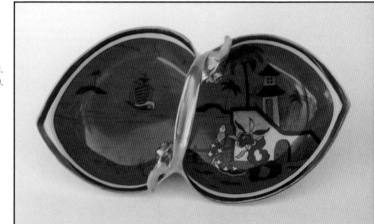

B.378 Basket bowl. 2.75"h x 7.5"w x 5.25"d. Backstamp: 27.1. $60-110.

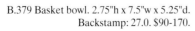

B.379 Basket bowl. 2.75"h x 7.5"w x 5.25"d. Backstamp: 27.0. $90-170.

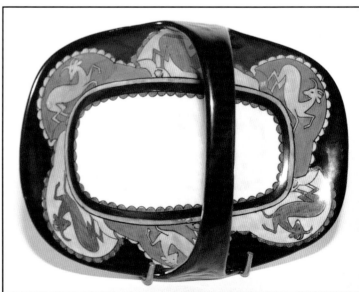

B.380 Basket bowl (handle is metal).
4.0"h x 4.5"w. Backstamp: 27.1. $120-180.

B.381 Bowl with figural handle. 4.88"h x 7.75"w
x 7.0"d. Backstamp: 27.0. $200-300.

B.382 Bowl with figural handle. 4.5"h x 7.0"w x 5.0"d. Backstamp, 27.1. $250-400.

B.382A Detail of B.382.

B.383 Bowl with figural handle. 3.5"h x 9.5"w x 9.0"d. Backstamp: 27.1. $400-500.

B.383A Alternate view of B.383.

B.384 Bowl with figural handle. 3.75"h x 6.5"w x 4.38"d. Backstamp: 27.0. $180-280.

B.385 Bowl with figural handle. 4.38"h x 4.0"w x 3.25"d. Backstamp: 27.1. $ 70-100.

B.386 Bowl with figural handle. 3.25"h x 7.75"w. Backstamp: 27.1. $80-120.

B.386A Top view of B.386.

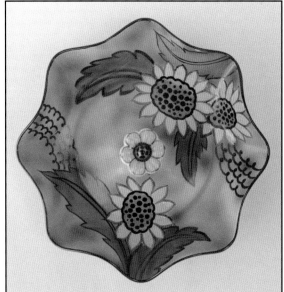

B.387 Bowl with figural handle. 3.25"h x 7.0"w x 6.0"d. Backstamp: 27.0. $80-120.

B.387A Detail of B.387.

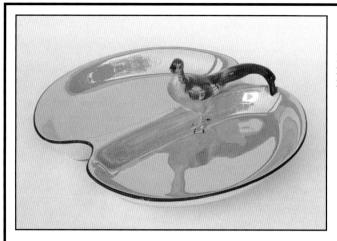

B.388 Bowl with figural handle.
2.75"h x 8.0"w x 7.25"d. Backstamp:
27.0. $90-170.

B.389 Bowl with figural handle. 2.25"h x 8.5"w.
Backstamp: 19.2. $100-200.

B.390 Bowl with figural handle. 2.25"h x
7.13"w x 5.75". Backstamp: 27.0. $90-140.

B.391. Bowl with figural handle. 1.75"h x
6.88"w x 6.13"d. Backstamp: 27.1. $40-90.

B.392 Bowl with figural handle. 2.75"h x 7.13"w x 4.6"d. Backstamp: 27.0. $30-50.

B.393 Bowl with one handle and three feet. 4.5"h x 9.75"w x 8.5"d. Backstamp: 19.1. $80-130.

B.393A Top view of B.393.

B.394 Bowl with one handle and three feet. 3.5"h x 8.0"w x 6.5"d. Backstamp: 271. $70-100.

B.395 Bowl with one handle and three feet. 2.88"h x 5.75"w x 4.38"d. Backstamp: 29.1. $80-120.

B395A Top view of B.395

B.396 Bowl with one handle. 2.0"h x 8.0"w x 7.5"d. Backstamp: 27.0. $20-50.

B.397 Bowl with one handle. 2.0"h x 8.0"w x 7.5"d. Backstamp: 25.1. $20-50.

B.398 Bowl with one handle. 1.38"h x 6.63"w x 6.25"d.
Backstamp: 27.1. $20-50.

B.400 Bowl with one handle. 2.25"h x 10.5"w x 9.0"d. Backstamp:
27.0. $50-90.

B.399 Bowl with one handle. 1.38"h x 6.0"w x 5.63"d.
Backstamp: 27.1. $30-70.

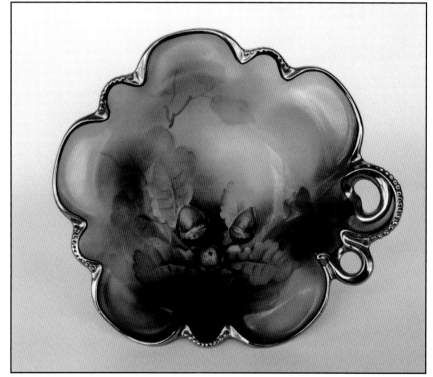

B.401 Bowl with one handle. 1.5"h x 8.13"w x 7.25"d. Backstamp: 27.0. $40-80.

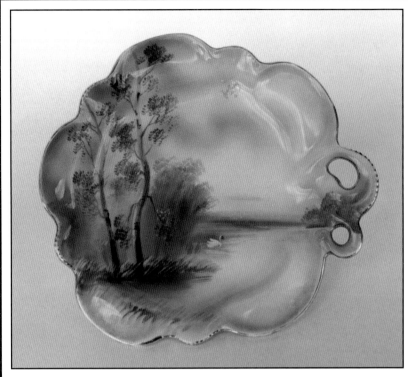

B.402 Bowl with one handle. 1.38"h x 7.25"w x 6.75"d. Backstamp: 27.0 $40-80.

B.403 Bowl with one handle. 1.75"h x 7.25"w x 6.75"d. Backstamp: 25.1. $70-120.

B.404 Bowl with one handle. 1.38"h x 7.25"w x 6.75"d. Backstamp: 27.0. $40-80.

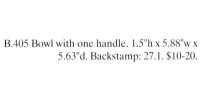

B.405 Bowl with one handle. 1.5"h x 5.88"w x 5.63"d. Backstamp: 27.1. $10-20.

B.406 Oval bowl with two handles. 2.25"h x 12.0"w x 7.0"d. Backstamp: 25.1. $20-60.

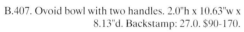

B.407. Ovoid bowl with two handles. 2.0"h x 10.63"w x 8.13"d. Backstamp: 27.0. $90-170.

B.408 Ovoid bowl with two handles. 1.88"h x 9.63"w x 6.5"d. Backstamp: 27.0. $80-160.

B.409 Ovoid bowl with two
handles. 2.0"h x 10.75"w x
8.13"d. Backstamp: 27.0.
$90-180.

B.409A Detail of B.409.

B.410 Oval bowl with two handles.
1.63"h x 10.5"w x 7.5"d. Backstamp:
19.1. $30-60.

B.411 Oval bowl with two handles.
1.63"h x 10.5"w x 7.5"d. Backstamp:
27.0. $20-40.

B.412 Oval bowl with two handles. 1.63"h x
10.5"w x 7.75"d. Backstamp: 19.1. $30-60.

B.413 Oval bowl with two handles.
2.25"h x 10.25"w x 6.88"d.
Backstamp: 29.1. $70-120.

B.413A Detail of B.413.

B.414 Ovoid bowl with two handles. 1.63"h
x 7.13"w x 5.5"d. Backstamp: 27.0. $10-20.

B.415 Round bowl with two handles, molded in relief. 3.25"h x 7.5"w x 6.25"d. Backstamp: 27.0. $100-170.

B.416 Round bowl with two handles. 3.0"h x 8.0"w x 5.5"d. Backstamp: 19.0. $80-140.

B.417 Round bowl with two handles. 3.63"h x 7.0"w x 6.0"d. Backstamp: 27.0. $100-200.

B.418 Round bowl with two handles. 1.5"h x 5.5"w x 4.5"d. Backstamp: 27.0. $20-30.

B.419 Round bowl with two handles. 1.5"h x 8.25"w x 6.25"d. Backstamp: 27.0. $80-130.

B.419A Detail of B.419.

B.420 Round bowl with two handles. 2.75"h x 8.75"w x 7.13"d. Backstamp: 27.0. $50-90.

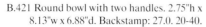

B.421 Round bowl with two handles. 2.75"h x 8.13"w x 6.88"d. Backstamp: 27.0. 20-40.

B.422 Round bowl with two handles. 2.75"h x 8.13"w x 6.88"d. Backstamp: 27.0. $40-80.

B.423 Round bowl with two handles. 2.5"h x 9.88"w x 9.0"d. Backstamp: 27.1. $40-80.

B.423A Detail of B.423.

B.424 Round bowl with two handles. 2.5"h x 9.88"w x 9.0"d. Backstamp: 27.0. $40-80.

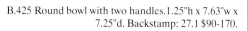
B.425 Round bowl with two handles.1.25"h x 7.63"w x 7.25"d. Backstamp: 27.1 $90-170.

B.426 Round bowl with two handles. 1.25"h x 7.63"w. x 7.25"d. Backstamp: 27.1.$90-170.

B.427 Round bowl with two handles. 2.5"h x 9.75"w. Backstamp: 27.0. $30-60.

B.428 Round bowl with two handles. 2.5"h x 9.75"w x 8.13"d. Backstamp: 27.0. $30-60.

B429 Round bowl with two handles. 2.0"h x 7.0"w x 6.0"d. Backstamp: 27.0. $20-40.

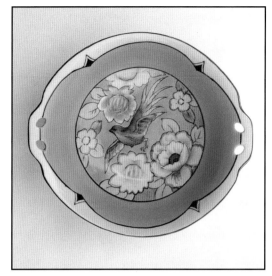

B.431 Round bowl with two handles. 2.0"h x 7.0"w x 6.0"d. Backstamp: 27.1. $30-50.

B.431A Detail of B.431.

B.430 Round bowl with two handles. 2.0"h x 7.0"w x 6.0"d. Backstamp: 19.2. $20-40.

B.432 Round bowl with two handles. 2.0"h x 7.0"w x 6.0"d. Backstamp: 27.0. $30-50.

B.433 Round bowl with two handles. 2.0"h x 7.0"w x 6.0"d. Backstamp: 27.1. $30-50.

B.434 Round bowl with two handles. 2.0"h x 9.38"w x 8.13"d. Backstamp: 19.0. $40-60.

B.432A Detail of B.432.

B.435 Round bowl with two handles. 2.0"h x 8.0"w x 7.0"d. Backstamp: 27.0. $30-50.

B.436 Round bowl with two handles. 2.0"h x 7.0"w x 6.0"d. Backstamp: 27.0. $30-50.

B.438 Round bowls with two handles. 1.5"h x 7.75"w x 6.75"d. Backstamp: All, 27.1. Each, $30-50.

B.437 Round bowl with two handles. 1.63"h x 8.5"w 7.5"d. Backstamp: 27.0. $30-50.

B.437A Detail of B.437.

B.439 Round bowls with two handles. 2.13"h x 8.0"w x 7.25"d. Backstamp: 27.0. Each, $20-40.

B.441 Round bowls with two handles. 2.0"h x 7.0"w x 6.0"d. Backstamp: 27.0. Each, $20-30.

B.440 Round bowls with two handles. 2.0"h x 7.0"w x 6.0"d. Backstamp: *Top,* 27.1. *Bottom,* 27.0. Each, $10-20.

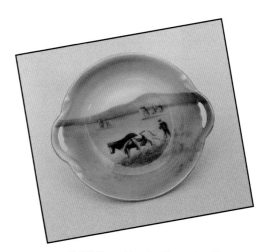

B.442 Round bowl with two handles. 1.5"h x 5.5"w x 4.88"d. Backstamp: 14.0 (39539). $10-20.

B.443 Round bowl with two handles. 1.5" x
5.5"w x 4.88"d. Backstamp: 14.0 (41885).
$40-80.

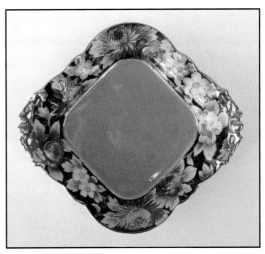

B.445 Four-sided bowl with two handles. 2.0" x 10.0"w
x 9.13"d. Backstamp: 27.0. $40-80.

B.444 Four-sided bowl with two handles. 2.0"h x 8.5"w x
6.75"d. Backstamp: 27.1. $140-190.

B.444A Detail of B.444.

B.446 Four-sided bowl with two handles. 2.25"h x 10.0"w x 8.5"d.
Backstamp: 19.2. $30-60.

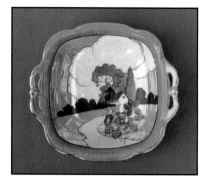

B.448 Four-sided bowl with two
handles. 2.0" h x 8.0"w x 7.25"d.
Backstamp: 27.1. $40-80.

B.447 Four-sided bowl with two handles. 2.25"h x 10.0"w x 8.5"d.
Backstamp: 27.0. $30-60.

B.448A Closeup of B.448.

B.449 Four-sided bowl with two handles.
2.38"h x 9.0"w x 6.63"d. Backstamp: 16.0.
$150-250.

B.451 Four-sided bowl with two handles. 3.0" h x 6.5"w.
Backstamp: 27.1. $40-90.

B.450 Four-sided bowl with two handles.
2.38"h x 9.0"w x 6.64"d. Backstamp: 27.1.
$150-250.

B.451A Interior detail of B.451.

B/452 Four-sided bowl with two handles. 1.63"h x 8.38"w x 7.25"d. Backstamp: 27.0. $50-100.

B.454 Four-sided bowl with two handles. 1.75"h x 6.5"w. Backstamp: 25.1. $40-80.

B.453 Four-sided bowl with two handles. 2.25"h x 8.13"w x 7.63"d. Backstamp: 27.1. $30-60.

B.455 Four-sided bowl with two handles. 1.88"h x 7.63"w x 7.63"d. Backstamp: 25.1. $30-60.

B.456 Four-sided bowl with two handles. 1.88"h x 7.63"w x 7.63"d. Backstamp: 27.0. $30-60.

B.458 Four-sided bowl with two handles. 2.75"h x 9.25"w x 8.0"d. Backstamp: 27.1. $50-90.

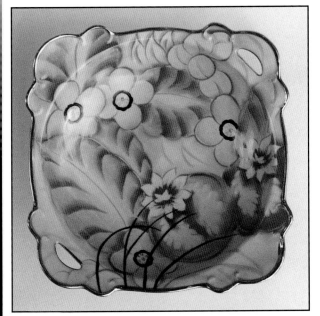

B.457 Four-sided bowl with two handles. 1.88"h x 7.38"w x 7.38"d. Backstamp: 27.1. $80-140.

B. 458A Detail of B. 458.

B.459 Four-sided bowl with two handles. 2.75"h x 9.25"w x 8.0"d. Backstamp: 19.1. $40-80.

B.462 Four-sided bowl with two handles. 2.38"h x 8.25"w x 6.88"d. Backstamp: 27.0. $20-40.

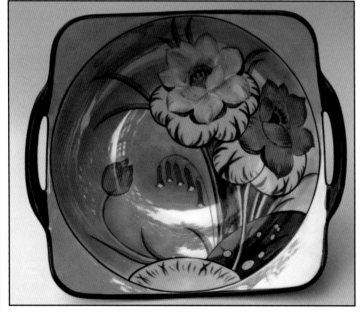

B.460 Four-sided bowl with two handles. 2.75" h x 9.25"w. Backstamp: 27.0. $40-80.

B.462A Detail of B.462.

B.461 Four-sided bowl with two handles. 2.0"h x 7.0"w x 6.0"d. Backstamp: 27.1. $30-50.

B.463 Four-sided bowl with two handles. 2.0"h x 6.63"w x 5.5"d. Backstamp: 27.1. $40-70.

B.465 Four-sided bowls with two handles. 1.63"h x 5.63"w x 4.63"d. Backstamp: *Top*, 27.1. *Bottom*, 25.1. Each, $10-20.

B.464 Four-sided bowl with two handles. 2.0"h x 6.63"w x 5.5"d. Backstamp: 27.1. $20-40.

B.466 Four sided bowl with two handles. 3.5"h x 6.5"w x 4.25"d. Backstamp: 27.1. $80-150.

B.466A Top view of B.466.

B.467 Four-sided bowl with two handles. 1.0"h x 6.0"w. Backstamp: 27.0. $10-20.

B.468 Six-sided bowl with two handles. 3.5"h x 9.38"w x 8.5"d. Backstamp: 27.0. $200-300.

B.468A Detail of B.468.

B.469 Six-sided bowl with two handles. 3.5"h x 9.38"w x 8.5"d. Backstamp: 27.0. $40-80.

B.470 Six-sided bowl with two handles. 2.0"h x 7.75"w x 7. 5"d. Backstamp: 27.1. $100-200.

B.471 Six-sided bowl with two handles. 2.0"h x 7.75"w x 7.5"d.. Backstamp: 29.1. $80-160.

B.472 Six-sided bowl with two handles. 2.0"h x 7.75"w x 7.5"d. Backstamp: 27.1. $80-160.

B.474 Six-sided bowl with two handles. 2.25"h x 8.0"w x 8.0"d. Backstamp: 25.1. $40-80.

B.473 Six-sided bowl with two handles. 2.25"h x 8.0"w x 8.0"d. Backstamp: 25.1. $100-200.

B.475 Eight-sided bowl with two handles. 3.88 "h x 10.75"w x 8.5"d. Backstamp: 27.0. $80-160.

B.476 Eight-sided bowl with two handles. 3.5"h x 9.88"w. Backstamp: 27.0. $80-160.

B.478 Eight-sided bowl with two handles. 2.5"h x 9.5"w x 8.13"d. Backstamp: 25.1. $100-170.

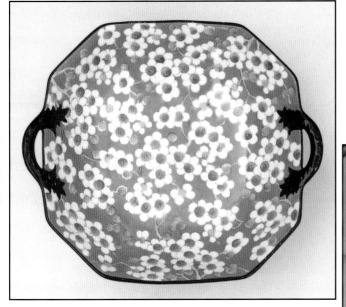

B.477 Eight-sided bowl with two handles. 2.13"h x 9.25"w x 8.5"d. Backstamp: 27.0. $60-100.

B.478A Detail of B.478.

B.479 Eight-sided bowl with two handles. 2.75"h x
11.0"w x 10.13"d. Backstamp: 27.0. $40-80.

B.481 Eight-sided bowl with two
handles. 2.25"h x 8.75"x.
Backstamp: 27.1. $100-150.

B.482 Eight-sided bowl with two
handles. 2.0"h x 9.0"w. Backstamp:
21.0. $30-40.

B.480 Eight-sided bowl with two handles. 1.63"h x
6.13"w x 4.5"d. Backstamp: 27.0. $30-60.

B.483 Eight-sided bowl with two
handles. 2.0"h x 9.88"w x 9.13"d.
Backstamp: 16.0. $100-200.

B.484 Eight-sided bowl
with two handles. 2.0"h x
9.88"w x 9.13"d. Backstamp:
27.0. $120-180.

B.485 Eight-sided bowl with
two handles. 2.0"h x 9.88"w
x 9.13"d. Backstamp: 27.1.
$100-160.

B.484A Detail of another
example of B.484. Look
carefully and you will see
distinct differences in the way
the flowers were (hand)
painted.

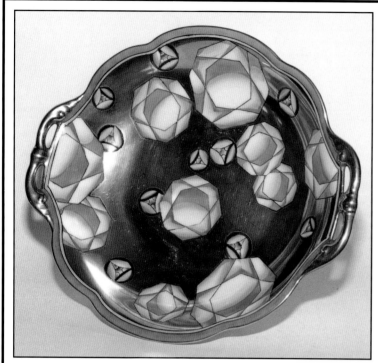

B.486 Eight-sided bowl with two handles. 2.0"h x 9.88"w x 9.13"d. Backstamp: 16.0. $900+

B.488 Eight-sided bowl with two handles. 1.75"h x 7.75"w x 6.5"d. Backstamp: 27.0. $40-80.

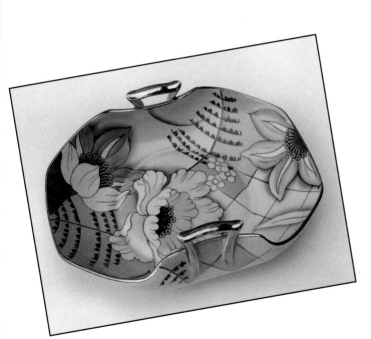

B.487 Eight-sided bowl with two handles. 3.0"h x 8.38"w x 5.38"d. Backstamp: 27.1. $80-130.

B.489 Eight-sided bowl with two handles. 2.13"h x 8.0"w x 5.75"d. Backstamp: 27.1. $30-40.

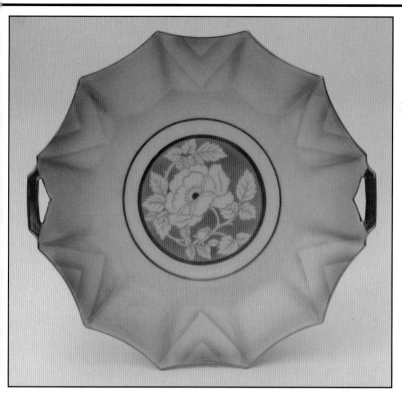

B.490 Twelve-sided bowl with two handles. 1.5"h x 10.0"w x 9.5"d. Backstamp: 25.1. $150-250.

B.493 Bowl with two handles and feet. 3.5"h x 7.88"w. Backstamp: 19.1. $60-100.

B.491 Bowl with two handles and feet. 3.25" x 6.5"w. Backstamp: 27.1. $30-50.

B.492 Bowl with two handles and feet. 5.0"h x 12.63"w x 8.25"d. Backstamp: 27.0. $40-60.

B.493A Top view of B.493.

B.494 Bowl with three handles. 2.0"h x 8.38"w. Backstamp: 27.0. $60-90.

B.495 Bowl with three handles. 1.38"h x 7.25"w. Backstamp: 27.1. $40-60.

B.496 Bowl with three handles. 1.38"h x 7.25"w. Backstamp: 27.1. $20-30.

B.497 Bowl with three handles. 1.38"h
x 7.25"w. Backstamp: 27.1. $40-80.

B.499 Bowl with three handles. 1.75"h x 6.25"w. Backstamp:
27.0. $20-30.

B.498 Bowl with three handles. 1.13"h x 6.0"w. Backstamp: 27.1.
$20-40.

B.500 Bowl with three handles. 1.63"h x
7.13"w. Backstamp: 27.0. $30-60.

B.501 Bowl with three handles. 1.5"h x 6.25"w. Backstamp: 27.1. $30-50.

B.504 Bowl with four handles. 2.7"h x 8.5"w x 8.5"d. Backstamp: 27.1. $40-80.

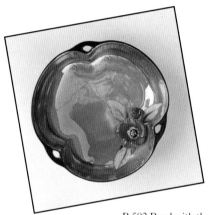

B.502 Bowl with three handles. 1.5"h x 6.25"w. Backstamp: 27.1. $30-50.

B.503 Bowl with four handles. 1.25"h x 5.38"w. Backstamp: 16.4. $90-140.

B.505 Bowl with four handles. 2.7"h x 8.5"w x 8.5"d. Backstamp: 27.1. $40-80.

B.506 Bowl with four handles. 2.5"h x 8.5"w x 8.5"d. Backstamp: 27.1. $50-100.

B.507 Bowl with four handles. 1.88"h x 8.13"w x 8.13"d. Backstamp: 27.1. $40-80.

B.508 Bowl with four handles. 1.75"h x 7.25"dia. Backstamp: 27.0. $20-30.

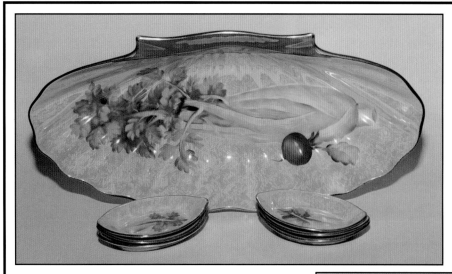

B.509 Celery or relish set. Bowl, 1.5"h x 13.0"w x 6.0"d. Individual salts, .63"h x 3.75"w x 2.25"d. Backstamp: 27.1. Set, as shown, $120-180.

B.510 Celery or relish set. Bowl, 2.5"h x 12.75"w x 5.38"d. Individual salts, .63"h x 3.75"w x 2.25"d. Backstamp: 27.0. Set, as shown, $100-150.

B.511 Celery or relish bowl. 2.75"h x 12.75"w x 5.38"d. Backstamp: 27.1. $50-80.

B.511A Detail of B.511.

B.512 Celery or relish set. 2.0"h x 11.88"w x 5.5"d. Backstamp: 27.0. Set, as shown, $50-80.

B.513 Celery or relish bowl. 1.88"h x 12.5"w x 5.63"d. Backstamp: 27.1. $30-60.

B.514 Celery or relish bowl. 2.5"h x 12.38"w x 5.5"d. Backstamp: 27.0. $40-80.

B.515 Celery or relish bowl. 1.63"h x 11.5"w x 5.63"d. Backstamp: 27.1. $20-40.

B.516 Celery or relish bowl. 1.5"h x 11.25"w x 5.38"d. Backstamp: 29.1 (39560). $20-40.

B.517 Relish bowl. 1.63"h x 8.75"w x 4.5"d. Backstamp: 27.1. $10-20.

B.518 Relish bowl. 2.0"h x 10.0"w x 5.75"d. Backstamp: 27.1. $40-80.

B.519 Relish bowl. 2.0"h x 8.38"w x 4.75"d. Backstamp: 54.0. $20-40.

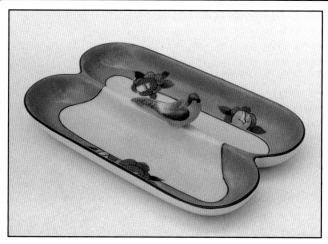

B.520 Relish bowl. 1.75"h x 6.5"w x 4.0"d. Backstamp: 27.0. $40-60.

B.521 Relish bowl. 1.25"h x 6.5"w x 4.13"d. Backstamp: 19.0. $40-80.

B.523 Centerpiece bowl. 7.0"h x 12.0"w x 9.25"d. Backstamp: none on either piece. With backstamp, $400+

B.522 Relish bowl. 3.0"h x 10.38"w x 7.88"d. Backstamp: 19.1. $20-40.

B.523A Interior detail of B.523.

B.524 Centerpiece bowl. 3.25"h x 12.13"w. Backstamp: 25.1. $100-150.

B.524A The backstamped base for the centerpiece bowl in B.524. 1.25"h x 5.25"dia.

B.524B The non-backstamped top piece of the centerpiece bowl in B.524. 2.0"h x 12.13"w.

B.525 Compote with two handles. 5.25"h x 10.38"w x 8.25"d. Backstamp: 27.1. $160-220.

B.525A Top view of B.525.

B.526 Compote with two handles. 3.38"h x 11.5"w x 9.5"d. Backstamp: 19.1. $60-100.

B.526A Detail of B.526.

B.527 Compote with two handles.
3.38"h x 11.5"w x 9.5"d. Backstamp:
19.0. $50-90.

B.529 Compote with two handles. 2.75"h x 9.5"w x 7.88"d. Backstamp:
27.0. $40-60.

B.528 Compote with two handles.
2.75"h x 9.88"w x 8.0"d. Backstamp:
27.1. $60-100.

B.528A Detail of B.528.

B.530 Compote with two handles.
2.63"h x 8.25"w x 7.0"d. Backstamp:
27.0. $50-90.

B.531 Compote with two handles. 2.63"h x
8.63"w x 7.0"d. Backstamp: 27.1. $40-80.

B.532 Compote with two handles. 2.63"h x 8.25"w x 7.0"d.
Backstamp: 27.0. $20-40.

B.530A Detail of another example of B.530. Look carefully and you will see
distinct differences in the way the flowers were (hand) painted.

B.533 Compote with two handles. 2.13"h x 7.0"w
x 5.75"d. Backstamp: 27.1. $30-60.

B.534A Top view of B.534.

B.534 Compote. 6.63"h x 9.13"w.
Backstamp: 19.0. $140-200.

B.535 Compote. 5.0"h x 7.0"w.
Backstamp: 27.0. $50-100.

B.536 Compote. 5.0"h x 7.0"dia. Backstamp: 27.0. $50-100.

B.537A Top view of B.537.

B.537 Compote. 5.0"h x 7.0"w. Backstamp: 27.0. $80-140.

B.538 Compote. 2.75"h x 6.5"dia.
Backstamp: 27.1. $300+

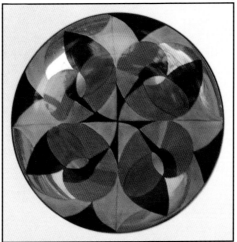

B.538A Top view of B. 538.

B.539 Compote. 2.63"h x 6.63"w. Backstamp: 27.0.
$300-400.

B.539A Detail of B.539.

B.540 Compote. 2.75"h x 6.5"w. Backstamp: 29.1.
$150-250.

B.540A Detail of B.540.

B.541 Compotes. 2.88"h x 6.5"w. Backstamp: 25.1.
Each, $100-150.

B.541A Detail of compote on
left in B.541.

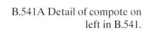

B.541B Detail of compote on
right in B.541.

B.542 Covered bowl. 7.0"h x 7.0"d. Backstamp: 27.1. $50-100.

B.543 Covered bowl. 5.0"h x 6.75"w. Backstamp: 27.0. $250-350.

B.543A Detail of B.543.

B.544 Covered bowl. 5.0"h x 6.75"w. Backstamp: 27.0.
$250-350.

B.545 Covered bowl. 5.0"h x 6.75"w. Backstamp:
27.0. $250-350.

B.544A Detail of B.544.

B.546 Covered bowl with two handles. 4.5"h x
8.13"w x 6.25"d. Backstamp: 16.0. $150-250.

B.547 Covered bowl. 6.0"h x 5.75"d. Backstamp: 27.1.
$40-80.

B.548 Covered bowl with underplate. 4.75"h x 5.5"w x 4.75"d. Backstamp: 27.0. $40-60.

B.550 Covered bowl. 4.5"h x 5.13"w. 27.1. $150-200.

B.549 Covered bowl. 4.5"h x 4.5"w. Backstamp: 25.1. $70-120.

B.551 Nut bowl, molded in relief. 3.13"h x 8.5"w. Backstamp: 27.0. $150-250.

B.551A Top view of B.551.

B.552 Nut bowl set, molded in relief.
Master bowl, 3.0"h x 7.5"w x 6.63"d.
Individual bowls, 1.0"h x 3.0"w x 1.63"d.
Backstamp: 27.0. Set, with 6 individual
bowls, $130-200.

B.553 Nut bowl, molded in relief. 2.38"h x
6.0"w x 6.0"d. Backstamp: 27.0. $100-200.

B.553A Top view of another
example of B.553.

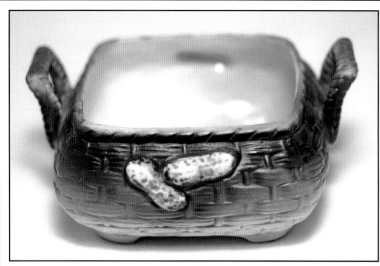

B.554 Nut bowl. 2.5"h x 5.0"w.
Backstamp: 27.0. $20-30.

B.555 Punch bowl set. Master bowl,
12.25"h x 13.25"w. Cups, 2.75"h x 3.5"w.
Backstamp: 27.0. $1500+

B.556 Salad bowl with serving utensils and individual
plates. Bowl, 4.0"h x 8.5"w; fork and spoon, 8.0" long
x 1.63"w; individual plates, 7.75"w. Backstamp: 27.1.
Set, as shown, $150-250.

B.557 Salad bowl with serving utensils. 4.5"h x 10.25"w x 8.0"d. Backstamp: 29.1. $200-300.

B.557A Top view of B.557.

B.558 Salad bowl with utensils. Bowl, 4.5"h x 10.25"w x 8.0"d. Fork and spoon, 7.25" long x 1.88"w. Backstamp: 27.1. $200-300.

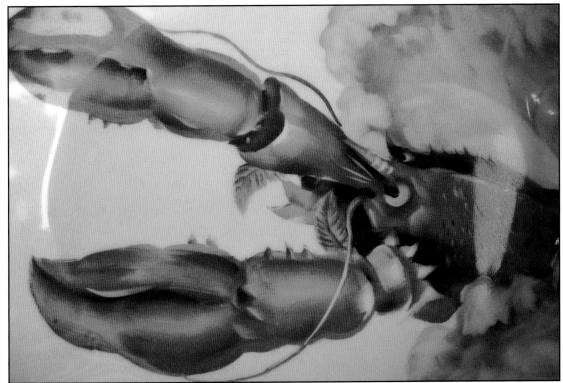

B.558A Interior detail of B.558

B.559 Seafood salad bowl with utensils. Overall, 4.5"h x 10.25"w. Backstamp: 54.0. $200-300.

B.561 Covered box 7.0"h x 5.0"w x 4.0"d. Backstamp: 29.1. $5000+

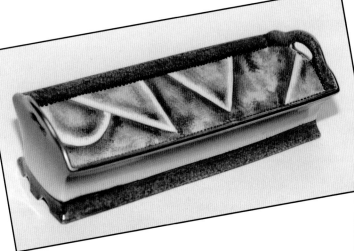

B.560 Cracker bowl. 2.5"h x 8.5"w x 3.5"d. Backstamp: 27.1. $150-250.

B.562 Covered box. 6.5"h x 5.13"h x 2.75"h Backstamp. 27.1. $1200+

B.563 Covered box. 5.5"h x 3.63. Backstamp: 27.0.
$3000+

B.564 Covered box. 4.25"h x 6.25"w.
Backstamp: 27.0. $150-200.

B.563A Detail of B.563.

B.565 Covered Box. 4.25"h x 6.25"w. Backstamp: 27.0. $180-250.

B.566 Covered box. 3.88"h x 6.0"w x 6.0"d. Backstamp: 19.1. $150-200.

B.566A Top view of B.566.

B.567 Covered box. 4.0"h x 6.0"w x 4.5"d. Backstamp: 25.1. $80-150.

Chapter C
Condiment Sets and Related Items

The items shown in the photos of this chapter have this in common: they all were intended, or are thought by most collectors and dealers to have been intended, for the storing and/or serving of condiments—i.e., things one normally eats *with* food, not *as* food. Specifically, one will find:

Berry sets (pp. 143-147)
Butter dishes (pp. 147-148)
Condiment sets (pp. 148-153)
   figural condiment sets or sets with figural elements (pp. 148-149)
   other non-figural condiment sets (pp. 150-153)
Honey pots (pp. 153-154)
Jam jars and sets (pp. 154-156)
Mayonnaise and sauce sets (pp. 156-157)
Mustard pots (p. 158)
Oil and vinegar set (p. 158)
Salt and pepper sets (pp. 158-165)
   figural salt and pepper sets (pp. 158-161)
   other non-figural salt and pepper sets (pp. 162-165)
Salt sets (pp. 165-166)

Condiment sets seem to be the Rodney Dangerfield of Noritake collectibles—they never quite get the respect they deserve. This is so even though some of the most amazing items in each of my previous books were shown in the chapter devoted to such items. In fact, in my second book, one of the top pieces in the entire volume, a jam set, was shown in Chapter C and held center stage all by itself on the cover. The trend continues in this third volume. Of the many excellent items shown throughout, several of the most outstanding are in this Chapter C. Indeed, as with the last volume, one of the most compelling of these exceptional items is a jam set (C.200). But there are at least a dozen other outstanding items; indeed, *all* the others shown are interesting and

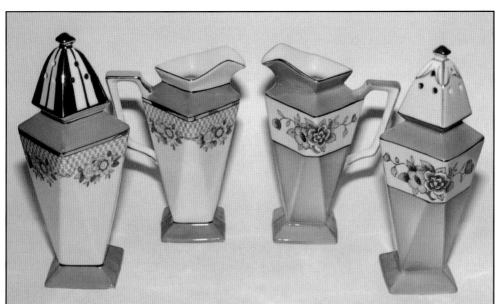

C.168 Berry sets. Sugar, 7.0"h x 3.25"w. Creamer, 5.75"h x 4.38"w. Backstamp: Green sugar, MIJ.1; Others, 27.1. Each set, $100-150.

worthy of attention for one reason or another (and often for several of them).

For various reasons, condiment items can be one of the more difficult areas of Noritake collecting. One of the principal reasons is that these items often have (or *had*, and that is the point) *many* rather small and fragile parts. Because small and fragile parts would have been the easiest to lose or break during the 75 or so years these sets have existed, it is difficult to find *complete* condiment sets. Consequently, collectors and dealers generally pay a lot of attention to the completeness of condiment sets. Although the values given for the items shown in this chapter reflect this, it is not easily seen in the figures by themselves. I have attempted to highlight the issue, therefore, by repeatedly inserting phrases like "set as shown" or "complete set" prior to the values estimate. It is almost impossible to put a dollar figure on the impact of a missing spoon or lid or toothpick holder but, if forced to give one (if nothing else as a starting point for discussion of the matter), I would say it is at least 40%. And in some instances, it could be much more. For example, consider the very last item shown in this chapter (C.247). For the sake of discussion, let's suppose that $130-190 seems to you like a reasonable estimate of the value of a *complete* set like the one shown in that photo. Now, suppose further that just one of the spoons is missing and that you want to sell the set. What do you think the fair asking price is for a set with only 5 of 6 tiny spoons? Given my "40% rule-of-thumb," the answer (in round numbers) would be about $80-120. Does this seem reasonable? Frankly, I think it may well be an amount that most sellers would not expect to receive very soon. For some other kinds of items, the impact of missing parts may be even greater. A fine example is the oil and vinegar set in C.215. Items like these are often seen without the porcelain stoppers. What is the impact of these missing pieces on value? Because it would be almost impossible to find these items, I think the impact is far more than 40%. Again, it is quite difficult to put a number on it, or at least a number that most people would accept, because opinions on this vary considerably. For the sake of discussion, though, I would say the impact of this sort of missing part is *at least* 60%. Thus, the value of the oil and vinegar without the stoppers would drop from the suggested $100-150 to around $40-60.

Some collectors and dealers will buy incomplete sets with the hope that they will find the missing pieces down the road. As just noted, the likelihood of succeeding will vary with the kind of part this is missing. Although this strategy is almost certainly counter-factual, the option remains viable in part because virtually every collector has had or has heard of a success story (I myself reported one in the introduction to Chapter C in my second Noritake book). Moreover, with the advent of Internet auctions, this approach becomes even more plausible because collectors know they probably will see more items of interest in a month than they would have previously in a year. Also, it can be very exciting when one finds a missing piece—a fact made all the more memorable because the piece often will not be expensive. Even so, I continue to think that buying parts is not something that one ought to do routinely or casually.

Sometimes it is not obvious that pieces are missing from certain sets. The butter tub shown in C.177 is an example. This 4-piece set is complete; in my first book, however, a similar butter tub was shown (C.14) without the underplate. I simply did not realize at the time that such a plate was standard for that sort of thing. Or, consider two of the jam sets shown in this chapter,

C.169 Berry set. Sugar, 6.75"h x 3.0"w. Creamer, 5.75"h x 4.0"w. Backstamp: 27.1. Set, $130-170.

C.202 and C.203. It can be argued, plausibly, that jam sets would have an underplate in order to catch any jam that might drip from the spoon or the lip of the bowl during use. And in fact, virtually every jam set shown in every book on Noritake collectibles that I know of has an underplate—*except* for the set with the large apple finial on the lid, as is found on the set in C.203. What are we to make of this? Are we to conclude that this sort of set had an underplate but that a truly complete set has not turned up? Or is it, perhaps, not a jam set? I do not know the answer but, *for now*, will accept the general view of dealers and collectors: this particular item is a jam set that, almost uniquely (for Noritake fancyware from the 1921-1931 era, at least), did not have an underplate.

From these more technical matters, let us consider some of the remarkable pieces shown in this chapter. Although it seems unfair to skip over the berry sets and butter dishes (because each is worthy of a comment), I begin with the condiment set shown in C.178. This set, with its many carefully fitted parts, is a marvel of design and craftsmanship. The next set (C.179) is very rare, especially when complete with a small porcelain mustard spoon. It may be noted, also, that we can be confident that the tray shown is the correct one because the tray color matches the trim at the base of the little buildings. Figural Noritake items, as I note in several other places in this book, are in much greater demand, other things equal, than non-figural Noritake items. As a result, we can predict that many collectors will be strongly attracted to the condiment sets shown in C.181-C.182. Even so, some exceptionally strong non-figural sets are shown in this chapter. The Deco cottage motif on the set shown in C.183 is superb and makes this set very desirable. The elements of the decoration on the sets shown in C.187 and C.195 are quite simple but their effect, given the shape of the items in these sets, is quite powerful.

There are other ways for seemingly simple sets to be quite extraordinary. A great case in point is the condiment set shown in C.184. What makes it unusual is not the stacking open salt and pepper shaker shown on the right in the photo. Although uncommon, such salt and pepper sets are not rare. Indeed, they can be found in many shapes and sizes. What makes this condiment set unusual is that it comes with a mustard pot (indeed, it is the mustard pot that makes it a condiment set). This pot almost certainly goes with the other items because all the pieces have the same (rather uncommon) blue trim. Also, the finial on the mustard seems like the flower on the salt in bud form. Because of this set, we now must wonder whether the small trays with pepper shaker and a matching (unstacked) open salt and are, in fact, incomplete versions of a set like the one shown in C.184. Two other examples are the honey pots (or honey houses as they also are called) shown in C.198. They may not look like it on first glance, but they are smaller than the comparably shaped ones in C.197. In my experience, the smaller ones are far less common than what I now think of as the "standard" sized items in C.197 and the suggested values reflect this.

The green basket weave jam set shown in C.200 is a marvelous example of Noritake artistic and technical competence. It also is, at the moment, a very rare set. This item, like so many others in this book, is far more impressive when seen in person. In terms of style or general character, this set seems to have been

C.170 Berry set. Sugar, 7.0"h x 3.0"w. Creamer, 6.25"h x 3.5"w. Backstamp: 27.1. Set, $100-150.

inspired by Majolica ware (the same may be said regarding the nut bowl shown in B.553). Another excellent molded set is shown in C.201—one made all the more elegant by the vertical stripes on the jar. It is nice that alphabetical considerations lead to mayonnaise (or sauce) sets being placed next in the chapter because they are broadly similar to jam sets in terms of both basic shape and the items in these sets. All of the sets shown are quite extraordinary. The set shown in C.209 is both rare and particularly elegant for Noritake fancyware items from the 1921-1931 era. The next set, which utilizes the same blanks, has an unusual motif. Perhaps the rarest and most compelling set from a design standpoint in the group is shown in C.211. Notice that the underplate has the same basic shape as the bowl; indeed, it almost looks like a flattened bowl. Notice also that the motif on the spoon melds perfectly with the motif on the inside of the bowl. The spoon was placed in the way you see it to show this but what is significant, I think, is that this was both quite an obvious way to display it and the spoon rested in that spot without having to do anything special to achieve the effect. The backstamp on this item appears to have been registered in about 1940. The sets in C.212 are of interest because a set just like these, except with a yellow basket-weave exterior, was shown in C.129 of my second Noritake book. It would appear these three items constitute a nice example of a "conceptual set"—a group of items, usually three but sometimes two or four (or perhaps more), that are related in some artistic or aesthetic way. In this instance, they are related by the use of three very basic and common colors in the Noritake fancyware palette of this period: blue, green and yellow (or tan). The set in C.213 is a fairly common basic shape, but the colors on it are unusual in my experience. Although quite attractive, the combination is also a bit unconventional. This unconventional quality, however, is precisely the feature that will appeal to many collectors of Noritake fancyware.

C.171 Berry set. Sugar, 7.0"h x 3.0"w. Creamer, 6.25"h x 3.5"w. Backstamp: 27.1. Set, $90-140.

Of the many kinds of condiment items, salt and pepper sets may seem to be the most prosaic and, consequently, ignorable. As with so many such assumptions, however, those who would accept it would be making a big mistake. Some of the most desirable items in the chapter are in this group. Figural salt and pepper sets are in great demand. Quite a few terrific and rather varied figural salt and pepper sets are shown in this chapter (see C.216-C.229). Although it is tempting to say something about them all, I will restrict myself to two sets shown in C.216 and C.217 and two others in C.235 and C.236. Regarding the first two sets, there are two facts that help establish that each pair is indeed a set. First, although the costumes of the pair in C.216 are not exactly the same, they clearly are related and comparable. Second, in neither pair are the sizes of the pouring holes the same—a fact of significance because, in true salt and pepper sets, one item will have smaller holes than the other (for salt and pepper, respectively). The simple fact that these sets, and particularly the first one, are very rare would warrant comment. What is most noteworthy, however, is that (so far as we know) the shaker on the right in C.216 is one of the very few, if not only, Noritake figural items that has a two-dimensional counterpart. A nearly identical version of the motif of the lady figural in C.216 ("nearly" because there are noticeable color differences) appears on a Noritake ashtray and on a cigarette box (see A.176 and A.183 in Chapter A of this book). Although the other two sets are quite attractive, in their different and individual ways, what should be noted are the backstamps on these items. Both of the items shown in C.235 have two backstamps (J.1 and MIJ.1). It is the only example of this particular double backstamp that I know of at this point. The backstamp on the items in C.236 shows that, originally, these were part of a larger set with backstamp 29.1 (see Chapter 3 for details).

Finally, we come to various salt sets. Immediately, it must be acknowl-

C.172 Berry sets. Sugar, 6.5"h x 2.63"w. Creamer, 5.63"h x 3.38"w. Backstamp: Blue sugar, MIJ.1, others, 27.1. Each set, $120-150.

edged that at least some of these items may not have been intended, originally, as salt sets (e.g., C.243 and C.244). It is possible, and sometimes claimed, that these were for mints or nuts. They have been placed in this chapter, instead of Chapter B (in the special purpose bowls section) because, in my experience anyway, most collectors and dealers refer to these items as salt sets. These sets illustrate a point made at the outset of this chapter—namely, that complete sets are difficult to find. They illustrate another point as well. Sets like these often do not bring prices that are comparable to what the items will bring when sold separately. Thus, one frequently will see small baskets like those shown in C.243 and C.244 being sold for $25 each. With 6 in a complete set, this would translate to a value for the set of $150 plus whatever would be reasonable for the (so-called) "master salt." If that item is pegged at a minimum of $50, this would put the value for the set at around $200—a "reasonable" figure given the logic just outlined, but not a realistic one in today's market. The values given for these items reflect this view. It is, by the way, a view that applies to other sets—notably coffee, snack and tea sets (see Chapter T).

Although my words here will not, alone, accomplish what I wish—namely, to bring greater or more appropriate respect to condiment items, I am confident the photos in this chapter will. Therefore, I invite you to savor them, as they richly deserve to be!

C.173 Berry set. Sugar, 6.5"h x 2.63"w. Creamer, 5.63"h x 3.38"w. Backstamp: 27.0. Set, $140-170.

C.175 Butter dish. 3.0"h x 6.5"w. Backstamp: 27.1. $90-110.

C.174 Berry set. Sugar, 6.5"h x 2.63"w. Creamer, 5.63"h x 3.38"w. Backstamp: 29.1. Set, $100-130.

C.176 Butter dish. 3.25"h x 6.5"w.
Backstamp: 27.0. $80-100.

C.177 Butter dish. Plate, 5.38"dia. Tub, 3.5"h x 5.0"w.
Inside of butter tray, 3.13"dia. Backstamp: Tub only,
27.0. Set, complete, $30-60.

C.178 Condiment set. Overall, 4.5"h x 4.13"w x
4.13"d. Salt (square tower), 1.63"h, pepper (round
tower), 2.0"h. Backstamp: C20.1. $100-170.

C.179 Condiment set. Tray, .5"h x 6.88"w x
2.88"d. Large building, 2.63"h x 2.0" w x 2.0"d.
Medium building, 2.25"h x 1.5"w x 1.38"d. Small
building, 1.25"h x 1.38"w x 1.0"d. Backstamp on
large building: 27.1; backstamp on small
buildings, J.1; tray has no backstamp. Complete
6 piece set, $320-420.

C.180 Condiment set. 5.0"h x 6.88"w x 2.88"d. Backstamp: 27.1. $280-400.

C.182 Condiment set. Tray, .75"h x 4.88"w x 3.38"d. Large duck, 1.88"h x 3.0"w x 1.5"d. Small ducks, 1.25"h x 1.88"h. x 1.13"d. Backstamp: 27.0. Complete set, $190-320.

C.181 Condiment set. Tray, .88"h x 6.5"w x 2.25"d. Mustard, 2.38"h x 1.75"w. Salt and pepper, 1.38"h x 2.0"w. Backstamp: Backstamp on tray: C22.0 (30040); on salt and pepper: J.0; on mustard, none. Set, as shown, $50-100.

C.181A Alternate view of C.181.

C.183 Condiment set. Tray, 1.25"h x 7.5"w x 3.0"d. Mustard, 3.0"h x 2.75"w. Salt and pepper, 3.0"h x 1.5"w. Backstamp: 27.1. Complete set, $300-400.

C.185 Condiment set. 3.0"h x 5.5"w x 4.75"d. Backstamp: 27.1. Complete set, $100-150.

C.184 Condiment set. Tray, 4.38"w x 2.75"d. Mustard, 2.13"h. Open salt and pepper, stacked, 2.63"h. Backstamp on tray: 27.0; on other items, MIJ.0. Complete set, as shown, $60-90.

C.186 Condiment set. Tray, 5.0"w x 3.88" d. Mustard, 2.63"h. Salt and pepper, 2.5"h. Toothpick holder, 1.75"h. Backstamp: C21.0. $20-40.

C.187 Condiment set. 3.38"h x 7.38"w. Backstamp: 16.0. Complete set, $120-190.

C.188 Condiment set. Tray, 1.5"h x 6.63"w x 2.25"d. Mustard, 2.25"h. Salt and pepper, 2.13"h. Backstamp on tray and mustard: C21.5; on salt and pepper, J.5. Complete set, $30-50.

C.189 Condiment set. Tray, 1.5"h x 6.88"w x 2.13"d. Mustard, 3.0"h. Salt and pepper, 2.5"h. Backstamp on tray and mustard: C21.0; on salt and pepper, MIJ.0. Complete set, $40-60.

C.190 Condiment set. Tray, 1.5"h x 6.88"w x 2.13"d. Mustard, 3.0"h. Salt and pepper, 2.5"h. Backstamp on tray and mustard, C23.1; on salt and pepper, MIJ.1. Complete set, $40-60.

C.191 Condiment set. Mustard, 3.0"h x 2.5"w x 1.63"d. Salt and pepper, 2. 5"h x 1.5"w. Toothpick holder, 1.75"h x 1.25 "w. Tray, 3.5" h x 4.38"w. Backstamp: 27.0. Complete set, $110-180.

C.193 Condiment set. Overall, 3.5"h x 5.5"w x 5.13"d. Mustard, 2.5"h x 2.25"d. Salt and pepper, 3.0"h x 1.5"w. Backstamp: 25.1. Complete set, $70-100.

C.192 Condiment set. Overall, 3.5"h x 5.5"w x 5.13"d. Salt and pepper, 3.0"h x 1.5"w. Mustard, 2.5"h x 2.25"w. Backstamp: 25.1. Complete set, $70-100.

C.194 Condiment set. 3.0"h x 5.5"w x 4.75"d. Backstamp: 27.0. Complete set, $110-180.

C.195 Condiment set. Tray, .25"h x 4.0"w x 4.0"d.
Mustard, 2.75"h x 1.5"w. Salt and pepper, 2.0"h x
1.0"w. Backstamp: Salt and pepper, J.1, Others, 27.1.
Complete set, $190-220.

C.197 Honey pots. 4.63"h x 4.13"w. Backstamp: 27.1.
Each set, with matching porcelain spoon, $150-250.

C.196 Condiment set. Tray, .63"h x 6.88"w. Mustard,
2.5"h x 2.0"w. Salt and pepper, 1.88"h x 1.75"w.
Backstamp: 27.1. $130-190.

C.198. Honey pots (note: these *are* smaller than those shown in C.197). 3.75"h x
3.38"w. Backstamp: 27.0. Each set, with matching porcelain spoon, $180-270.

C.199 Honey pot. 3.88"h x 2.75"w x 2.5"d.
Backstamp: 27.1. With matching porcelain spoon,
$190-250.

C.200 Jam set. Pot, 5.5"h x 3.75"w. Overall,
6.0"h x 5.5"w. Backstamp: 27.0. $400+

C.201 Jam set. 5.63"h x 4.88"w. Backstamp: 27.1.
$130-190.

C.202 Jam set. Plate, 5.5"dia. Pot, 5.25"h x 4.25"w.
Backstamp: Pot, 29.1 (39556). Underplate unmarked.
$100-150.

C.203A Double
backstamp on C.203.

C.203 Jam set. 5.25"h x 5.0"w x 4.25"d.
Backstamp: Jar has double backstamp, 16.0
& 19.1. Spoon, 19.1. $70-100.

C.204 Jam set. 5.25"h x 4.25"w.
Backstamp: 27.1. $80-140.

C.205 Jam sets. *Left*, 4.88"h x 5.75"w. *Right*, 5.25"h x
5.88"w. Backstamps: *left,* 19.0; *right,* 27.0. Each, $60-100.

C.206 Jam set. 4.63"h x 8.0"w. Backstamp: 19.2. Complete set, $90-140.

C.207 Jam set. 5.0"h x 5.5"w. Backstamp: 27.1. $150-190.

C.208 Jam set, with attached underplate and metal handle. 4.25"h x 5.38"w. With handle up, 6.0"h x 5.38"w. Backstamp: 27.1. Complete, as shown, $90-150.

C.209 Mayonnaise set. 3.5"h x 6.25"w. Backstamp: 27.0. $80-100.

C.210. Mayonnaise set. 3.5"h x 6.25"w.
Backstamp: 27.1. $60-90.

C.213 Sauce set. Unusual colors. Bowl, 2.88"h x 6.25"w. Plate, 1.0"h x
6.25"w. Backstamp: Bowl, 27.0, underplate not marked. $70-100.

C.211 Sauce set. 2.75"h x 6.88"w. Backstamp:
39.019. $130-180.

C.212 Sauce sets. 2.5"h x 6.63"w. Backstamp: 27.1 (All pieces marked). Each complete set, $170-220.

C.214 Mustard pots. 3.38"h x 4.25"w x 3.38"d. Backstamp: *front row,* 27.0; *back row,* 27.1. Each complete set, $20-40.

C.216 Salt and pepper set. 4.25"h x 1.5"w. Backstamp: J.1. Each, $180-380.

C.215 Oil & vinegar set. 3.5"h x 5.88"w. Backstamp: 27.1. Complete, with matching porcelain stoppers, $100-150.

C.217 Salt and pepper set. 3.5"h x 1.25"w. Backstamp: J.2. Each, $50-80.

C.218 Salt and pepper set.
3.63"h x 1.38"w. Backstamp:
MIJ.1. Each, $150-250.

C.219 Salt and pepper set. 3.63"h x 1.63"w.
Backstamp: MIJ.0. Each, $60-100.

C.218A Detail of C.218.

C.220 Salt and pepper set. Tray, .5"h x 4.63"w x 3.25"d. Figural
Dutch girl, 3.75"h x 1.63"w. Swan, 2.0"h x 2.5"w x 1.75"d.
Backstamp: figural girl, J.1; swan, 27.1; tray unmarked. Set, as
shown, $150-200.

C.221 Salt set. 3.25"h x 2.38"w. Backstamp: MIJ.1. Each, $80-130.

C.223 Salt and pepper set. Tray, .25"h x 4.25"w x 2.38"d. Salt and pepper, 2.0"h x 1.38"w. Backstamp: salt and pepper, J.1; tray unmarked. Set, as shown, $250-350.

C.222 Salt and pepper set. 3.25"h x 2.25"w. Backstamp: MIJ.1. Each, $80-130.

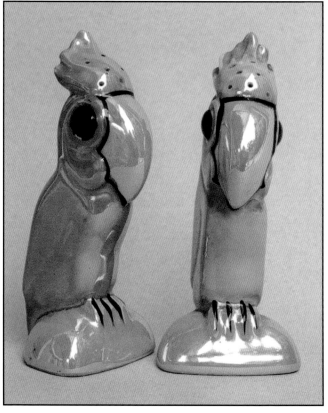

C.224 Salt and pepper set. 4.25"h x 1.88"w x 1.63"d. Backstamp: MIJ.1. Each, $80-100.

C.225 Salt and pepper set. 2.13"h x 1.88"w x 1.75"d. Backstamp: MIJ.1. Each, $70-90.

C.228 Salt and pepper set. 2.88"h x 3.0"w. Backstamp: 27.1. Set, as shown, $70-90.

C.226 Salt and pepper set. 3.38"h x 3.38"w x 2.5"d. Backstamp: 19.0. Set, as shown, $70-90.

C.229 Salt and pepper set (two pieces; pepper sits on open salt). 3.0"h x 2.25"w. Backstamp: 27.1. $70-90.

C.227 Salt and pepper set. 2.0"h x 1.75"w. Backstamp: J.1. Each, $50-70.

C.230 Salt and pepper set. Overall, 3.0"h x 5.25"w. Salt and pepper, 2.5"h x 1.5"d. Backstamp: salt and pepper, J.1; holder unmarked. $80-100.

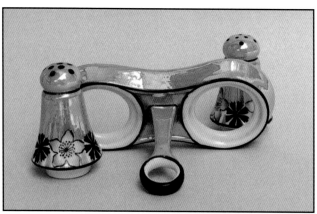

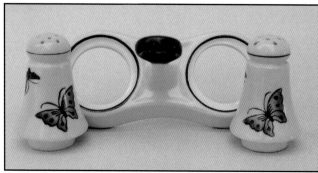

C.232 Salt and pepper set. 3.0"h x 5.25"w x 2.25"d. Backstamp: 27.1. Set, $70-90.

C.231 Salt and pepper set. Overall, 3.0"h x 5.25"w. Salt and pepper, 2.5"h x 1.5"d. Backstamp: salt and pepper, J.1; holder unmarked. $80-100.

C.233 Salt and pepper set. Tray, 4.38"w x 2.63"d. Salt, 1.5"h x 1.5"w. Pepper, 2.5"h x 1.0"w. Backstamp: salt and pepper, MIJ.1; tray unmarked. Set, with spoon (not shown) $100-150.

C.234 Salt and pepper set. 5.38"h x 2.38"w. Backstamp: MIJ.1. Each, $20-40.

C.236 Salt and pepper set. 4.0"h x 1.5"w. Backstamp: MIJ.1w. Each, $70-90.

C.235 Salt and pepper set. 4.75"h x 1.5"w. Backstamps: J.1 *and* MIJ.1. Each, $20-40.

C.235A Backstamps on the items in C.235.

C.237 Salt and pepper set. 3.88"h x 1.88"w. Backstamp: J.1. Each, $20-40.

C.238 Salt and pepper sets. 3.5"h x 1.75"w. Backstamp: J.1. Each, $20-40.

C.239 Salt and pepper set. 2.75"h x 1.88"w.
Backstamp: J.1. Each, $20-40.

C.240 Salt and pepper sets. 2.63"h x 1.88"w. Backstamp: MIJ.0.
Each, $20-40.

C.241 Salt and pepper set. 2.75"h x 2.38"w.
Backstamp: MIJ.1. Each, $20-40.

C.242 Salt and pepper set (the lettering on the
item to the right says "Niagra Falls"). 2.63"h x
1.5"w. Backstamp: MIJ.0. Each, $20-40.

C.243 Salt set. Large basket,
5.5"h x 6.5"w x 4.38"d. Small
baskets, 2.25"h x 2.25"w x 1.75"d.
Backstamp: 27.1. Set, as shown,
$120-180.

C.244 Salt set. Large basket, 5.5"h x 6.5"w 4.38"d. Small baskets, 2.25"h x 2.25"w x 1.75"d. Backstamp: 27.0. Set, as shown, $140-190.

C.246 Salt set. Large swan, 2.25"h x 6.0"w x 3.5"d. Small swans, 1.75"h x 2. 5"w x 1.88"d. Backstamp: 27.1. Set, as shown, $170-230.

C.245 Salt set in original box. Originally, there was a plastic master spoon with this set. It fit into the long space on the right of the box. A very incomplete set with this decoration (and not in its box) was shown in C.102. Box, 2.63"h x 9.13"w x 7.0"d. Large swan, 2.25"h x 6.0"w x 3.5"d. Small swans, 1.75"h x 2.5"w x 1.88"d. Backstamp: 27.1. Set, as shown, $190-290.

C.247 Salt set in original box. Box, 1.88"h x 7.13"w x 4.5"d. Baskets, 1.75"h x 2.0"w x 1.5"d. Backstamp: 27.1. Set, as shown (with all spoons), $130-190.

Desk and Dresser Items

In this chapter, one will find photos of the following kinds of items meant for use in the home on and around desks and dressers:

Desk items
    Ink wells (pp. 168-170)
    Desk set (p. 170)
Dresser items
    Dresser dolls (pp. 171-172)
    Dresser sets (pp. 172-173)
    Dresser trays (pp. 173-174)
    Hair receiver (p. 174)
    Perfume bottles (pp. 175-176)
    Pin trays (pp. 176-177)
    Powder boxes and jars (pp. 177-179)
    Powder puff boxes (pp. 179-182)
    Rouge (or cosmetic) boxes (p. 182)
    Talcum powder shaker (p. 182)
    Trinket dishes (p. 183)

Figural lady dresser dolls and powder boxes, figural inkwells, clown trinket dishes and powder puff boxes and dresser trays with Deco lady motifs are, without a doubt, the most widely recognized "glamour stocks" of the entire Noritake fancyware collecting world, even for those who do not seek them. Because of this and because such items were a sizable portion of all the pieces shown in the Chapter Ds of my two previous books, it may safely be predicted that most readers familiar with Noritake fancyware will have picked this chapter, more than any other, to look into first. Indeed, most of you now reading these words have probably already looked at the photos in this chapter, perhaps several times.

Given this, it is appropriate to ask: You saw some pretty amazing pieces in this chapter, didn't you? I thought so. When you looked through the photos, I expect you noticed that, in this book, as in both previous ones, the emphasis in Chapter D is decidedly on dresser items. This is not a product of biases in photo selection. Noritake-marked desk items simply are not very common—a fact apparently attributable to consumer-driven trends in the Noritake-

D.162 Ink well. 4.13"h x 4.88"w. Backstamp: 16.0. $2200+

marked fancyware products of the period covered by this book.. Even so, the shapes of and decorative work on some of these items are exceptional. A great example is the very first item shown in the chapter, the inkwell in D.162. The head and collar comprise the lid that covers the inkwell cavity. The Maruki backstamp on this one-of-a-kind item (so far) tells us that this piece originally was exported to Great Britain. Its decoration fairly shouts 1920s. All the other inkwells are also unusual, however. The suited penguin-like figural inkwell in D.164 and D.164A will of course appeal to many collectors, but the inkwell in D.165 and D.165A may well be rarer and certainly is exceptionally well-decorated. Because it is such an unusual piece and has only an MIJ.1 backstamp on it, some readers may wonder whether the Noritake Company really made it. It is a reasonable question. It is nice, therefore, to be able to report that its provenance was established recently by the discovery of a Noritake salesman sample page showing this inkwell. The MIJ.1 backstamp does suggest, however, that this item *may* have come with a tray or some other matching piece with the full backstamp.

Although some collectors refer to virtually any Noritake-made two-piece human figural form as a dresser doll, this designation (while often useful) is less precise than we sometimes can and should be. For example, from the size and shape, we sometimes can say fairly confidently that a two-piece human figural is a powder jar (D.188-D.189, are examples). By the same token, we probably are right to think of fairly similar sized two-piece figurals depicting a woman holding a cigarette as cigarette jars (and, hence, they are shown in Chapter A). But these are not hard-and-fast rules. Thus, even though the lady in the two-piece figural Noritake figural piece known as the "Seated Lady" is depicted holding a cigarette, these items are shown in the Bowls and Boxes chapter (Chapter B; for an example of this piece in this book, see B.562).

Moreover, we sometimes simply can not tell from the size and shape alone what the function of a piece might have been. For example, there are two-piece figurals that are not all that different in size from some powder boxes but because they seem too small for powder they tend to be known, simply, as dresser dolls (e.g., D.168-D.170). Our uncertainties regarding function are even greater for the items shown in D.167 and D.167A. How were they used? It has been suggested by some fairly well-informed collectors of cosmetic items from the 1920s that the tall two piece figurals were meant to be used for storing plain glass bottles of cologne. By essentially the same logic, it is said that the small figurals were meant for the storage of plain bottles of perfume that were, of course, likely to be much smaller than cologne bottles. As appealing as these viewpoints are, we are not yet in a position to confirm them.

One of the great appeals of dresser trays is that they are flat and relatively large surfaces. This means that some of the images depicted on them are relatively large and very well-executed versions of motifs usually seen on much smaller pieces. A superb example is the tray shown in D.175. A dresser tray with a very closely related motif is shown in D.128 in my second Noritake book. These motifs are also found on other dresser items—notably powder puff boxes (D.79 in the first book and D.142 and D.143 in the second). Diane Kovarik was the first to establish and report publicly (in July 2000) that these three lady motifs are also found on bridge tally cards produced in the 1920s by the Buzza Company of Craftacres, Minnesota. Since the tally set has four different ladies (one more than the three known on Noritake items), it seems likely that the inspiration for the Noritake motifs came from this source and not the reverse (see also Chapter E, below).

I know of few Noritake collectors who make a special effort to seek and collect hair receivers. One can imagine various reasons for this. Most telling,

D.163 Ink well. 4.25"h x 2.25"w.
Backstamp: 27.1. $200-300.

D.163A Alternate view of D.163.

perhaps, is that Noritake dresser sets from the 1920s generally did not have hair receivers and those that do are rather plainly decorated. The hair receiver shown in D.177, then, is a dramatic exception to this "rule." The decoration, which seems to have affinities with motifs from the American southwest, is not seen all that frequently but it is found on a rather wide variety of items. In this book, for example, there is a large vase with it (V.331) and, in *Collecting Noritake A to Z* a very large and spectacular Noritake punch bowl with this design is shown in B.304. This hair receiver is of interest not only for its bold motif but also because its existence suggests quite strongly that a complete dresser set with this decoration awaits discovery, and what a discovery this will be!

Little figural pin dishes, such as those shown in D.183-D.187 have four undeniable virtues: they are genuinely *cute*, they come in many colors, they display easily (no display stands are required) and they are small, which means there *always* is room for one more. Consequently, these items are in much demand but, as a result, they have lost one virtue they had a few years ago: no longer can they be had for small change. The alert collector will have noticed that there are at least three different kinds of figural dog pin dishes, as shown in D.183.

Noritake powder puff boxes have always been of considerable interest to collectors but, recently, the demand for these items has skyrocketed. Within just a few months, the auction prices for some boxes that used to be thought of as "expensive" at $400 have more than doubled. The currently more desirable boxes have one thing in common: they feature a well-executed Deco lady motif. The examples shown in this book are in D.197-D.201. Fortunately for collectors, few of these seem to be truly "rare" and, if their values continue to increase, we may expect more will show up on the secondary market. What that will do to values remains to be seen, of course. Much rarer, in my experience, are the figural rouge jars shown in D.203 and D.204. Even so, their values currently are lower than lady powder puff boxes simply because they are not in as much demand. The figural lady talcum shaker shown in D.205 is somewhat unusual in having a full #27 backstamp. Many similar items that are clearly Noritake-made have an MIJ backstamp. Because of this, one keeps expecting to see these items as part of a larger set but, so far as I know, no such set is known—*yet!*

This chapter ends with as strong a note as it began. Just as the inkwells shown in this chapter are eye-popping wonders, so are the trinket dishes. All of those shown in this chapter undoubtedly *deserve* comment, because each one is a special piece. Even so, I limit my comments to the trinket dish shown in D.209 and D.209A. This piece is, without a doubt, one of the most dramatic and exceptional Noritake pieces shown in this or any other Noritake book (disclosure: this is not, alas, a part of my collection). Trinket dishes in this shape have been known to collectors for some years. The first one I ever saw, in 1990, was purchased at auction that year for $1000, a then virtually unheard of amount for a single piece. A duplicate of it is shown in D.160 *Collecting Noritake A to Z* and, at the time (1999), was assigned a value of "at least" $800. The slumped posture and poignant facial expression are incredibly expressive in these pieces. These features are retained in the trinket dish shown in D.209. The overall power of this piece is heightened considerably, however, by the complex and colorful costume, and by the addition of a painted ball and cap in the dish cavity. In addition, the purple color on the rim of the dish is both unusual for Noritake fancyware and a superb complement to the color of the costume. All in all, it is a superb and fitting conclusion to what surely will be one of the most frequently examined chapters of this book.

D.164 Ink well. 3.25"h x 2.25"w. Backstamp: 27.1. $450-650.

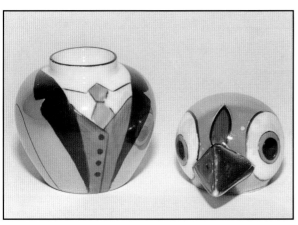

D.164A Alternate view of another example of D.164.

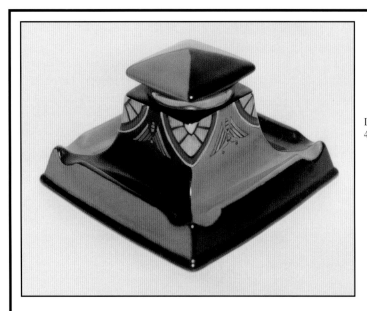

D.165 Inkwell with pen rests. 3.0"h x
4.5"w. Backstamp: MIJ.1. $280-430.

D.165A Alternate view of D.165.

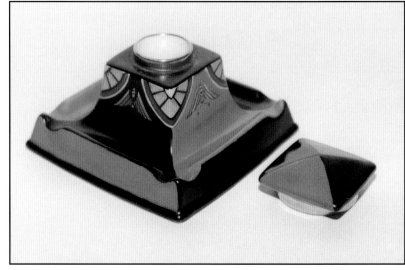

D.166 Desk set. 2.0"h x 6.5"w. Backstamp: 27.1.
$300-450.

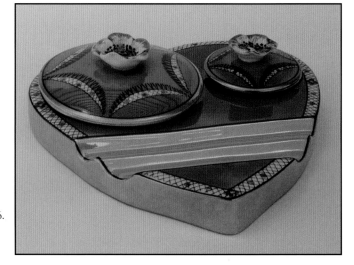

D.166A Alternate view of D.166.

D.167 Dresser dolls. *From the left,* 9.0"h x 3.5"w; 4.5"h x 1.5"w; 4.25"h x 1.5"w; 8.75"h x 3.75"w. Backstamp: small clown, MIJ.1; others, 27.1. *Left and right,* each, $1300-1800; *two small center items,* each, $300-400.

D.168 Dresser doll. 6.5"h x 4.0"w. Backstamp: 27.1. $1300-1800.

D167A. Alternate view of center items in D.167.

D.169 Dresser doll. 6.0"h x 3.5"w. Backstamp: 29.0 (25920). $900-1400.

D.170 Dresser doll. 6.0"h x 3.5"w.
Backstamp: 29.0 (25920). $900-1400.

D.172 Dresser set. Tray, .63"h x 12.25"w x 8.88"d. Small tray,
.38"h x 4.5"w x 3.25"d. Candlesticks, 5.13"h x 3.13"w. Large
powder, 2.75"h x 3.75"w. Small powder, 2.13"h x 2.25"w.
Backstamp: 16.2. $400-600.

D.171 Dresser set. Tray. .63"h x 11.63"w. Doll,
6.25"h x 3.5"w, Powder puff, 3.88"dia.
Backstamp: 27.1. $1100-1600.

D.173 Dresser set. Tray, .5"h x 10.75"w x 7.5"d. Overall
dimensions of powder puff box, 4.25"h x 3.88"w.
Backstamp: 27.1. $600-800.

D.174 Dresser set. Tray, 10.5 "w x 5.5"d. Large cosmetic, 2.5"h x 3.75"w. Powder puff, 1.5"h x 4.0 "dia. Small cosmetic, 2.0 "h x 2.75"dia. Backstamp: 25.1. $190-290.

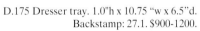

D.175 Dresser tray. 1.0"h x 10.75 "w x 6.5"d. Backstamp: 27.1. $900-1200.

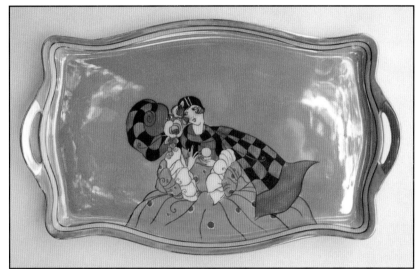

D.175A Detail of D.175.

D.176 Dresser tray. .63"h x 6.75"dia.
Backstamp: 27.1. Each, $650-850.

D.176A Detail of D.176.

D.177 Hair receiver. 3.25"h x 3.5"w.
Backstamp: 29.0 (25920). $80-120.

D.178 Perfume bottle. 6.0"h x 1.5"w. Backstamp: 27.1. $350-550.

D.179 Perfume bottle. 6.0"h x 1.5"w. Backstamp: 27.1. $270-370.

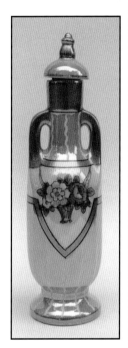

D.180 Perfume bottle. 6.0"h x 1.5"w. Backstamp: 27.1. $170-270.

D.178A Detail of D.178.

D.181 Perfume bottles. 2.0"h x 2.5"w. Backstamp: 27.1. Each, $120-200.

D.184 Pin tray. 2.0"h x 3.0"w.
Backstamp: 27.1 $150-250.

D.182 Perfume bottle. 2.0"h x
2.5"w. Backstamp: 27.1. $120-200.

D.185 Pin tray. 2.0"h x 3.0"w. Backstamp: 27.0. $130-230.

D.183 Pin trays. *Left rear*, 2.88"h x 2.75"w; *right rear*, 2.0"h x 2.75"w; *front left & right*, 1.63"h x 2.75"w. Backstamp: *left rear,* 27.0; *others,* 27.1. Each, $80-180.

D.186 Pin tray. 2.0"h x 3.0"w.
Backstamp: 27.1. $120-220.

D.187 Pin trays. 2.0"h x 4.0"dia.
Backstamp: 27.0. Each, $190-260.

D.188 Powder box. 6.25"h x 3.5"w.
Backstamp: 29.0 (25920). $1200-1700.

D.189 Powder boxes. 5.5"h x 4.0"w. Backstamp: *left,* 29.0 (25920); *center,* 27.0; *right,* 29.0 (25920). Each, $1200-1700.

D.189A Detail of D.189.

D.189B Detail of D.189.

D.189C Detail of D.189.

D.190 Powder box. 3.13"h x 5.88"w x 4.25"d. Backstamp: 25.1. $180-280.

D.190A Top view of D.190.

D.192 Powder box. 3.0"h x 4.63"dia. Backstamp: 27.1. $130-190.

D.192A Top view of D.192.

D.191 Powder box. 3.0"h x 4.63"dia. Backstamp: 35.1. $60-90.

D.193 Powder puff box. 3.0"h x 3.5"w. Backstamp: 27.1. $200-250.

D.194 Powder puff box. 3.0"h x 3.5"w.
Backstamp: 27.1. $200-250.

D.195 Powder puff
box. 1.38"h x 4.0"dia.
Backstamp: 27.1.
$200-250.

D.196 Powder puff box. 1.38"h
x 4.0"dia. Backstamp: 27.1.
$200-250.

D.197 Powder puff box. 1.0"h x 4.0"dia. Backstamp: 27.0. $450-700.

D.198 Powder puff box. 1.0"h x 4.0"dia.
Backstamp: 27.1. $450-700.

D.200 Powder puff box. 1.0"h x
4.0"dia. Backstamp: 27.1. $500-750.

D.199 Powder puff box. .63"h x 3.25"dia.
Backstamp: 27.1. $500-750.

D.201 Powder puff box. 1.0"h x 4.0"dia.
Backstamp: 27.0. $450-700.

D.202 Powder puff box. .63"h x
3.25"dia. Backstamp: 27.0. $190-230.

D.204 Rouge jar. 3.0"h x
2.13"w. Backstamp: 27.1.
$450-650.

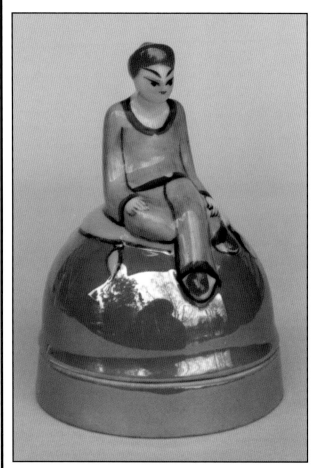

D.203 Rouge jar. 3.0"h x 2.13"w. Backstamp: 27.1. $450-650.

D.205 Talcum shaker. 6.5"h x 2.0"w.
Backstamp: 27.1. $290-390.

D.206 Trinket dish. 4.25"h x 6.5"w x 5.5"d. Backstamp: 27.1. $450-750.

D.208 Trinket dish. 3.5"h x 5.0"w. Backstamp: 27.1. $1300-1600.

D.207 Trinket dish. 4.0"h x 5.75"w x 5.25"d. Backstamp: 27.0. $400-600.

D.209 Trinket dish. 3.5"h x 5.0"w. Backstamp: 27.1. $2200+

D.209A Detail of D.209.

Chapter E

Ephemera Pertaining to Noritake Fancyware Designs

"Ephemera" derives from a Greek word meaning "lasting a day." It is an apt word for the materials that are central to this chapter. They are paper items which were intended to be used once and then thrown away. Fortunately for us, some of the people who had these items did not follow this "rule" (although in some cases, the items were never used). Items similar to these were shown in my first two books on Noritake fancyware collectibles. In *Noritake Collectibles A to Z* (1997), they were all in Chapter 2 (see pages 14-15 and 19-23) where they appeared in connection with a discussion of the history of the Noritake Company and of the Noritake collecting field. Those two groups of photographic materials were very kindly provided by, respectively, Margaret Hetzler and Dr. and Mrs. Dennis and Susan Buonafede (plus, there were photographs of mine of similar items from the collection of Fred Tenney). I am still most grateful to these individuals for this support. In *Collecting Noritake A to Z* (1999) these items were, in a sense, promoted to their own chapter in Part Two of the book, "Chapter S: Salesman Sample Pages and Other Paper Items" (pp.147-155). As the title of that chapter indicates, the focus was on those amazing and but unfortunately all too rare pages from notebooks that Noritake sales people carried around as they visited various stores and other potential outlets for their fancy line items—i.e., those more decorative pieces that complemented their dinnerware products.

Although no salesman sample pages were slated for this book, I knew of other very important paper items that pertained directly to the Noritake collecting field and arranged for them to be included (on which more in a moment). In the meantime, I was faced with an organizational problem, one derived from the use of mnemonically selected letters to designate the chapters in Part Two, where I wanted these materials to appear. Since there were no salesman pages, it made no sense to put the new materials just mentioned into another Chapter S. A chapter called "Paper Items" would have been fine, of course, but there already is a very useful Chapter P. Fortunately, the Chapter E slot was vacant and so, quite happily, here we are.

As the title of Chapter S tells us, there were paper items shown other than salesman sample pages. Specifically, there was one magazine cover from France in the 1920s with an image that reminded Brian Hurst, the person who found it, of a well-known Noritake fancyware dresser tray (D.129 and D129A in *Collecting Noritake A to Z*) known to collectors as "Susy Skier"—a name that Howard Kottler gave the motif. Although a very plausible claim (indeed, so plausible that the photograph was included in the chapter), it also is very clear that the motif on the magazine cover was modified in some rather important ways if it was, in fact, the source for Susy Skier. For one thing, the lady on the French magazine cover is bare breasted and, although she clearly is skiing, she is not using poles. Susy Skier is, needless to say, not bare-breasted and she is using ski poles. The case is weakened further by comments that appear in the catalogue accompanying the exhibition of Kottler's Noritake fancyware (see Coddington et al in *Bibliography*). These comments were offered by Ronny Cohen who, at the time, was an art historian in New York. Cohen suggests (p.28) that the Susy Skier motif may well have been inspired by a layout in the January 1925 issue of *Vogue*.

I mention all of this to indicate that, in general, the search for artworks and other materials that could be the inspirational source of Noritake fancyware designs often depends on very subjective judgments, which often generate considerable debate. This may be illustrated by considering the Susy Skier case a bit more. Before including the French cover in Chapter S of *Collecting Noritake A to Z*, I examined the 1925 *Vogue* layout. I must say, I was unimpressed. The images were *very* simple, almost mundane drawings. Indeed, to me the images (there were several) seemed so weak, I began to look at other issues of *Vogue* from around that time, expecting to discover that Cohen had accidentally mentioned the wrong month. Needless to say, the search was fruitless. But there are grounds for doubting the relevance of the image on the French magazine, too. Thus, Susy Skier has an Argyle sweater and long wool ski socks rolled over at the knees. The French skier is wearing a red jacket with ermine trim and nylons held up by a partially visible garter belt. Her face is turned to the right and her open lips subtly but fully reveal her teeth. Susy Skier, on the other hand, is looking straight down the hill where she is skiing and has a rather serious expression on her face. On the other side of the ledger, however, both Susy Skier and her ostensible French counterpart have a long scarf and short skirt. Moreover, they both are being blown back by the wind in a very similar way. Also, their skis are not shown full length in either image and their downhill angles are essentially identical. So are the boots they are wearing.

Fortunately, not all cases are as uncertain or complex as this one. The images shown in Chapter 2 of *Noritake Collectibles A to Z*, are, as it were, open and shut cases. Indeed, one of them (Photo 2.13, p.15) actually offers the chance to test the hypothesis that is, in a sense, presented by the image. Three bridge tally cards from the 1920s are shown, each with a woman with a fashionably short 1920s hair style. The three tally cards are numbered and most significantly for our purposes, the number two tally card is missing. One tally card image, that on the number 1 card, matches *very* closely a well-known Noritake fancyware image found on a napkin ring (Z.31, *left* on p.199 of *Collecting Noritake A to Z*). The photo in Z.31 shows a second Noritake napkin ring, as does the photo in 2.13 of *Noritake Collecting A to Z*. Although the images on these two napkin rings are obviously similar to each other, the second one does not match either of the ladies shown on the other two tally cards. From my point of view, this is good news because it is this that makes possible a predictive "test" of the claim inherent in the photo. What we can predict, with considerable (but by no means total) confidence I think, is that when an example of the missing bridge tally from that particular set is found, the image on it will match rather closely the motif on the second lady napkin ring.

Although the other cases offered by Margaret Hetzler on those two pages are equally strong, I will not review them here. Instead, I want to bring another voice into this discussion, along with about a dozen *very* impressive images. Margaret Hetzler provided some of these and I provided others. Most of them, however, were provided by Diane Kovarik, who like Margaret, is a very experienced collector of both Noritake fancyware and selected 1920s ephemera. At a recent Noritake Collectors' Society convention, Diane gave a beautifully illustrated and highly informative presentation on the subject of 1920s ephemera and designs found on Noritake fancyware. A written version of her lecture-presentation appeared later in *Noritake News*. With my urging and her consent, the remainder of this chapter is an updated and more heavily illustrated version of that article.

Noritake Designs and 1920s Ephemera

by Diane Kovarik

Ever since I first learned about Homer Conant and his "Mme Pompadour" prints (e.g., see the Hetzler image in E.1 that links a Noritake plate and a Conant print, an image that also appeared in *Collecting Noritake A to Z*; see 2.10), I have been fascinated by the idea that there are design inspirations for the items Noritake produced during the Art Deco era. We know from past research by Howard Kottler and others that the Noritake Company had a sales office and design studio in New York City in the 1920s. The design studio somehow created designs suited to western tastes and then sent them to Japan where they were painted, by hand, onto the china. With this as a starting point, I started to look for items that would have been available as inspirations for those designers during the 1920s. To date, the items I have found all seem to have the following characteristics: they were inexpensive, they were made out of paper, they were readily available, and they were small. In general, they were made between 1924 and 1928.

E.1 Noritake plate and a 1920s print by Homer Conant. Plate 8.5" dia. Backstamp 27.0; Print, 13.75"h x 10.0"w.

Various artists and companies made the items. A striking example is an undated print entitled "Moths," a work signed by an artist named Marygold (see E.2 and E.2A). The print is of special interest because it probably was the design source for a Noritake cake plate, one shown in *Collecting Noritake A to Z* (page 124, P.138; also shown below in E.3 and E.3A). A rather different example is the booklet "How to Make Crepe Paper Costumes" (E.4). The Dennison Mfg. Co. published it in 1925. Dennison's was a hugely popular company that sold crepe paper that was used to make a wide variety of party accessories. They provided helpful guides, like the booklets pictured here, so the 1920s hostess could deliver the most successful parties and dances. The lady on the cover of the booklet shows up on a variety of Noritake items in both a red floral as well as a yellow and black striped dress (see the Hetzler image in E.5).

E.2A Detail of print by Marygold.

E.2 Print by Marygold entitled "Moths." Size unframed, 15.0"h x 6.13"w.

E.3 Noritake cake plate. 1.0"h x 10.5"w x 9.75"d.
Backstamp: 27.1.

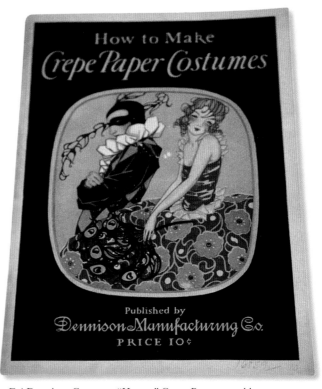

E.4 Dennison Company "How to" Crepe Paper pamphlet
from the 1920s.

E.3A Detail of plate in E.3. S

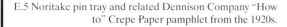

E.5 Noritake pin tray and related Dennison Company "How to" Crepe Paper pamphlet from the 1920s.

Many items have to do with a pastime that was extremely popular in the 1920s: playing bridge. There was a lot of ephemera associated with playing bridge, including items such as tallies, score pads, paper name cards and, of course, the playing cards (e.g., compare the bridge tally shown in E.6 with the Noritake tea tile shown in E.7 and E.7A). Such items were sold in five and dime stores across the country. Given our interest in materials from the 1920s, it is important to note that the game of bridge changed significantly during that period. Prior to that time—i.e., from 1904 until 1925, there was one standard way to play bridge in the U.S. It was commonly referred to as "auction bridge." Then, in 1925, Ely Culbertson created a new form of bridge. He called it "contract bridge" and it became an immediate hit. Indeed, by 1928, it had overtaken auction bridge as the most popular form of bridge in America. This date (1928) is important because, so far, all the bridge ephemera with scoring rules that I have found that can be linked to Noritake designs refer to auction bridge. This strongly suggests they were published prior to 1928-1929—a point of interest given our desire to know the age of the items in our collections.

E.7 Noritake tea tile from the 1920s. 6.5"dia. Backstamp 27.1.

E.7A Detail of tea tile shown in E.7

E.6 Bridge tally card from the 1920s.

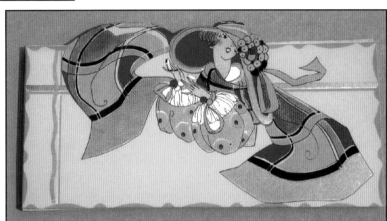

The four rectangular items shown in photos E.8-E.11 are bridge score cards. I found them as a complete boxed set. Although undated, they were published by the Henderson Line of Cincinnati, Ohio. Noritake collectors will recognize them instantly as the "scarf ladies" that decorate Noritake powder puff boxes and dresser trays (see D.175 and D.175A in this book; for other examples, see D.128, D.142, D.143 in *Collecting Noritake A to Z*). If you compare the tallies to the Noritake items, you will see that the Noritake designers felt it was necessary to fill in the rest of their dresses, probably to add

E.8 Henderson Line bridge score card from the 1920s.

E.9 Henderson Line bridge score card from the 1920s.

E.10 Henderson Line bridge score card from the 1920s.

E.11 Henderson Line bridge score card from the 1920s.

more impact to the overall look of the items. In E.12, another score card is shown. To Noritake collectors, she is known as the "Lady in Red." She shows up virtually unchanged on Noritake compotes, plates (e.g., P.92 in *Noritake Collectibles A to Z*) and a covered bowl (as shown in E.12). Two other bridge score cards from the 1920s that match Noritake fancyware motifs by Noritake are also shown here (see the Hetzler images in E.13 and E.14; the powder puff box in E.14 is also shown above in D.201)

E.12 Bridge score card from the 1920s with a covered bowl from the 1920s by Noritake. Bowl, 4.5"h x 8.5"w x 6.25"d. Backstamp: 27.1.

E.13 Bridge score card from the 1920s with a 1920s oval dresser tray by Noritake. Tray, .38"h x 8.5"w x 5.75"d. Backstamp: 27.1.

E.14 Bridge score card from the 1920s with a 1920s powder puff box by Noritake. Box, 1.0"h x 4.0"dia. Backstamp: 27.0.

Another set of bridge accessories relevant to Noritake derives from the popular 1924 film "Dorothy Vernon at Hadden Hall." This film was produced by United Artists and starred Mary Pickford in the title role. Based on a novel of the same name published in 1908 by Charles Major, the film is set in Elizabethan England. Accordingly, very large ruffled collars and wristbands are featured prominently in the costumes of the women who are central in the motifs on these bridge items which, once again, were produced by The Henderson Line. These ladies appear on three relatively rare but still well-known Noritake dresser trays. One is shown in E.13 (previous page); another appears in D.22 of *Noritake Collectibles A to Z.* The third may be seen in Van Patten's second (1994) Noritake book (plate 1207)

One of the most popular and prolific manufacturers of bridge ephemera was the Buzza Company of Craftacres, Minnesota. Craftacres was not a real town but actually a city block in downtown Minneapolis where the Buzza factory was located. George Buzza started his company in the early part of the 1900s. Its major output was small, framed prints with inspirational or comical verses called mottoes but it also created bridge items, sometimes in partnership with the US Playing Card Company. So far, I have several Noritake-related items made by The Buzza Company including the "Turban Ladies" found on powder puff boxes (see E.15; this powder puff box is also shown above in D.200) and tobacco jars (e.g., A.93 in *Noritake Collectibles A to Z*). The Buzza Company also produced a score card with an image they named "Crinoline Girl" (see E.16; many Noritake collectors refer to the motif on the ashtray as the "Spanish Lady").

Finally, no game of bridge would be possible without a deck of cards. In E.17, a card from an exquisite deck with a design named "Bubbles" is shown next to a Noritake cigarette box with a very similar motif. The card is signed by an artist named Mollie MacMillan. The US Playing Card Company of

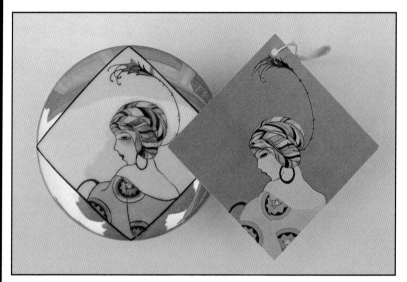

E.15 Bridge score card from the 1920s with a 1920s powder puff box by Noritake. Box, 1.0"h x 4.0"dia. Backstamp: 27.0.

E.16 Bridge score card from the 1920s with a 1920s ash tray by Noritake. Ash tray, 1.0"h x 4.0"w. Backstamp: 27.1.

Cincinnati, Ohio, published this deck of cards during 1927 and 1928 (see E.18). The US Playing Card Co. is still in business today and has its own in-house art department. They report that they do not have any more information on who Mollie was or how long she worked for them. It is interesting that the Noritake Co. designers deleted Bubbles's bubble pipe and the bubbles she has produced and replaced them with a cigarette and smoke (see E.19 and E.20).

In closing, it has been a fascinating journey for me so far. I know there must be many more items out there. To find them, all we need to do is look.

E.18 Deck of U.S. Congress playing card ("Bubbles") from the 1920s, with box.

E.17 U.S. Congress playing card ("Bubbles") from the 1920s with a 1920s cigarette box by Noritake. Box 1.75"h x 3.5"w x 2.75"d. Backstamp: 27.1.

E.19 Detail of "Bubbles" motif on playing cards shown in E.17 and E.18.

E.20 Detail of Noritake motif on cigarette box shown in E.17.

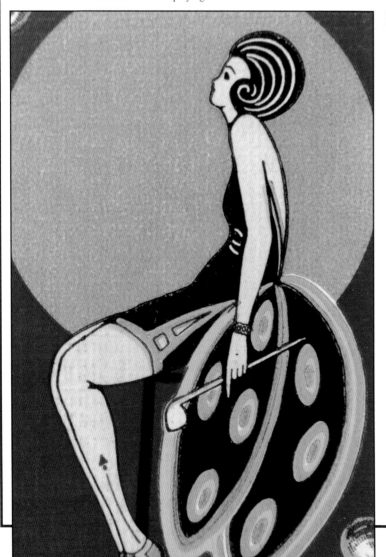

Chapter F

Figurines

In this chapter are photos of seventeen remarkable Noritake backstamped figurines, sequenced as shown below. Defined by their basic forms, these groups are arranged alphabetically.

Birds (pp. 193-195)
Dragon (p. 195)
Fish (pp. 195-196)
Humans (pp. 196-198)
Mammals (p. 198)

There are two parts to this brief introduction. First, I offer a few comments on some of the amazing figurines that are shown in this chapter. Second, and in keeping with a theme introduced in Chapter 2, above, I use a letter from a fellow collector to discuss an interesting backstamp issue that arises with these figurines more than almost any other Noritake-made fancyware.

Most of the Noritake figurines available on the collector market were made after World War II. Demand for these seems to vary quite a bit and so do prices. As a result, some of the estimated value ranges for items in this chapter are fairly broad. Often, these are for items not seen all that often but which, for one reason or another, seem to vary greatly in selling price when they do show up. One thing that is so amazing about these figurines is how diverse they are. This becomes all the more evident when the entire array of figurines shown in this and my two previous Noritake books are considered as a set. One can find everything from insects to trucks, from women posed and dressed in an extremely modern manner (F.41 in this book, for example) to others that seem quite traditional (F.45) and from familiar animals like dogs (F.47 is a stunning example in this book) to mythical beasts (the rare dragon figurine shown in F.37). This diversity is, I think, at least partly why the values trends are so unclear. Although there are a few collectors who are interested in almost any Noritake figurine, others will focus only on certain kinds: birds or cats or dogs, for example, or the sometimes Mother's Day-related figurines featuring mother-offspring pairs (not unlike the very cute pair shown in F.36).

In terms of rarity, four items stand out in this chapter. I have mentioned two of them already (the dragon in F.37 and the Art Deco pair in F.41). Another very unusual and, I believe, quite rare item is the lady carrying the mirror and basket shown in F.42. A different version of this 1920s or early 1930s piece was shown (including a back view) in *Noritake Collectibles A to Z* (F.21). It has long been a matter of speculation among collectors as to how many of any one fancyware item the Noritake Company made. So far, we have very little information on this although some figurines and holiday collectibles (Easter eggs, for example) do have backstamps that indicate the edition size.

F.34 Bird figurine. 7.5"h x 3.13"w. Backstamp: 65.019. $90-150.

This is the case for the Arnold Palmer figurine shown in F.43 and F.43A. Only 600 of this particular item were made.

Finally, in terms of visual drama, three items particularly catch my eye. For motion and grace, I doubt that any Noritake figurine can top the one shown in F.47, although there will be some close contenders. The woman depicted in the figurine shown in F.45, on the other hand, is just the opposite—all is serene and quiet, almost as though she has been hit by some cosmic pause button. The feeling is similar with the woman in F.46, although in so many ways she is just the opposite of F.45 (but notice the coy angle of their heads).

From these more aesthetic issues, we turn now to matters of chronology and value, as introduced through a letter I received. As with the other letters used in this way in this book, I have edited the original slightly and, of course, left out the sender's name. My response, which also has been edited and so is not exactly the same as the one that originally published in *Noritake News*, follows the letter which (to make it easy to identify) is in Italics.

In your book Noritake Collectibles A to Z, *you have several pages with the typically white animal figurines—e.g., the deer and its fawn, a horse and colt, etc. You list that they have backstamp 65.5. Are they older than the same figurines with backstamp 70.7 which say Mother's Day 1977 (1 of 2800)? I thought they were all produced in the 1970s. Are the more recent ones worth less than the ones with the #65 backstamp?*

The dates given in my books for some of the items in Chapter F were supplied by the Noritake Company. They are the date when the item was *first released*. Such a date cannot be taken as the actual date of manufacture for a particular piece shown but, rather, only indicates its *potential maximum age*. There is a different ambiguity with the dates given for the backstamps (see Chapter 3) even though these were provided by the Noritake Company. It is not always clear from the context whether the year dates when the backstamp was *registered* or when it was first *used*. Generally, or at least so it appears, Noritake backstamps were registered prior to their use, sometimes by at least several months and sometimes by as much as several years. To complicate matters further, some backstamps appear to have been used for a fairly short time span while others were used for many years, sometimes not continuously. Consequently, the backstamp dates also can tell us only the *approximate* maximum age of a piece. This point is an important one for *all* collectors of or dealers in Noritake fancyware of all kinds.

For many collectors, one of the more pertinent matters, however, will be the question about the *relative* ages of the two apparently identical pieces with the 65.5 and 70.7 backstamps. As it happens, it is particularly difficult to say precisely what the year of first use was for these two backstamps. Without offering the many but still rather meager reasons for saying so, I simply will state that backstamp 65.5 apparently began to be used in *about* 1946. As for backstamp 70.7, the initial year appears to be *about* 1950. Thus, we have two identical pieces with backstamps that *probably* were registered within a few years of each other prior to or around 1950. It is more significant, however, that I do not know how long either of these backstamps was used. On the piece with the 70.7 backstamp, however, there is other factory-applied information—specifically the year 1977. Even with all the uncertainties alluded to, it seems likely that pieces with a backstamp accompanied by a 1977 date are newer than pieces with a backstamp that began to be used in about 1946.

Even in the absence of definite solutions to these chronological matters,

F.35 Bird figurine. 6.38"h x 2.38"w. Backstamp: 65.019. $70-130.

the question of the impact of age on the value of porcelain items can be discussed. For Noritake fancyware, in my view, the impact usually will be trivial to non-existent *unless* the age differs by at least 25 years. Why 25 years? Well, mostly this figure is a proxy indicator of the likely rarity of the two pieces. If we assume that the same quantities of an item were produced each of the (hopefully only) two times they were made, the current relative rarity of the two items can then only be influenced by their rate of destruction (for this discussion, we ignore potential issues of workmanship and artistic merit on value simply by assuming they are equal). Over time, some pieces inevitably are going to be destroyed. With more time, there ought to be more breakage. Assuming that the quality of the porcelain is the same (a reasonable assumption with Noritake Company items), the difference in the amount of breakage is not likely to be great enough to effect values unless there is a "fairly large gap in years" between the two production dates. I know of no grounds for saying with authority how many years this should be. Above, I suggest "at least 25 years" simply because that seemed a reasonable estimate to me. I am quite well aware, however, that it is just one opinion. Since the two items mentioned in the letter *could* differ in age by more than 25 years (1946 vs. 1977), the proposed rule of thumb suggests they might well differ in value, with the older one being worth more because it is likely to be rarer. How much more is it worth? I am really not sure but, if forced to put a number on it, I would say not more than about 1% per year.

F.36 Bird figurine. 6.0"h x 4.25"w x 3.0"d. Backstamp: 65.019. $250+

F.37 Dragon figurine. 3.25"h x 13.0"long. Backstamp: 55.3. $300+

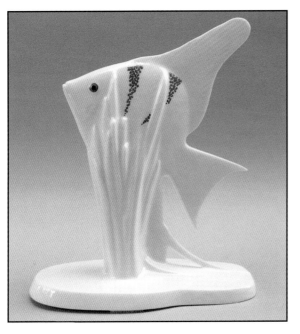

F.38 Fish figurine. 5.38"h x 6.38"w. Backstamp: 67.019. $80-140.

F.39 Fish figurine. 4.75"h x 12.0" long. Backstamp: 66.57. $280-380.

F.40 Fish figurines. *Left*, 3.75"h x 12.0" long; *right*, 3.75"h x 10.25" long. Backstamp: 65.019. Larger fish, $150-250; smaller fish, $110-220.

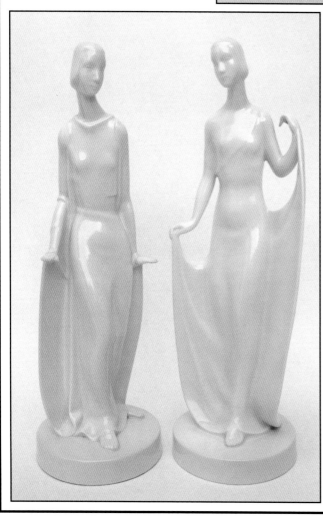

Left: F.41 Figurines. *Left*, 10.5"h x 3.0"w; *right*, 10.5"h x 3.38"w Backstamp: 25.1. Pair, as shown, $900-1400.

Right: F.42 Figurine. 7.25"h x 2.75"w. Backstamp: 27.0. $400-600.

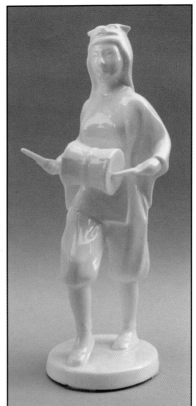

F.44 Figurine. 8.75"h x 3.13"w. Backstamp: 65.5. $140-220.

F.43 Figurine. Overall, 10.0"h; wooden base, 8.0"w x 5.25"d. Backstamp: AP75.5 (Arnold Palmer Collection. A Limited Edition of 600 pieces). $300+

F.45 Figurine. 8.0"h x 4.75"w. Backstamp: 65.5. $240-320.

F.43A Figurine in F.43 shown in presentation box.

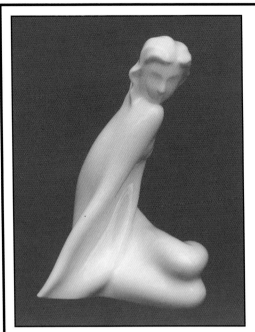

F.46 Figurine. 4.25"h x 8.75"w x 4.25"d.
Backstamp: 67.019. $150-250.

F.47 Figurine. 6.5"h x 9.0"w x 3.88"d.
Backstamp: 65.5. $250+

F.48 Figurine. 5.88"h x 4.25"w x 3.25"d.
Backstamp: 67.019. $100-200.

Chapter H
Holiday Items

H.12 Christmas Bell, 1972, in original box (Holly). Bell, 3.25"h x 2.5"w. Box, 2.88"h x 3.75"w x 4.25"d. Backstamp: 70.7 (Bone China Limited Collectors Series No 1). $10-20.

The thirteen bone china porcelain bells shown in this particular Chapter H are all part of a single limited-edition series produced by the Noritake Company between 1972 and 1984. Except for the first one, which in effect, announces the series, each of the others depicts a line of the famous "Twelve Days of Christmas" song. One bell was issued each year. They were meant to be presented as gift items for display or, because they are not heavy, for use as Christmas tree ornaments.

As with the Valentine heart and Easter egg series, fewer of each edition were made as the years went by, presumably because of changing levels of interest. Lou Ann Donahue, in her vital little book on Noritake collectibles (see *Bibliography* for details), reports that 28,000 of the 1972 Christmas bell were made, with a suggested retail price of $14.50. By the very next year, this figure had dropped considerably. Nearly ten thousand *fewer* bells (18,200, to be precise) were made that year—the initial year of the "Twelve Days of Christmas" series (1973). For the next four years (1974-1977), the production run was ten thousand for each bell. In 1978, that figure dropped again to 8,600 for the Six Geese a Laying bell, which had a suggested retail price of $25.

Although Donahue's account ends with that bell, it is likely that the quantities produced dropped two or three more times as was the case with all the other limited edition series. From a collector's perspective, this is very important because when other things are equal, as they are in the case of not only these bells but the other holiday and special occasion series produced by the Noritake Company, the quantities produced will (or should) be the most significant factor bearing on value. To some, this may seem almost too elementary and obvious to warrant mention. I am mentioning it, however, because I frequently have seen sellers on eBay describing the first edition of the Noritake Easter eggs and valentine hearts as being "very rare." Just as frequently and far more surprisingly, bidders often respond with very hefty bids even though the Donahue account shows very clearly that the first edition was not rare—a fact I also noted when introducing these items in Chapter H of *Noritake Collectibles A to Z*; see page 186).

I attempted to take these quantity figures into account when assigning values for the items in this chapter. But, because there is not much demand for these bells at the moment, the size of the value range is small. Also small is the difference in the average value of the most common bell and the rarest bell (the last one produced presumably). Consequently, the actual differences in values shown in the captions are correspondingly small. This may change in the future.

Largely because demand for these bells is not yet very strong, there does not seem to be much premium associated with being able to purchase a complete thirteen bell set even though one can see why there ought to be at least some (except from the perspective of those who prefer "the hunt"). It also should be emphasized in this context that the full set is thirteen bells, even though only twelve of them pertain to the song. This fact is established by noticing the words that accompany the backstamp on the bell that has the first line of the song. The words, located inside the bell, state that it is the "Second Edition." Some collectors may be confused by these words on Noritake items, perhaps because of the importance of "first editions" in book collecting. Thus, it may be thought that a phrase like "Second Edition" shows that an item was made *after* the initial production run; that it was, as it were, a "second printing." For Noritake fancyware, this is incorrect. The phrase simply refers to the position of an item in a series.

The words from the song do not appear on the bells. On the outside of each bell, there is only the word "Christmas" followed by a year. In the box with each bell, there was a small pamphlet more-or-less naming the bell, mostly by using the familiar lyrics depicted graphically on the bell. In the captions, therefore, the names based on the song lyrics that are provided are from that source, not from anything written on the bell. It is from such a pamphlet that we learn the first bell was called, simply, "Holly." Finally, the different figures for the bell heights shown in the captions are not typographical errors. They are different because, in fact, the bells do differ in that respect (and that one only as far as size is concerned). These variations are caused by differences in the sizes of the image incorporated into the porcelain handles which, by the way, are pierced to facilitate use as a tree ornament.

H.14 Christmas Bell, 1974, in original box (Two Turtle Doves). Bell, 3.25"h x 2.5"w. Box, 2.88"h x 3.75"w x 4.25"d. Backstamp: 70.7 (Third Edition). $10-20.

H.15 Christmas Bell, 1975, in original box (Three French Hens). Bell, 3.5"h x 2.5"w. Box, 2.88"h x 3.75"w x 4.25"d. Backstamp: 70.7 (Fourth Edition). $10-20.

H.13 Christmas Bell, 1973, in original box (Partridge in a Pear Tree). Bell, 3.25"h x 2.5"w. Box, 2.88"h x 3.75"w x 4.25"d. Backstamp: 70.7 (Second Edition). $10-20.

H.18 Christmas Bell, 1978, in original box (Six Geese a Laying). Bell, 3.5"h x 2.5"w. Box, 2.88"h x 3.75"w x 4.25"d. Backstamp: 70.7 (Seventh Edition). $20-30.

H.16 Christmas Bell, 1976, in original box (Four Colly Birds [blackbirds]). Bell, 3.5"h x 2.5"w. Box, 2.88"h x 3.75"w x 4.25"d. Backstamp: 70.7 (Fifth Edition). $10-20.

H.17 Christmas Bell, 1977, in original box (Five Golden Rings). Bell, 3.25"h x 2.5"w. Box, 2.88"h x 3.75"w x 4.25"d. Backstamp: 70.7 (Sixth Edition). $10-20.

H.20 Christmas Bell, 1979, in original box (Seven Swans a Swimming). Bell, 3.5"h x 2.5"w. Box, 2.88"h x 3.75"w x 4.25"d. Backstamp: 70.7 (Eighth Edition). $20-30.

H.21 Christmas Bell, 1980, in original box (Eight Maids a Milking). Bell, 3.25"h x 2.5"w. Box, 2.88"h x 3.75"w x 4.25"d. Backstamp: 70.7 (Ninth Edition). $20-30.

H.22 Christmas Bell, 1981, in original box (Nine Ladies Dancing). Bell, 3.63"h x 2.5"w. Box, 2.88"h x 3.75"w x 4.25"d. Backstamp: 70.7 (Tenth Edition). $20-30.

H.23 Christmas Bell, 1982, in original box (Ten Lords a Leaping). Bell, 3.75"h x 2.5"w. Box, 2.88"h x 3.75"w x 4.25"d. Backstamp: 70.7 (Eleventh Edition). $20-30.

H.24 Christmas Bell, 1983, in original box (Eleven Pipers Piping). Bell, 3.63"h x 2.5"w. Box, 2.88"h x 3.75"w x 4.25"d. Backstamp: 70.7 (Twelfth Edition). $20-40.

H.25 Christmas Bell, 1984, in original box (Twelve Drummers Drumming). Bell, 3.75"h x 2.5"w. Box, 2.88"h x 3.75"w x 4.25"d. Backstamp: 70.7 (Thirteenth Edition). $20-40.

Chapter L
Lamps, Night Lights and Other Related Items

The items shown in this chapter are clustered into two unlabeled subgroups: those that need candles in order to be lights and those that need bulbs. Within each of those tacit subgroups, the items are sorted into two alphabetically sequenced sets:

Candlesticks (pp. 203-206)
Chambersticks (pp. 206-207)
Lamps (pp. 207-208)
Night lights (pp. 209-211)

Some Noritake collectors and dealers may think of candle- and chambersticks as fairly common items and, in a sense they may be. *Pairs* of these items, however, are not so easy to find. Because singles of these items are fairly common, values are given on a "for each" basis. Although a group of single candlesticks and chambersticks can be an enjoyable and attractive display, I think pairs can be expected to sell for a bit more than twice the "for each" value. It is difficult to say what the premium should be, however, and sellers should be aware that not all buyers prefer pairs.

Two of the items shown in this chapter are among the rarest and most spectacular items in the entire book. The items I have in mind are the night lights shown in L.55 and L.56. These items are rarely seen on the secondary, collectors' market for at least two reasons. First, they are two-piece items, with the upper piece tending to be not only quite thin and fragile but also a bit top-heavy and not firmly attached to the base. As a result, we can be sure that many of these lamps must have been broken accidentally over the years. Second and partly in view of what was just said, the two-piece Noritake porcelain night lights from the 1920s that have survived probably do not get to the secondary market very often. Instead, they have become treasured heirlooms that pass from generation to generation within families. There are small holes in the taller of the two lamps, it should be noted, indicating that this item could be used as a perfume lamp. The holes allow heat from the lighted bulb to come through to warm a bit of cotton soaked in perfume. Heated thus, the perfume's fragrance would be more noticeable.

It would be an oversight not to mention some of the unusual candlesticks (they have no handles) and chambersticks (they usually have only one or sometimes two handles) shown in this chapter. The motif on the pair shown in L.38 can be found on other items, including a centerpiece bowl. This suggests that these candlesticks and the bowl were meant to be used together. Sometimes this combination of items is referred to as a mantle set. The pair in L.40 are similar in decoration to a pair shown

L.38 Candlesticks. 8.25"h x 4.88"w. Backstamp: 27.0. Each, $100-120.

in *Collecting Noritake A to Z* (L.23) but they have a rather different shape. Although not visible in the photo, inside of each of the items shown in L.41 there is a small cavity to hold the candle tightly. They function a lot like the next item (L.42) which, in my experience is a not at all commonly seen blank. It is interesting to me that the motif on the chamberstick shown in L.46 is found on such a wide array of items, including a spooner shown in Chapter Z (Z.56), a tea set and various rather elaborate bowls and serving items as well. Another unusual blank, as uncommon as L.42, is the chamberstick in L.47. Yellow is a strong color and it has been used to great effect, I think, on the chambersticks in L.48-L.50. The motif on the pair in L.51 is both uncommon and uncommonly minimalist, for Noritake items especially.

Finally, we turn to various items that have been made into lamps by the addition of various (mostly metal) parts (see L.52-L.54). Vases and candlesticks are the items of choice for such conversions. Sometimes the holes for the cords are drilled after having been sold to the customer; sometimes the holes were drilled at the factory. The most reliable method for deciding what was done is to look for glaze on the inside edge (as it were) of the hole. If there is no glaze, it very probably was drilled after the Noritake Company made it. In terms of value, I think it matters little where or when the drilling was done. The key is how well it was done. After the porcelain has been fired, attempts to drill holes for cords can (for obvious reasons) produce hairlines, cracks and rough edges or chips (and worse). In these instances, the effect on value can be substantial. Although brief, I hope my commentary about these brilliant items has enlightened you (sorry; I couldn't resist).

L.40 Candlesticks. 7.0"h x 4.25"w. Backstamp: 27.0. Each, $80-110.

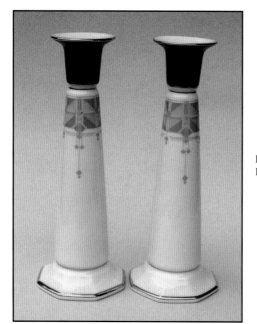

L.39 Candlesticks. 8.0"h x 3.0"w. Backstamp: 86.5. Each, $40-80.

L.41 Candlesticks. 5.5"h x 3.5"w. Backstamp: 19.0. Each, $30-50.

L.43 Candlesticks. 3.75"h x 4.25"w. Backstamp: 27.1. Each, $90-120.

L.42 Candlestick. 4.25"h x 4.5"w. Backstamp: 27.1. $60-100.

L.44 Candlesticks. 3.75"h x 4.25"w. Backstamp: 27.1. Each, $90-120.

L.45 Candlesticks. 2.5"h x 5.38"w. Backstamp: 27.1.
Each, $90-120.

L.47 Chamberstick. 3.13"h x 4.25"w. Backstamp: 27.1. $80-100.

L.46 Chamberstick. 6.0"h x 5.63"w. Backstamp:
27.0. $90-120.

L.48 Chamberstick. 3.0"h x 4.75"w.
Backstamp: 27.0. $80-100.

L.49 Chamberstick. 1.88"h x 4.5"w.
Backstamp: 27.1. $50-80.

L.50 Chambersticks. 1.75"h x 4.25"w.
Backstamp: 27.0. Each, $50-80.

L.51 Chambersticks. 1.75"h x 2.75"w. Backstamp: 27.1.
Each, $30-50.

L.52 Lamp. Overall: 23"h; lamp vase:
8.88"h x 5.38"w. Backstamp: 27.0. Lamp
vase alone, $100-200.

L.53 Lamp (candlestick). Overall, with fixture, 8.0"h; candlestick, 6.13"h x 4.5"w. Backstamp: 27.0. As shown, $140-180.

L.54 Lamp bases (candlesticks with pre-drilled cord holes). 6.13"h x 4.5"w. Backstamp: 27.0. Each, $100-140.

L.55 Perfume night light. 9.75"h x 5.0"w. $2500+

L.55B. Lamp in L.55 illuminated. The head and hands are dark because in those parts of this piece the porcelain is much thicker and so less light comes through.

L.55A Detail of L55.

L.56A Detail of lamp in L56.

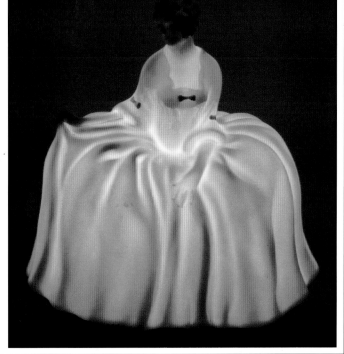

L.56B Lamp in L56 illuminated. The
head and one of the hands are dark
because in those parts of this piece the
porcelain is much thicker and so less
light comes through.

Opposite page: L.56 Night light (after Royal Doulton's
"Polly Peachum"). 8.0"h x 5.25"w. Backstamp: 27.0.
$2500+

Plaques, Plates, Trays and Other Flat Items

In this chapter, the many plates, plaques, trays, serving plates and other basically flat items shown in it are grouped as follows:

Cake plates (pp. 212-220)
Children's plate (p. 221)
Chip and dip, and other combination or multi-piece serving sets (pp. 222-225)
Lemon plates (pp. 225-228)
   loop center-handled lemon plates (p. 225)
   side-handled lemon plates (pp. 226-228)
   solid center-handled lemon plates (p. 228)
Plaques (pp. 229-231)
Plates, round and without handles (pp. 231-235)
Plates, sided and without handles (p. 236)
Plates with one side handle (p. 237)
Plates with two handles, other than cake plates (pp. 237-238)
Plates with three handles (p. 238)
Platter (p. 239)
Sandwich and other large center-handled serving plates (pp. 239-240)
Trays (pp. 241-242)

In the introduction to Chapter P in *Collecting Noritake A to Z*, I suggested, partly in jest, that there were basically only two kinds of Noritake plates: (1) lemon plates and (2) all the others. This debatable remark was offered as wry commentary in the face of a seemingly indisputable fact: the Noritake Company produced lemon plates in huge quantities. One lamentable consequence of this is that too many dealers and collectors seem unable to utter the phrase "Noritake lemon plate" without inserting the word "lowly" in front of it. Although it doesn't show (of course), I have a big ironic grin on my face as write these words. This is because, in this chapter, which is loaded with photographs of wonderful pieces, the most amazing and rare of all these terrific items is a lemon plate! It isn't a lady piece nor does it have a Deco motif; in fact, it is really quite plain. The item I have in mind, a *complete* (to my knowledge, uniquely so) lemon set, is shown below in P.229. What makes it special is that it is *all* there: original box, pack-

P.198 Cake plate with bolted pedestal. (Note: The plate shown in P.3 in *Noritake Collectibles A to Z* is not on a pedestal.) 2.88"h x 10.75"w x 10.0"d. Backstamp: 27.1. $450-600.

P.199 Cake plate with bolted pedestal. 2.75"h x 11.0"w. Backstamp: 27.1. $120-170.

P.199A Detail of P.199.

ing material, bone fork, the wrapper for the fork and, of course, the "lowly" lemon plate. Or is it, in fact, a *lemon* plate?

One thing we know for sure is that virtually all collectors and dealers *refer* to these items as "lemon plates." If asked (and it is always a good idea to start this way), collectors and dealers will support their view by noting that lemon motifs are very common on these plates. They also are likely to show you how simple it would be to serve lemons on such plates. "See," they will demonstrate, "by holding the side handle, one can so easily and politely hold the plate out so your guest can take a slice for their tea" (if I had a dollar for every time this has been demonstrated in my presence, I could buy any lemon plate shown in this book). As widespread and plausible as these views are, it may also be that they are at least incomplete and maybe even invalid.

Although I have not tallied the relevant numbers, I am confident that while lemon motifs are commonly seen they are almost rare as a percent of all known motifs on such plates. Only 1 of the 17 shown in this book has a lemon motif. None of the 17 shown in *Collecting Noritake A to Z* has a lemon motif and just 10 of the 56 shown in *Noritake Collectibles A to Z* has such a motif. In total, that is only about 12%. More significantly, when one examines Larkin Company catalogs from the 1920s, one most frequently finds these plates referred to as *pickle* sets. Most of the ones I have seen in these catalogs have the side handle and come with a bone fork just like the one shown in P.229 (but without the paper wrapper—omitted from the picture in Larkin catalogs, one presumes, because it would virtually hide the fork). In some instances, they are described as a "pickle or lemon set"—but note that it is pickle that comes first. With the bone fork, they typically were priced at about $1 to $1.25 each.

Even in the face of these facts, I am sure most dealers and collectors will continue to refer to these items as lemon plates and, in keeping with the goal of organizing the book so it is *easy* for collectors and dealers to use it, I will continue referring to these items as lemon plates even though, at one time, they may have been thought of primarily as pickle plates. For the same reason, I also will continue to include relatively large (up to 8" dia.) center and side-handled plates in the lemon plate section (e.g., see P.230, P.239 and P.240 in this book or P.31 in *Noritake Collectibles A to Z*).

The motifs on all of the lemon plates shown in this book are striking, but I cannot resist directing your attention to three that I think are particularly unusual. One of these is the lemon plate with a very bold, abstract geometric motif (see P.225). It contrasts dramatically with a lemon plate shown in P.228 that is unusual because of its yellow luster, an uncommon color for Noritake wares. Finally, the lemon plate shown in P.239 should be noted because it is unusual in both overall motif and shape (although P.240 does repeat the shape).

There are, of course, many other kinds of items in this chapter with features and qualities of special interest to the collector. For example, the pancake server shown in this book (P.221) has a particularly bold and well-executed motif. This fact is made all the more significant by another one—namely, that it has a Cherry Blossom backstamp, a mark linked in the minds of many (often quite erroneously, I think) with less well-produced pieces. Sweetmeat sets, such as the one shown in P.224, are difficult to find complete and even more difficult to find with a box that is in good condition—a variable that has considerable impact on their value. Condition is always a consideration, of course, but sometimes it becomes particularly important. Children's cereal dishes, such as the one shown in P.216, are often very worn. So, when one finds such an item in fine or better condition, it adds greatly to its value.

Sometimes two items that differ in seemingly small ways will differ greatly in value. For example, there are two so-called "chip and dip" serving sets shown in this book (P.219 and 220). The figural handle on one, coupled with the fact that it is a figural lady, makes a *huge* impact on the value. I refer to these as "so-called" chip and dip sets because the term probably post-dates the piece. Another "what is the right term" question can be raised regarding the super "sandwich set" shown in P.222. Some may wonder why it is not listed as an ice cream set. The two main reasons are the shape of the plates and the length of the tray. In the 1920s, fancy boxed ice cream often came in long blocks with a square cross-section shape. Consequently, individual ice cream serving plates are basically square, not round. Also, while these ice cream blocks were relatively long (a 12.5" long plate is shown in P.27 in *Noritake Collectibles A to Z*), they were a lot shorter than the 17.25" long tray shown here in P.222.

Although the four plaques shown in this book are quite different, they are all rather rare. Usually, the Indian plaque shown in P.244 has a backstamp from the pre-1921 Nippon era. Given this, it is not surprising that the one shown in this book has backstamp 27.0, one of the first backstamps used by the Noritake Company after 1921 for fancyware exported to the United States. Much the same can be said for the dog plaque (P.243) but there is more: typically (if not always), the Nippon era version of this plaque had fewer colors. The *exquisite* framed plaque shown in P.245 is also, stylistically, more typical of the Nippon era. From the backstamp on it (which was registered in 1912), we know that this plaque was not originally intended for export, but, rather, was for the domestic (i.e., Japanese) market. Appropriately enough, this piece is in the hands of a collector in Japan.

The remaining plaque (P.242) not only has a particularly striking and unusual motif but also is rather unusual in other respects. It too has a domestic market backstamp—a magenta version of the backstamp found on the previously discussed plaque. What is of particular interest, however, is the inscription in the middle left (see P.242C). It both dates the piece quite precisely (in itself an unusual feature of any Noritake item from the period) but also suggests (according to Company sources) that the piece was decorated expressly for Mike Kenzie. It has been suggested to me, again by sources in Nagoya, that whoever Mr. Kenzie was (or is), he must have been a rather significant visitor to the Company because it was anything but common to produce such an elaborately decorated item. In this context, please note the artist's signature (N. Hayashi) on the right (see P.242D).

In contrast to these plaques, cake plates are rather plentiful and, as with lemon plates, are very often seen as less desirable as a result. And, as with lemon plates (and bowls and many other Noritake items), I think such opinions ought to be re-evaluated. Cake plates offered several advantages to the designers and to the painters who decorated them, the main one being that they are relatively large and flat and, hence comparatively easy to decorate well. As a result, the sharp-eyed collector can find some *very* striking cake plates that are, because demand is weak, often quite reasonably priced. Of the many excellent cake plates shown in this chapter, the first two (P.198 and 199) are particularly noteworthy. Pedestal cake plates are both

P.200 Cake plate. 1.38"h x 10.75"w x 10.25"d. Backstamp: 27.0. $120-170.

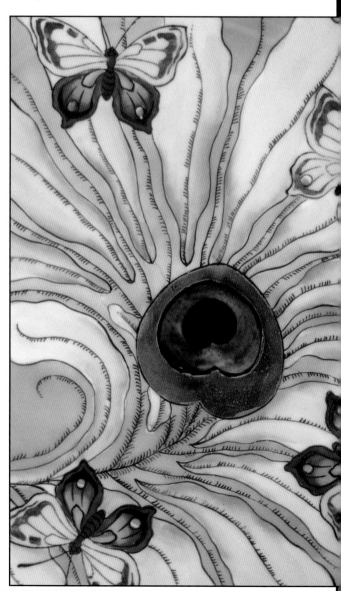

P.200A Detail of P.200.

striking and uncommon. The motif on P.198, known to most collectors as "The Plantation Lady," is found on a *wide* variety of Noritake blanks (see Chapter 2, above) and is in great demand. By contrast, the cake plate shown in P.201, which happens to be on one of the most common cake plate shapes, is one of the rarest motifs in this book. I know of no other piece with that motif or even one like it, although surely they exist. A plate in that shape also was used to record the unusual motif shown in P.202. From the backstamp on it, which was registered in 1926 in Bombay, we know that this piece was originally intended for export to India.

As far as we know, any cake plate with handles will have two of them. Not all two-handled plates, however, are cake plates. Some two-handled plates seldom would be taken for cake plates because they are relatively small (5-7 inches in diameter). Others, however, are as large as cake plates (and in some cases larger). Four such plates are shown in this book. They are not in the cake plate section because the shapes of these plates are quite unlike the typical Noritake cake plate. Of course, these plates (or perhaps they are trays; it is not always obvious which is the more appropriate designation) could be used for serving cakes. As with the lemon plates (and various other items), determining an item's function is an inexact "science." These three plates are all quite different and, in their various ways, beautiful examples of Noritake creativity and artistic excellence. Of particular note, however, is the plate shown in P.262. The marble-like square in the center is smooth and flat while the roses around this square are molded-in-relief.

Most Noritake plates without handles are round. In this book, there are several that are artist-signed, a feature that, while not rare, is certainly not common with Noritake items (see P.246 and P.247). Although some collectors are now making a special effort to seek artist-signed items, it cannot be said, at this time, that such pieces are commanding exceptional prices (see above, Chapter 2, for more on this). Instead, the plates that command top dollar are various so-called "Lady Plates."

There are quite a few "Lady" motifs on Noritake items and a good selection of them have been shown in my first two books. Few if any of the known "Lady Plates," however, are currently in greater demand than the ones shown in P.255. Plates with these motifs come in two sizes. The ones shown are 6.25" in diameter; the larger plates are 7.75" in diameter. The values given for these plates will perhaps seem out of line with many seemingly similar items shown in my other books. Two things need to be said about this. First, the values on those sorts of items in my previous books are now much lower than current market values. Second, there simply seems to be *tremendous* demand for these particular motifs. How long this will last, of course, is impossible to say. The larger plates, by the way, do not seem to be commanding prices that are all that much higher than the smaller ones.

Although the women depicted on these plates are obviously quite different from each other, they are also similar in certain important ways. Their most striking common feature, I think, is the treatment of their eyes. Nearly as striking are the similar renderings of their lips and noses; all have a pink glow from what one presumes represents facial make-up. There also is one difference that seems greater than it actually is, at least in my opinion. I refer to the fact that one of them does not have a hat. This is the lady in the plate on the left, known to collectors variously as "The Spanish Lady" or "The Fan Lady." Although she is hatless, there is, in the motif, a design element that, as I see it anyway, corresponds rather well with the other two plates. This element is the fan. It, like the two hats, has a prominent, long curved edge.

Males and/or masculinized (androgynous) females are essentially "rare"

P.201 Cake plate. 1.38"h x 9.75"w x 9.5"d. Backstamp: 27.0. $500+

motifs on Noritake items from the 1920s. The most frequently seen and most obviously male motif is the one on the plate shown below in P.250. This is known to collectors as the "Man in Cape" motif, for obvious reasons. Two other plates within this motif category are P.248 and P.249—both highly desirable items. Also worthy of special attention are the trays and sandwich plates shown in this chapter. Most happen to have superb floral motifs that, so far, are still not commanding prices commensurate with their artistic merit. The motifs on two of these items (P.271 and P.277) deserve a closer look than they are usually given. At first glance, they seem to have the same "Lady in the Garden" motif. In one, however (P.271), the woman is holding a bouquet of yellow roses; in the other (P.277), she is looking at an uncaged bird sitting on her left hand. Many different Noritake items have one or the other of these obviously related motifs. Finally, the large, three-section tray shown in P.275 deserves to be singled out because it is a very unusual blank.

P.202 Cake plate. 1.38"h x 9.75"w x 9.5"d. Backstamp: RC26.2. $70-100.

P.202A Detail of P.202.

P.203 Cake plate. 1.13"h x 10.63"w x 10.13"d. Backstamp: 27.0. $20-40.

P.203A Detail of P.203.

P.205 Cake plate. 1.25"h x 9.75"w x 9.5"d. Backstamp: 27.1. $20-40.

P.205A Detail of P.205.

P.204 Cake plate. 1.25"h x 9.75"w x 9.5"d. Backstamp: 27.1. $20-40.

P.204A Detail of P. 204.

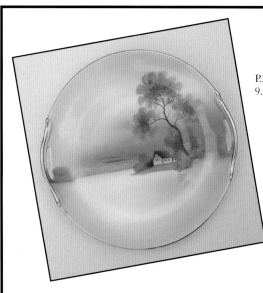

P.206 Cake plate. 1.25"h x 9.75"w x 9.5"d. Backstamp: 27.1. $20-40.

P.207 Cake plate. 1.25"h x 9.75"w x 9.5"d. Backstamp: 27.0. $20-40.

P.208 Cake plate. 1.0"h x 10.88"w x 10.25"d. Backstamp: 27.1. $30-50.

P.209 Cake plate. 3.25"h x 10.5"w x 9.63"d. Backstamp: 27.1. $30-50.

P.210 Cake plate. 1.0"h x 10.25"w x 9.75"d.
27.1. $30-50.

P.210A Detail of P.210.

P.212 Cake plate. 1.38"h x 9.63"w.
x 9.5"d. Backstamp: 27.1. $30-50.

P.211 Cake plate. 1.25"h x 10.13"w x 9.5"d.
Backstamp: 27.1. $40-80.

P. 211A Detail of P.211.

P.213 Cake plate. 1.5"h x 10.88"d. x
10.38"d. Backstamp: 27.0. $30-50.

P.214 Cake plate. 1.5"h x 9.5"w x
9.0"d. Backstamp: 27.0. $40-70.

P.215 Cake plate. 1.75"h x 9.38"w x 8.88"d.
Backstamp: 29.1. $60-90.

P.215A Detail of P.215.

P.216 Child's cereal dish. 1.25"h x 7.0"dia.
Backstamp: 27.1. $110-180.

P.216A Detail of P.216.

P.216B Detail of P.216.

P.216C Detail of P.216.

P.217 Cheese server. 4.63"h x 7.88"w x 5.88"d.
Backstamp: 27.1. $90-140.

P.218 Cheese server. 4.63"h x 7.88"w x
5.88"d. Backstamp: 27.1. $100-160.

P.219 Covered chip and dip (2 pieces). Figural lady handle is 2.5"h; overall,
4.5"h x 9.5"w. Backstamp: 27.1. $600-800.

P.219A Detail of P.219.

P.220 Covered chip and dip (2 pieces). 2.5"h x 5.63"d. Backstamp: 16.0. $60-90.

P.221 Pancake server. Plate, 9.0"dia. Cover, 3.75"h x 6.88"w. Backstamp: 19.2. $190-250.

P.222 Sandwich set. Serving plate, 1.13"h x 17.25"w x 6.63"d. Individual plates, .75"h x 6.0"dia. Backstamp: 27.1. Set, as shown, $180-260.

P.223 Serving set with
sauce bowl. Sauce bowl,
3.5"h x 6.75" x 3.25"d. Plate,
1.5"h x 12.0"w x 9.5"d.
Spoons, 7.25"long x 1.88"w.
Backstamp: 27.1 $230-300.

P.223A Detail of P.223.

P.224 Sweetmeat set in original box. 2.38"h x 11.5"dia. Backstamp: 27.0. $190-250.

P.225 Loop center-handled lemon plate. 2.5"h x 5.25"dia. Backstamp: 27.1. $70-100.

P.226 Loop center-handled lemon plate. 2.63"h x 6.5"dia. Backstamp: 25.1. $20-40.

P.224A The box lid of P.224.

P.227 Round loop center-handled lemon plate. 2.5"h x 5.25"dia. Backstamp: 27.1. $20-40.

P.228 Round loop center-handled lemon plate. 2.63"h x 5.13"dia. Backstamp: 27.1. $30-50.

P.229 Round side-handled lemon plate in
original box with fork wrapped in original paper.
Box, 1.5"h x 6.13"w x 6.13"d. Plate, 1.25"h x
5.5"dia. Fork, 4.75" long. Backstamp: 25.1. As
shown, $130-160.

P.231 Round side-handled lemon plate. 1.5"h x 6.25"dia.
Backstamp: 27.1. $30-50.

P.230 Round side-handled lemon plate. 2.0"h x 7.63"dia.
Backstamp: 27.0. $30-50.

P.232 Round side-handled lemon plate.
1.5"h x 6.25"dia. Backstamp: 27.1. $20-40.

P.233 Round side-handled
lemon plate. 1. 5"h x 6.25"dia.
Backstamp: 27.0. $30-50.

P.235 Round side-handled lemon plate.
1.25"h x 5.75"dia. Backstamp: 27.1. $20-40.

P.234 Round side-handled lemon plate.
1.25"h x 5.75"dia. Backstamp: 27.0. $20-40.

P.236 Round side-handled lemon
plate. 1.25"h x 5. 5"dia. Backstamp:
27.1. $20-40.

P.237 Round side-handled lemon plate. 1.25"h x
5.5"dia. Backstamp: 27.1. $20-40.

P.240 Solid center-handled lemon plate. 2.75"h x 7.5"dia.
Backstamp: 25.1. $40-70.

P.238 Side-handled sided lemon plate.
1.5"h x 6.0"w. Backstamp: 27.1. $30-50.

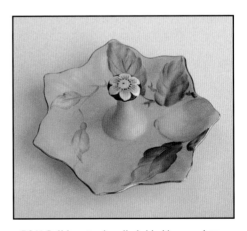

P.241 Solid center-handled sided lemon plate.
3.13"h x 6.0"w. Backstamp: 27.1 $40-50.

P.239 Solid center-handled lemon plate. 2.75"h x 7.5"dia.
Backstamp: 27.1. $40-70.

P.242 Plaque. Signed by N. Hayashi. 1.25"h x
10.25"dia. Backstamp: 07.3. $400+

P.242A Detail of P.242.

P.242C Detail of P.242.

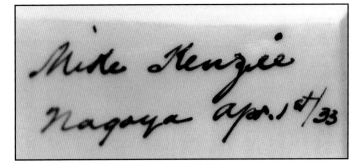

P.242B Detail of P.242.

P.242D Detail of P.242.

P.243 Plaque. 1.13"h x 10.5"dia.
Backstamp: 27.0. $800+

P.243A Detail of P.243.

P.244 Plaque. 1.38"h x 10.63"dia.
Backstamp: 27.0. $500+

P.246 Plate. Signed B.
Fushimi. 1.25"h x 10.0"dia.
Backstamp: 27.0. $50-80.

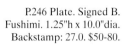

P.245 Plaque in frame. Plaque, 7.75"dia. Frame 11.5"h
x 11.5"w. Backstamp: 07.0 $400+

P.246A Detail of P.246.

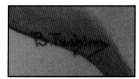

P.246B Detail of P.246.

P.247 Plate. Signed M. Wana. 1.0"h x 8.63"dia. Backstamp: 27.0. $40-70.

P.247A Detail of P.247.

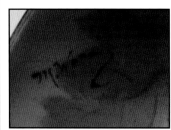

P.247B Detail of P.247.

P.248 Plate. 1.0"h x 7.75"dia.
Backstamp. 27.0. $450-600.

P.248A Detail of P. 248.

P.249 Plate. 1.0"h x 7.75"dia. Backstamp: 27.1. $450-600.

P.250 Plate. 1.0"h x 7.75"dia.
Backstamp: 27.1. $400-550.

P.250A Detail of P.250.

P.249A Detail of P.249.

P.251 Plates. .88"h x 7.75"dia.
Backstamp: *left,* 27.1; *right,* 26.1.
Each, $40-70.

P.252 Plates. .88"h x 7.75"dia.
Backstamp: 27.0. Each, $40-70.

P.254 Plate .75"h x 5.75"dia.
Backstamp: 27.0. $40-70.

P.253 Plate. .75"h x 6.25"dia. Backstamp:
27.0. $40-70.

P.255 Plates. .75"h x 6.25"dia. Backstamp: All,
27.1. *Left and right,* Each $600-900; *Center,*
$700-1000.

P.256 Sided plate. 1.0"h x 8.5"w x 8.13"d. Backstamp: 27.0. $30-40.

P.257 Sided plate. 1.0"h x 8.5"w x 8.13"d. Backstamp: 27.0. $30-40.

P.256A Detail of P.256.

P.257A Detail of P.257.

P.258 Plate with one side handle. 1.13" h x 7.5"w x 7.13"d. Backstamp: 27.0. $20-40.

P.261 Plate with two handles. 1.63"h x 10.5"w x 9.75"d. Backstamp: 27.1. $170-240.

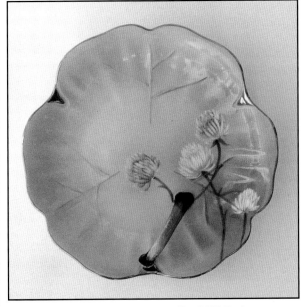

P.259 Plate with one side handle. 1.5"h x 8.0"d. Backstamp: 25.1. $40-70.

P.262 Plate with two handles. 1. 5"h x 10.25"w x 9.25"d. Backstamp: 25.1. $170-240.

P.260 Plate with side handle. 2.25"h x 7.5"w x 6.3"d. Backstamp: 27.0. $40-70.

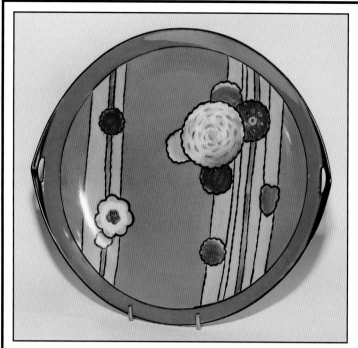

P.263 Plate with two handles. 1.0"h x 10.0"w x 9.5"d. Backstamp: 27.0. $90-140.

P.265 Plate with three handles. 1.25"h x 9.38"w. Backstamp: 27.0. $60-100.

P.264 Plate with two handles. 1.75"h x 10.25"w x 8.88"d. Backstamp: 19.1. $80-110.

P.266 Plate with three handles. 1.25"h x 9.38"w. Backstamp: 27.1. $50-90.

P.267 Platter. Weighs nearly four pounds. 1.63" x 16.0"w x 12.0"d. Backstamp: 28.1 (Roseara). $180-230.

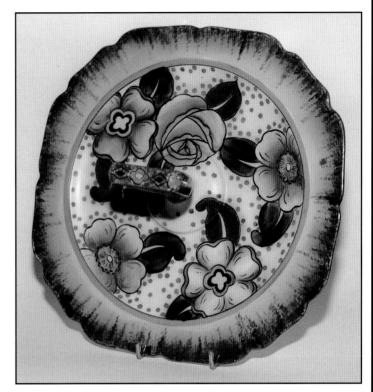

P.269 Sandwich plate. 3.75"h x 9.38"w x 9.38"d. Backstamp: 27.1. $160-210.

P.268 Sandwich plate. 4.0"h x 9.75"dia. Backstamp: 19.1. $100-160.

P.270 Sandwich plate. 3.0"h x 7.5"dia. Backstamp: 25.1. $160-210.

P.271 Sandwich plate with figural element. 3.0"h x 8.25"dia.
Backstamp: 27.1. $370-520.

P.271A Detail of P.271.

P.272 Sandwich plate with figural element. 5.0"h x 8.0"dia.
Backstamp: 19.2. $210-260.

P.273 Sandwich plate with figural element. 5.0"h x 8.0"dia. Backstamp:
27.0. $210-260.

P.274 Tray. 1.0"h x 13.0"w x 10.13"d.
Backstamp: 19.1. $130-190.

P.274A Detail of P.274.

P.275 Tray. 1.5"h x 11.5"w x 6.0"d.
Backstamp: 25.1. $120-170.

P.276 Tray. .88"h x 9.0"w x 9.0"d. Backstamp: 27.0. $140-200.

P.277 Tray. .88"h x 9.0"w x 9.0"d. Backstamp: 27.1. $390-580.

P.276A Detail of P.276.

P.277A Detail of P.277.

Tea Sets and Other Items Pertaining to Beverages

Tea sets and related items are the focus of this chapter. The photographs of the items shown are grouped and sequenced as follows:

Breakfast set (p. 243)
Children's tea set (pp. 244-245)
Chocolate sets (pp. 246-247)
Coffee and demitasse sets (pp. 247-249)
Condensed milk container (p. 250)
Cream and sugar sets (pp. 250-252)
Cups and saucers (pp. 252-253)
Snack sets (pp. 253-254)
Tea caddy (p. 254)
Tea sets (pp. 254-256)
Tea strainers (pp. 256-257)
Tea tiles and trivets (pp. 257-258)

T.114 Breakfast set. Tray, .63"h x 10.75"w x 9.25"d. Egg cup, 3.5"h x 2.38"w. Creamer, 2.5"h x 3.0"w. x 2.5"d. Sugar, 2.0"h x 3.13"w. Salt and pepper, 1.38"h x 2.5"w. Backstamp: salt and pepper, MIJ.1; others, 27.1. $150-250.

Before sharing my thoughts on the interesting features of some of the elegant items in this chapter, I need to address, briefly, three other topics: terminology, set contents and function, and values (in that order). On eBay and in other contexts, one can expect to encounter words being used by sellers from Australia, Great Britain, and New Zealand that few American collectors would think of as familiar. Examples I have seen fairly often include "coffee can," "tennis set," "TV set" and "trio." My point here is not to foster the use of these words by American collectors (though of course I would have no objection), but, rather, to (as it were) "translate" them (whenever possible with reference to items shown in this chapter).

As I have seen the term "coffee can" used, it designates a straight-sided, cylindrical type of cup (along with its saucer) that Americans refer to as "demitasse" (e.g., such as the cups shown in T.119 and T.120). The terms "tennis set" and "TV set" appear to be equivalent and interchangeable. They are used to designate an item that Americans usually refer to as a "snack set"

T.114A Alternate view of T.114.

or "luncheon set" (e.g., T.140). The word "trio" could be especially confusing to collectors if they are familiar with a discussion (mostly in *Noritake News*) of an apparent artistic strategy utilized by the design team in the New York office. This strategy involved the creation of different but related items that, together, constituted a "conceptual set"—i.e., a set of items that belonged together not because of function (such as the items in a tea or dresser set) but because of some artistic theme or concept. It was proposed

T.115 Child's toy tea set. Part I. Pot, 3.5"h x 5.5"w x 3.75"d. Creamer, 2.0"h x 3.25" w x 2.75"d. Sugar, 2.63"h x 4.25"w x 3.0"d. Backstamp: 27.1. Items shown, $150-250.

that many of these conceptual sets had three items and so they were referred to, in that discussion, as "trios." I believe the only "trio" in this sense shown in this book is in P.255. How it is a conceptual set is discussed in the introduction to Chapter P. There also is a "quartet" (a four item conceptual set). It is in Chapter B, photo B.438. When those bowls are shown together as they are, it tends to be fairly obvious how their design elements are related, conceptually. The potential for confusion regarding the word "trio" arises because, for some years prior to its use in the discussion of conceptual sets, it was used to designate another type of set. In this usage, one seen frequently on eBay, the word designates a set of three specific pieces, matching exactly in décor: a cup (tea or coffee), a saucer and an individual serving plate. The only trios in this sense that are shown in this chapter are in the tea set shown in T.147.

Many of the items shown in this chapter, just as in Chapter C, are sets. Collectors or sellers of sets inevitably will be confronted with decisions on three important matters regarding sets. One of them has to do with the impact on value of a missing piece or pieces. Another pertains to the number of cups and saucers that make up a complete chocolate, coffee, demitasse, or tea set. A third issue is whether the item presented as a set is a true set or "marriage"—i.e., a pseudo-set. The impact of missing pieces on value usually is substantial. Even an elegant coffee set with just one missing saucer is likely to bring as much as 50% less at auction than a complete set. The reason is simple: it may be years, if ever, before one will find a replacement saucer. Of course, if the pattern on the items in the set is known to be fairly common, the chances of finding a replacement piece can be expected to go up. In that case, the impact of a missing piece on value goes down a bit. A different, but related, issue may be mentioned in this context. It often happens that a group of, say, 6 or 8 cup and saucer sets, will be sold at a lower average price per set than a single cup and saucer set. This is particularly true, in my experience, for snack (TV, tennis) sets like the one shown in T.140. An individual set like that one, although hardly common, regularly sells for from $150-$250. Although I have only a few cases to go on, the trend seems clear. When groups of 5 or more sets are offered, the average price of each set is lower than when a single set is offered. This happens, I think, because more buyers are looking for one example of an item than for a large group of them. Indeed, I think we can take this observation a step further. In general, coffee, tea, and demitasse sets, children's toy tea sets, and other multi-piece sets, even when complete, bring lower prices than one might expect given the number of pieces in the set. The exceptions are sets of exceptional beauty and rarity (Azalea children's tea sets, for example, or a demitasse set like the one shown below in T.119).

How many cups and saucers should a *complete* chocolate, coffee, demitasse or tea set have? The answer, I think, is that six is the minimum and most common number, but 8 is not unknown. Virtually all of the experts I consulted agreed that a set with from 1 to 4, or 7 cups and saucers would *not* be considered complete. Rather frequently, however, one will hear that a set with 5 cups and saucers is complete because, so the story runs, sets with an even number of cups and saucers (especially four items) are considered bad luck in some cultures. And indeed, I have seen some non-Euro-American buyers react quite negatively to the thought of buying a set with four cups and saucers. Even so, since most of these sets were meant to be exported to places where even numbers are not associated with bad luck, it seems almost certain that sets with 5 cups and saucers made for export are not complete. Rather, what they are (or may be) is not unlucky.

What items belong in a set? Sometimes this is fairly easy to establish; at other times, however, it can be difficult. For example, look at the cream and sugar set in T.126. This certainly is not the only Noritake cream and sugar set known to have a matching and appropriately sized tray (another one is shown in T.25 in *Noritake Collectibles A to Z*, for example; others are known). Because the blanks for the cream and sugar in this set are fairly common, one may wonder if other cream and sugar sets in that shape came with a matching tray. The short answer is that we do not know for sure. It seems to me, however, that whether a cream and sugar set would come with a matching tray would have more to do with the motif on the set

T.115A Child's toy tea set. Part II. Cup, 1.38"h x 2.88"w. x 2.38"d. Saucer, .5"h x 3.75"dia. Plate, .5"h x 4.38"dia. Backstamp: 27.1. Items shown, $200-300.

than the shapes of the pieces in it. Of the sets with trays that I know about, all have relatively formal motifs, a feature that somehow fits with the use of a tray, which, to me, conveys a bit more formality. Given this, I think we should expect that some cream and sugar sets will have trays while others will not. How is the collector or dealer to know which sets have trays? The answer to this, I am afraid (at this point, at least) is experience and, as most of us know, even that can be an unreliable guide. A different sort of example that forces us to consider what constitutes a set is presented by the items shown in T.114, the first photograph in this chapter. It is a rare and unusual breakfast set. The decoration on all the items shown match perfectly and they all have the same backstamp. The tray, as you will notice, has four indentations but there are five items on it. The two small circles would clearly seem to be for the salt and pepper shakers. Although the other three items fit into the two larger circles, only the eggcup seems to fit perfectly. Moreover, in the other breakfast sets I know of (which are different in the basic shape of the tray) all include a coffee or teacup that fits one of the indentations (e.g., see T.79 and T.80 in my second Noritake book). In light of this, can we say that the set in T.114 is a true and complete set or is it incomplete or a marriage? I simply do not know. What I do know is that it is a lovely group of items. I also know that mysteries like this are rather more common than we wish, especially for the items of the sort shown in Chapters C and T of my books. Because there are so many creative

T.115B Detail of teapot in T.115.

marriages on the secondary market, it is difficult to provide a small set of rules for the collector or dealer to use except for that old standby: *caveat emptor* (buyer beware).

Some wonderful and unusual items are shown in this chapter. The chocolate and demitasse sets (T.116-T.123) are a particularly strong group. Although they are diverse in style and detail, each was designed and decorated with exceptional skill. The motif on the set in T.119 will not appeal to all, of course, but I think it is one of the most exciting items shown in this book. Many would expect that cream and sugar sets would be almost too prosaic to bother with but, as a glance at those shown in this chapter will demonstrate, this would be a mistaken assumption. Sets like the one shown in T.125 were shown in my first Noritake book (see T.22 and T.23) with a note saying there was uncertainty as to the true function of these items. Some thought they were for serving melted butter, the tray being available to catch drips from the spout. Others thought it was a cream and sugar set, with the tray intended for sugar cubes. Recently, a fellow collector sent a copy of a portion of a catalog from the 1920s with a drawing of a set like these. There, it is referred to as a "Novelty Open Sugar & Creamer." The sugar, it states further, "holds loaf sugar." They were sold at the time for 85 cents per set. All the other cream and sugar sets shown in this chapter are excellent, desirable items. Perhaps the most unusual set, though, is the one shown in T.132. The shapes are unusual in my experience.

Not many Noritake collectors collect single cups and saucers. When it is realized, however, that some are as elegant as the ones shown in this chapter (T.136-T.139), this may change. The snack sets were discussed above but of those shown (T.140-T.143), the reader may wish to take note of T.143, for it is rather unusual in both shape and color. The tea caddy shown in T.144 is relatively rare and, curiously enough, is one of only two or three designs that I know of for this item. Surely there must have been more but, so far, they have not turned up. Tea pots, remember, are short and stout. As such, they contrast greatly with coffee and demitasse pots, which are tall and have spouts that are quite long, and with chocolate pots, which are tall but have very small spouts at the very top. The tea sets shown in T.145-T.148 are quite different and each

T.116 Chocolate set. Pot, 8.5"h x 6.88"w x 3.63"d. Cup, 2.75"h x 3.25"w. Saucer, 5.0"dia. Backstamp: 27.0. With 6 cups and saucers, $450-550.

T.117 Chocolate set. Pot, 8.5"h x 6.88"w x 3.63"d. Cup, 2.75"h x 3.25"w. Saucer, 5.0"dia. Backstamp: 27.0. $450-550.

is beautiful in its own way. The set in T.147, however, is likely to be the most amazing one to most collectors. Finally, consider the tea tiles and trivets shown at the end of the chapter (T.151-T.156). Although each one is a show-stopper, only one of them (T.151) is truly rare. As such, these items represent a collecting area with considerable growth potential.

T.118 Chocolate set. Pot, 8.5"h x 6.75"w. Cup, 2.75"h x 3.0"w. Saucer, .5"h x 4.75"dia. Backstamp: 27.1. Set of 6, $350-500.

T.119 Demitasse set. Tray, 1.0"h x 12.0" dia. Pot, 6.5"h x 6.38"w x 2.75"d. Creamer, 2.88"h x 4.38"w x 2.5"d. Sugar, 3.5"h x 5.25"w x 3.0"d. Cup and saucer, 5.25"h x 4.25"w. Backstamp: 27.1. Set as shown, $1000+

T.120 Demitasse set. Tray, 1.0"h x 16.0"w x 11.25"d. Pot, 6.5"h x 6.38"w x 2.75"d. Creamer, 2.88"h x 4.38"w x 2.5"d. Sugar, 3.5"h x 5.25"w x 3.0"d. Cup and saucer, 5.25"h x 4.25"w. Backstamp: saucer, no mark; others, 27.0. Set with 6 cups and saucers, $450-550.

T.120A Detail of T.120.

T.121 Demitasse set. Tray, 13.5"w. Pot, 7.13"h x 7.0"w. Creamer, 2.75"h x 3.75"w. Sugar, 4.0"h x 4.63"w. Cup and saucer, 2.38"h x 4.38"w. Backstamp: 16.0. With 6 cups and saucers, $500-700.

T.122 Demitasse set. Pot, 6.88"h x 7.25"w x 3.5"d. Creamer, 3.5"h x 4.0"w x 2.75"d. Sugar, showing back, 4.13"h x 5.25"w x 4.5"d. Cup and saucer, 2.5"h x 4.75"w. Backstamp: 27.1. With 6 cups and saucers, $450-550.

T.123 Demitasse set. Tray, 1.0"h x 12.0"dia. Pot, 7.0"h x 6.5"w x 3.5"d. Creamer, 2.5"h x 3.5"w. Sugar, 3.5"h x 3.75"w. Cup, 2.0"h x 3.0"w. Saucer, 4.25"dia. Backstamp: 25.1. With 6 cups and saucers, $300-400.

T.124 Condensed milk container. 5.25"h x 4.5"w. Backstamp: 19.2. $80-120.

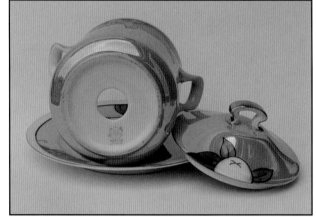

T.124A Alternate view of T.124.

T.125 Cream and sugar set. 4.0"h x 6.5"w x 5.5"d. Backstamp: 27.0. $80-130.

T.126 Cream and sugar set. Tray, 1.38"h x 11.38"w x 4.0"d. Creamer 3.25"h x 4.63"w x 1.63"d. Sugar, 4.0"h x 5.25"w x 2.75"d. Backstamp: 27.1. $100-150.

T.127 Cream and sugar set. Creamer, 3.38"h x 4.0"w x 2.25"d. Sugar, 2.25"h x 6.0"w x 3.5"d. Backstamp: 27.0. $200-300.

T.128 Cream and sugar set. Creamer, 3.38"h x 4.0"w x 2.25"d. Sugar, 2.25"h x 6.0"w x 3.5"d. Backstamp: 27.1. $90-130.

T.129 Cream and sugar set. Creamer, 5.0"h x 3.38"w x 2.75"d. Sugar 2.63"h x 3.75"w x 3.5"d. Backstamp: 27.0. $60-90.

T.130 Cream and sugar set. Creamer, 5.0"h x 3.38"w x 2.75"d. Sugar, 2.63"h x 3.75"w x 3.5"d. Backstamp: 27.1. $70-90.

T.131 Cream and sugar set. Creamer, 4.38"h x 4.75"w x 3.5"d. Sugar, 5.0"h x 5.25"w x 4.25"d. Backstamp: 27.3. $90-110.

T.132 Cream and sugar set. Creamer, 3.5"h x 3.5"w x 2.5"d. Sugar, 2.38"h x 3.5"w x 3.5"d. Backstamp: 27.0. $40-80.

T.135 Mustache cup and saucer. 2.25"h x 4.63"w. Backstamp: 27.0. $80-120.

T.133 Cream and sugar set. Creamer, 3.5"h x 3.63"w x 2.38"d. Sugar, 2.38"h x 5.13"w x 3.38"d. Backstamp: 25.1. $30-60.

T.136 Cup and saucer. 2.75"h x 5.75"w. Backstamp: 16.4. $80-120.

T.134 Cream and sugar set. Creamer, 3.5"h x 4.38"w x 3.25"d. Sugar, 4.5"h x 6.0"w x 3.75"d. Backstamp: 27.1. $40-80.

T.137 Cup and saucer. 2.38"h x 5.13"w.
Backstamp: 16.4. $80-120.

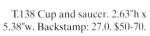

T.138 Cup and saucer. 2.63"h x
5.38"w. Backstamp: 27.0. $50-70.

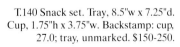

T.139 Cup and saucer. 2.38"h x
4.38"w. Backstamp: 16.4. $40-90.

T.140 Snack set. Tray, 8.5"w x 7.25"d.
Cup, 1.75"h x 3.75"w. Backstamp: cup,
27.0; tray, unmarked. $150-250.

T.141 Snack set. Tray, 8.5"w x 7.25"d. Cup, 1.75"h x 3.75"w. Backstamp: 27.0. $50-90.

T.142 Snack set. Tray, 8.5"w x 7.25"d. Cup, 1.75"h x 3.75"w. Backstamp: 27.0. $20-30.

T.144 Tea caddy. 4.0"h x 6.25"w x 3.5"d. Backstamp: 27.1. $200-300.

T.143 Snack set. Tray, .75"h x 7.25"dia. Cup, 2.25"h x 4.5"w x 3.5"d. Backstamp: 25.1. $20-40.

T.145 Tea set. Pot, 6.25"h x 9.13"w. Creamer, 3.75"h x 5.13"w. Sugar, 4.38"h x 5.75"w. Cup 2.38"h x 5.5"w. Saucer, 7.5"dia. Plate, 7.5" dia. Backstamp: 27.0. Set, as shown, $400-500.

T.146 Tea set. Pot, 5.25"h x 8.5"d x 3.63"d; Cup, 1.88"h x 4.5"w x 3.75"d; Saucer, .88"h x 5.5"dia.; Creamer, 3.13"h x 4.63"w x 2.38"d; Sugar, 4.25"h x 6.38"w x 2.75"d; Plate, .88"h x 7.5"dia. Backstamp: 27.0. Set, with 6 cups, saucers and serving plates, $450-550.

T.146A Detail of plate in T.146.

T.147 Tea set. Pot, 6.75"h x 6.75"w. Creamer, 5.13"h x 4.0"w. Sugar, 5.75"h x 4.75"w. Cup and saucer, 2.63"h x 5.13"w. Plate, 6.38" dia. Backstamp: 16.4. Set, as shown, $480-680.

T.148 Tea set. Pot, 6.25"h x 8.5"w x 4.5"d. Creamer, 3.0"h x 3.5"w. Sugar, 3.5"h x 4.63"w. Cup, 2.25"h x 4.5"w x 3.5"d. Saucer, 1.0"h x 4.25"dia. Plate, 1.0"h x 7.25"dia. Backstamp: 27.0. Set, with 6 cups, saucers and serving plates, $180-280.

T.149 Tea strainer. 1.0"h x 5.5"w x 3.75"d. Plate, 4.88"dia. Backstamp: 27.1. $80-140.

T.153 Tea tile. .5"h x 5.0"w x 5.0"d. Backstamp: 27.0. $30-60.

T.150 Tea strainer. 1.0"h x 5.5"w x 3.75"d. Plate, 4.88" dia. Backstamp: 27.1. $80-140.

T.151 Tea tile. .5"h x 6.5"dia. Backstamp: 27.1. $250-400.

T.152A Detail of T.152.

T.152 Tea tile .5"h x 4.88" x 4.88"d. Backstamp: 27.1. $40-90.

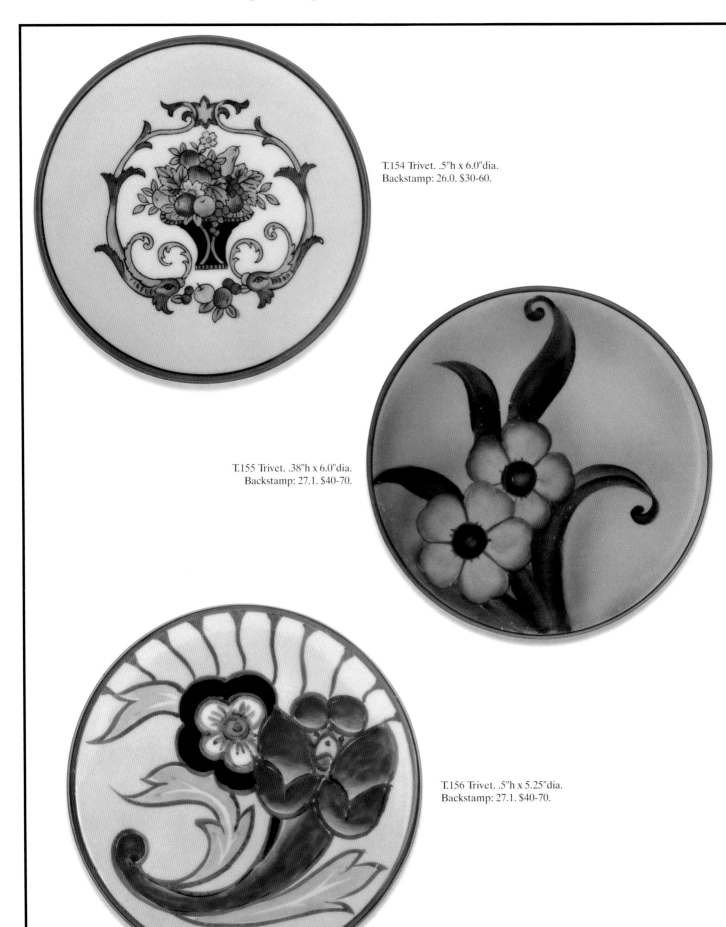

T.154 Trivet. .5"h x 6.0"dia.
Backstamp: 26.0. $30-60.

T.155 Trivet. .38"h x 6.0"dia.
Backstamp: 27.1. $40-70.

T.156 Trivet. .5"h x 5.25"dia.
Backstamp: 27.1. $40-70.

Chapter V
Vases and Other Items Pertaining to Flowers

In this chapter there are photos of various items which, in one way or another, pertain to flowers. They are clustered into the following categories:

Ferners (pp. 259-260)
Flower frogs (pp. 261-262)
Potpourris (pp. 262-263)
Urns (pp. 263-265)
Vases (pp. 265-291)
    figural vases and vases with a figural element (pp. 265-268)
    vases with no handles (pp. 268-281)
    vases with 1 handle (basket vases) (pp. 281-283)
    vases with 2 handles (pp. 284-290)
    vases with three or more handles (pp. 290-291)
Wall pockets (pp. 291-294)

In its basic structure this chapter is organized along the same lines as the others in this book. Thus, the basic categories (e.g., flower frogs, urns, wall pockets) are sequenced in alphabetical order. The vases group has subgroups that also are sequenced alphabetically. They are defined with reference to two features that are noticed almost instantly when anyone looks at any vase. These are (1) the number of handles it has and (2) whether the vase is in a figural form or has a figural element. Within these groupings, the vases generally are sequenced with reference to height. Because these groups and subgroups are defined in terms of simple, readily determined features, users of this book should be able to locate any vase of interest quite rapidly and easily. And that is the point.

By far the vast majority of the items shown in this chapter are vases (including wall pockets which, although a kind of vase, are placed in their own group). Indeed, in this particular Chapter V, vases outnumber non-vase items ten to one. If the Chapter Vs in my first two Noritake books are taken into account, the ratio drops only a little—to about nine to one. Although no data are as yet available to give the claim a solid numerical grounding (and due to the loss of records during the war, they may never be), I suspect that this ratio does not diverge very much from what the company actually produced during the pre-war period. As with other Noritake production trends, we may plausibly suggest that market considerations, not artistic ones, would have accounted for most of this.

V.293 Ferner. 4.75"h x 6.25"w x 5.0"d. Backstamp: 27.0. $90-140.

Although only a few of the items in this chapter are not vases, they are still of considerable interest, aesthetically and otherwise. The shape of the ferner shown in V.294 is so graceful, it would be desirable no matter what was painted on it. All Noritake bird flower frogs are very much in demand, but few garner more attention than those like the one shown in V.295. It is bold, powerful, and has considerable dramatic flair. Because the bases on these items are small, few have the full Noritake backstamp. Instead, they tend to have MIJ backstamps (as V.296 does). Because the differences between the lettering of Noritake and non-Noritake MIJ backstamps are often quite small, collectors and dealers need to examine very carefully the many figural flower frogs available on the secondary market before concluding that they were made by the Noritake Company. In addition to the character of the letters in the words "Made in Japan," both the quality of the painting and the porcelain needs to be considered. This set of comments applies to at least one other item shown in this chapter—the figural vases in V.307 and V.308. Again, because of lack of room, these items have only the words "Made in Japan" as a backstamp. Because there are quite a few non-Noritake versions of this vase, collectors and dealers need to examine these items very carefully before deciding whether they were made by the Noritake Company. This cautious approach should be taken with regard to all MIJ marked pieces, of course. (This vital issue is discussed at some length in Chapter 3.)

Noritake potpourris are not truly rare but great ones are hard to find. Few if any are more colorful or beautifully designed than the one shown in V.298. Although the two shown in V.297 are not nearly as colorful, they are excellent pieces. They also are unusual in that each still has its small inner lid (shown beside each piece). The lid was put on the jar when there was no need for the fragrance from the flower petals. This helped to make the aromatic effect of the contents of a potpourri jar last longer. Having these easily lost or broken inner lids adds considerably to the value of such items. Potpourris like the one shown in V.298, it should be noted in this context, are not known to have had such inner lids. Urns are the remaining non-vase type of floral item shown in this chapter. Most urns from the Noritake (post Nippon) era are fairly small, although usually superbly done (e.g., see V.300 or V.303). As impressive as these are, however, they pale when compared to certain very large and elaborately decorated Noritake urns that, for the most part, were made prior to the 1920s. A truly spectacular example is shown in V.299. From the style of the decoration and registration date of the backstamp (1908 in London, England), it may plausibly be surmised that this breathtaking urn was made some years prior to 1920.

Noritake vases, besides having been produced in large numbers, have several virtues as a collectible. Although some of these, such as their beauty and design diversity, are important, they are common to virtually all other types of Noritake as well. Some of their other virtues, however, are not only less general but also, for many collectors, of as much significance as beauty and diversity. For example, vases can be used with far less risk of damage than almost any other kind of Noritake collectible. Moreover, they are easy to display; no stands are required and the designs can easily be appreciated even when the item is on a high shelf. Even so, and somewhat to my surprise and continuing puzzlement, the general demand for vases among collectors is not all that strong (although some vases stand as notable exceptions to this trend). There

V.294 Ferner. 3.5"h x 6.13"w. Backstamp: 27.0. $90-140.

is no way to tell whether this trend will continue. As I have said with regard to bowls, however, those of us who enjoy Noritake vases will not mind if the trend does continue. If it does, it is reasonable to think that we can expect prices will not rise very fast and that great items will be somewhat more affordable.

It may seem that it is always fairly obvious whether something is a vase but there are some interesting and difficult cases, as there are with some items in almost all of the other chapter-groupings in this book. For example, some apparent vases are (or were meant to be) made into lamps. Thus, one will see an item from time to time that "clearly" is a vase but that also has a hole in the bottom or near the base. Obviously, since the typical user of a vase expects it to hold water, such items cannot be ordinary vases. The hole is for an electric cord. Our assumption, of course, is that various usually metal parts were to have been fastened to the top and bottom of the "vase" to form the lamp. There is an example of such a vase in this book (V.385), although the hole is not shown. Because of the hole, it would have been reasonable to show this item in Chapter L, the chapter on lamps and candlesticks. Since, however, I had other items of the same shape without a predrilled hole, I put the item shown in V.385 in this chapter where, I believe, most people will expect to find it or an item that looks like it.

There are other puzzling cases worth mentioning. Are all the basket-shaped items in this chapter (V.361-V.370) truly vases? Indeed, what are the grounds for thinking that *any* of them is a vase? Frankly, it is hard to say why they should be considered vases other than for the "fact" that it is fairly easy to see that they *could* be used as vases. It might be added, and it is not trivial, that there are few other functions that come to mind when one stops to consider the matter. On a par with this reason is another one—namely, the tendency of experienced collectors and dealers to *refer* to these items as vases (as "basket vases" to be precise), although this certainly does not "make" them vases. Indeed, these same people just as confidently think that certain other very similar baskets are *not* vases (see Chapter B, B.356-B.380). In this context, consider the items shown below in V.313 and V.313A. The mermaid flower frog clearly belongs in this chapter; indeed, a flower frog just like this one was shown in Chapter V *Noritake Collectibles A to Z* (see V.4). But what about the "bowl"? What makes it a "vase"? Or is it a vase? There are quite a few collectors and dealers, I suspect, who have seen that "bowl" being offered for sale as a "bowl." And yet, it seems clear that, with the flower frog, it is a vase, or at the very least, a bowl that also can be used as a vase if one also uses some sort of flower frog. But if that is all it takes to be a vase, then a most of the items in Chapter B *could* be vases, too.

Most errors of classification that could result from facts such as these are not all that significant, in my opinion, although I would grant that a few of them may mean that some users of this book will to have to hunt a bit longer before they find what they are looking for. Speaking of classification errors, in *Collecting Noritake A to Z*, I comment (p.170) on the motif on an item shown in V.245. To me, and to most people, it looks like a vase with a bunch of celery painted on it. Among other things, I said it should get some sort of prize for being one of the most wacky and whimsical Noritake vases ever. Not long after that book came out, a fellow collector informed me that that "vase" was not an ordinary vase (we agreed on that part!); rather, it was a celery crisper. It was meant to be used to keep celery fresh and crisp. One simply put celery stalks and cold water into the "vase" and the stalks would absorb the water, thereby, remaining crisp. In a case-clinching comment (this collector is an attorney, by the way), she mentioned that she had a "vase" just like the one in

V.295 Flower frog. 3.5"h x 3.25"w x 2.75"d. Backstamp: 27.0. $200-300.

V.245 but it came with six individual salt dips decorated to match. Had I known all this when preparing that book, I would have shown that "vase" in Chapter B, along with the other celery/relish *bowls*. In summary, we have two very instructive cases here. In one of them, we have something that looks like a bowl that is a vase (V.313, shown below and discussed in the previous paragraph). In the other, we have what looks like a vase but is a bowl or at least could be shown with them (V.245 in *Collecting Noritake A to Z*). For people like me, cases like these help make collecting loads of fun!

Do not misunderstand me, however. Even for people like me, the most fun as a collector comes from seeing and, from time to time, acquiring some of the interestingly diverse and aesthetically satisfying porcelain fancyware items made by the Noritake Company. In light of this, then, Noritake vases ought to be the source of considerable pleasure for Noritake collectors because no other basic type of Noritake collectible is more diverse or of higher overall quality. Most readers, I think, are likely to be convinced of this by even a casual glance at the many fine items shown in this chapter. Although it is tempting to do more, I comment on only a *few* of these items in the next few paragraphs.

Noritake figural vases, like other Noritake figural items, are much admired and in great demand. Two of those shown below that were made in the 1920s are particularly noteworthy, although for rather different reasons. One of these is the triple bud vase shown in V.309. Collectors will be interested to know that there is a monochrome glass vase by Steuben that is an exact duplicate in size, shape, and all other details (except for color). The other vase is shown in V.306. It is impressive in part because of its complex and delicate form. Not only would it and other vases like it have been difficult to make in quantity but also few of them can be expected to have survived to the present without damage. For these and other reasons, many collectors seek such vases and even those who do not would still acknowledge that they are very special items. Interestingly, however, vases like these have varied considerably in price, recently, when auctioned. Although the cases are few, my records show a range of $400 to $1400. We can be certain that some of this variation is attributable to differences in decoration, but only *some* of it. How to account for the rest remains a puzzle. We do know, however (and as I have pointed out in several other places in this book, but especially toward the end of the Introduction to Part Two), collectibles auction results are notoriously problematical sources of information for estimating values. In this book, the most surprising figural

V.296 Flower frog. 3.75"h x 2.5"w x 2.0"d. Backstamp: MIJ.1. $170-270.

V.297 Potpourris, showing interior lids. 6.0"h x 4.0"w. Backstamp: 27.0. Each set, when complete, $120-180.

vase is shown in V.304. Interestingly, given the bold subject matter, it bears a backstamp registered in 1946. It can be presumed, of course, that hundreds of these were made. So far, however, the one shown in V.304 is the only one I know of.

The vases without handles shown in this chapter are amazingly diverse. One of them (V.317) has a particularly bold almost surreal shape. For other items, shape also is a feature of great interest but they are more quietly dramatic (e.g., V.315, V.319, V.335 and V.335A). All of these are rather uncommon if not downright rare items. In terms of decoration, some are elegant and lavish to the point that words fail (e.g., V.316 and V.318). Some have amazingly abstract, others subtly compelling, modern "floral" motifs. The vases shown in V.329 and V.331 are among my favorites within the former category (and, alas, neither one is mine); the vase shown in V.337 is a fine example in the latter group. The motif on it is found on many different Noritake items, including an urn (V.300) in this chapter. Deco cottage motifs can be found on a wide variety of Noritake items also, particularly plates and bowls. A very fine example is shown in this chapter, however, in V.359. Collectors and dealers will want to take note of the flower frog shown with it. Since it fits perfectly into the vase, we can be virtually certain it was an original component and that others with this shape without the flower frog are, thus, incomplete sets.

Some of these vases have unusual surface treatments. The vase shown in V.328 has a rarely seen purple stone-like luster finish. Most Noritake-made dragonware items, featuring a writhing white moriage dragon with bulging blue eyes, are found on items bearing pre-1921 "Nippon" backstamps. The vase shown in V.333, therefore, is a somewhat unusual find. Another very fine vase with a distinctive surface is shown in V.345. The leaves on the trees are textured in a manner that is quite pleasing to the touch. The very next vase shown, which has the same shape (V.346), also has a subtly textured surface achieved with both enameling (the yellow floral elements) and by the application of numerous heavy dollops of yellow-orange paint (the splotches seen over the bulk of the surface). The fine, mist-like airbrushed blue highlighting on the interior, on the other hand, offers a pleasing but surprisingly modern contrast to the more traditional yet bold exterior.

As must be abundantly clear by this point, motifs featuring Deco ladies are very much admired and in demand by collectors. In this part of Chapter V, there are three fine examples (V.341, V.349 and V.324). The last mentioned example seems related, conceptually, to a vase just like this one in shape that was shown in *Noritake Collectibles A to Z*—namely, V.65. Since it appears that conceptual sets often contain three items, we can hope (and even expect) that a third very large lady vase like these two will be found. Moreover, if it can be said, as some of us think it can be, that the three three-footed vases shown in V.94 of *Noritake Collectibles A to Z* constitute such a conceptual set, then we can even "predict" what the motif on that yet-to-be-found vase will be. It can be expected that the motif will feature a lady in the pale blue beaded dress (this motif may be seen on the wall pocket shown below in V.404). Time will tell whether we are right. While on the subject of conceptual sets, consider the two vases shown in V.347 and V.348. May we not expect to see, someday, a similar vase in a third color (green or blue)? If so, we can expect that any collector in North America who has or obtains one probably will have gotten it from very far away since the backstamp shows that both of these vases originally were exported to Australia.

Of the many quite spectacular vases shown in this chapter, the one to be seen in V.371 and V.371A must be considered one of the very best. It is particularly impressive that the gold luster handles show virtually no wear what-

V.298 Potpourri. 8.0"h x 5.5"w. Backstamp: 27.1. $200-300.

soever. The same made be said of the handles on the next vase (V.372) which are most uncommon in both shape and location on the vase. The motif on the superb vase shown in V.374 is not at all common but it is known on a plaque (shown in P.172 of *Collecting Noritake A to Z*). For those who find bold floral motifs appealing, the vases shown in V.382, V.390 and V.391 should be of considerable interest.

I conclude with a few words about the wall pockets shown in this book. These items are among the few "love 'em or hate 'em" types of Noritake that I know of. I have no idea why this should be the case. What I do know is that because of this, prices for wall pockets tend to be rather unpredictable, especially when they are placed at auction. Accordingly, the value ranges given for these items are somewhat wider than for most of the other items in this chapter. In terms of artistic interest, those shown in V.399 and V.400 are noteworthy given the discussion (above) of conceptual sets. In what other colors will wall pockets like these be found? By the same token, can we not expect to find a fourth wall pocket like the three shown in V.401-V.403? Can we expect the background color to be orange (to pair up with the red one and as a complement to the purple and blue pair)? For the same reason, can we expect that the bird, which surely will be shown sitting on a branch, will have its breast facing left? Again, time will tell whether we are right to expect such a wall pocket to emerge from someone's attic. In the meantime, we can enjoy these and all the other items shown in this chapter.

V.301 Urn. 9.25"h x 4.25"w. Backstamp: 27.0. $100-180.

V.300 Urn. 10.5"h x 5.0"w. Base, 4.0"dia. Backstamp: 27.1. $280-380.

V.302 Urn. 9.25"h x 4.25"w. Backstamp. 27.0. $100-180.

V.299 Urn with two handles. 16.75"h x 8.25"w. Backstamp: 16.4. $3000+

V.303 Urn. 8.25"h x 6.38"w. Backstamp:
16.0. $210-260.

V.304 Figural vase. 11.5"h x 5.0"w.
Backstamp: 65.5. $400-500.

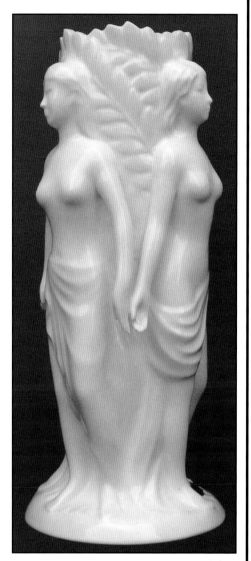

V.304A Side view of V.304.

V.305 Vase with figural element. 7.38"h x 5.5"w.
Backstamp: 27.1. $350-450.

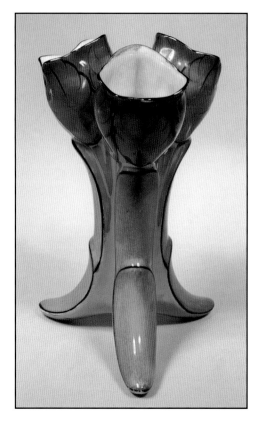

V.307 Figural vase. 6.0"h x
4.0"w. Backstamp: MIJ.1.
$100-150.

V.306 Vase with figural elements. 7.13"h x 7.25"w.
Backstamp: 27.1. $700-900.

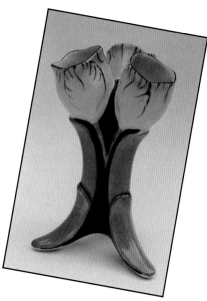

V.308 Figural vase. 6.0"h x 3.75"w.
Backstamp: MIJ.0. $100-150.

V.309 Figural vase. 5.88"h x 4.0"w. Backstamp: 27.1. $150-250.

V.311 Vase with figural element. 5.0"h x 3.0"w x 2.75"d. Backstamp: 27.0. $140-190.

V.310 Vase with figural element. 5.0"h x 3.0"w x 2.75"d. Backstamp: 27.1. $140-190.

V.312 Vase with figural element. 5.0"h x 3.5"w x 3.5"d. Backstamp: 27.0. $180-260.

V.313 Vase with flower frog.
3.63"h x 7.5"w. Flower frog,
3.5"h x 3.25"w. Backstamp:
bowl-vase, 27.1; flower frog,
MIJ.1. Set, as shown, $450-550.

V.313A Alternate view of V.313.

V.314 Vase with no handles. 13.13"h x
6.5"w. Backstamp: 19.0. $110-180.

V.315 Vase with no handles. 11.0"h x 4.88"w.
Backstamp: 67.019. $80-100.

V.316 Vases with no handles. 10.25"h x 5.0"w. Backstamp: 16.0. Each, $500-700.

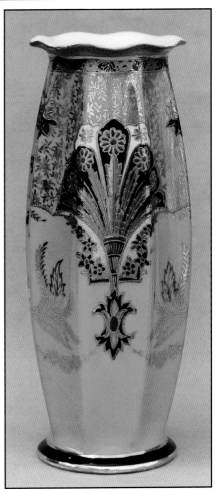

V.318 Vase with no handles. 9.5"h x 3.5"w x 3.5"d. Backstamp: 16.4. $150-200.

V.317 Vase with no handles. 10.0"h x 4.5"w. (large vase; height figure not a misprint). Backstamp: 27.1. $200-300.

V.318A Alternate view of V.318.

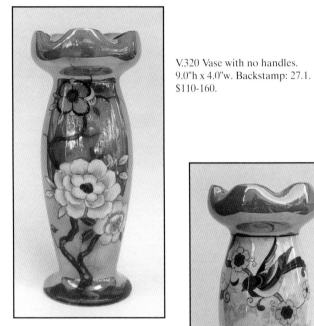

V.320 Vase with no handles. 9.0"h x 4.0"w. Backstamp: 27.1. $110-160.

V.321 Vase with no handles. 9.0"h x 4.0"w. Backstamp: 27.1. $110-160.

V.319 Vase with no handles. 9.5"h x 4.75"w. Base, 3.5" dia. Backstamp: 25.1. $170-220.

V.322 Vase with no handles. 9.0"h x 4.0"w. Backstamp: 27.1. $110-160.

V.323 Vase with no handles.
9.0"h x 4.0"w. Backstamp:
19.1. $130-200.

V.325 Vase with no handles.
8.5"h x 4.0"w. Backstamp:
27.0. $70-100.

V.324 Vase with no
handles. 8.88"h x 4.63"w.
Backstamp: 29.1 (29812),
$800-1200.

V.326 Vase with no handles. 8.5"h x
4.0"w. Backstamp: 27.0. $90-120.

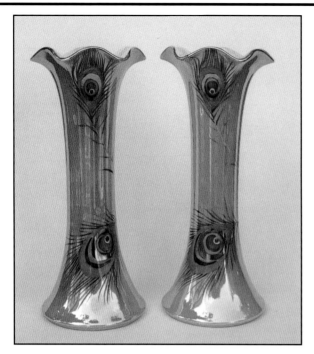

V.327 Vases with no handles. 8.5"h x 3.75"w. Backstamp: 27.1.
Each, $100-180.

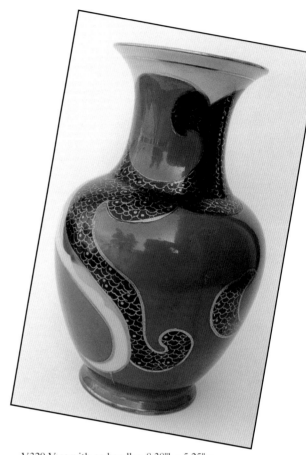

V.329 Vase with no handles. 8.38"h x 5.25"w.
Backstamp: 27.0. $90-170.

V.328 Vase with no handles. 8.38"h x
5.25"w. Backstamp: 27.0. $50-80.

V.330 Vase with no handles.
8.38"h x 5.25"w. Backstamp:
27.0. $100-150.

V.331 Vase with no handles. 8.13"h x 4.63"w. Backstamp: 27.0. $500+

V.333 Vase with no handles. 7.63"h x 3.63"w. Backstamp: 27.0. $200-300.

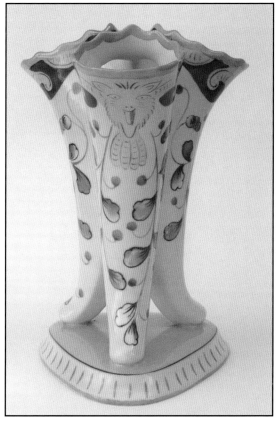

V.332 Vase with no handles. 8.0"h x 5.75"w. Backstamp: 27.1. $200-250.

V.334 Vase with no handles. 7.63"h x 3.63"w. Backstamp: 27.0. $100-150.

V.335 Vase with no handles. 7.75"h x 4.38"w x 2.75"d.
Backstamp: 25.1. $250-350.

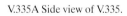

V.335A Side view of V.335.

V.336 Vase with no handles.
7.75"h x 4.0"w. Backstamp:
27.1. $160-220.

V.337 Vase with no
handles. 7.63"h x 3.5"w.
Backstamp: 27.1. $200-300.

V.340 Vase with no handles. 7.5"h x 4.0"w. Backstamp: 27.0. $70-110.

V.338 Vase with no handles. 7.5"h x 4.0"w. Backstamp: 27.1. $60-90.

V.341 Vase with no handles. 7. 5"h x 3.38"w. Backstamp: 27.1. $500+

V.339 Vase with no handles. 7.5"h x 4.0"w. Backstamp: 27.0. $60-90.

V.342 Vase with no handles. 7.5"h x 4.38"w.
Backstamp: 27.0. $60-90.

V.344 Vase with no handles. 6.75"h x 3.25"w.
Backstamp: 27.1. $130-190.

V.343 Vase with no handles.
7.13"h x 3.5"w. Backstamp:
27.1. $100-180.

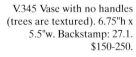

V.345 Vase with no handles
(trees are textured). 6.75"h x
5.5"w. Backstamp: 27.1.
$150-250.

V.346 Vase with no handles (much enameling).
6.75"h x 5.5"w. Backstamp: 27.1. $120-180.

V.348 Vase with no handles. 6.63"h x 5.5"w.
Backstamp: 54.0. $100-150.

V.347 Vase with no handles. 6.63"h x 5.5"w.
Backstamp: 54.0. $100-150.

V.349 Vase with no handles. 6.5"h x 4.13"w x 2.75"d.
Backstamp: 29.1. $350-450.

V.349A Back view of V.349

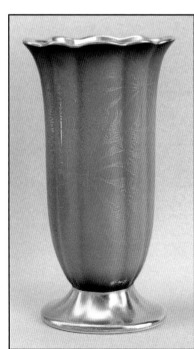

V.350 Vase with no handles (etched surface
design). 6.25"h x 3.25"w x 2.25"d. Backstamp:
31.7. $90-130.

V.351A Top view of V.351, showing interior flower supports.

V.351 Vase with no handles. 6.0"h x 6.75"w. Backstamp: 25.1. $100-150.

V.353 Vases with no handles. 6.0"h x 4.0"w. Backstamp: *third vase from left:* 19.0; *others,* 27.0. *Left,* $90-120; *left and right center,* $130-190; *right,* $150-250.

V.352 Vase with no handles. 6.0"h x 3.5"w. Backstamp: 68.7. $50-80.

V.354 Vase with no handles. 5.88"h x 5.38"w. Backstamp: 27.0. $90-140.

V.355 Vase with no handles. 5.88"h x 5.38"w. Backstamp: 27.0. $90-140.

V.358 Vase with no handles. 5.63"h x 5.0"w. Backstamp: 27.1. $130-180.

V.356 Vases with no handles. 5.75"h x 4.0"w x 1.75"d. Backstamp: *left,* 27.1; *center,* 31.7; *right,* 25.1. Left, $90-140; *center,* $80-120; *right,* $140-190.

V.357 Vases with no handles. 5.63"h x 5.0"w. Backstamp: 27.1. Each, $90-140.

V.359 Vase with flower frog. 4.5"h x 5.5"w. Flower frog, 2.5"h x 3.75"w. Backstamp: vase 27.1; flower frog, MIJ.1. Two-piece set, as shown, $230-270.

V.360 Vases with no handles. 4.38"h x 3.0"w. Backstamp: 27.1. Each, $60-100.

V.361 Basket vase. 8.0"h x 5.0"w. Backstamp: 27.0. $90-130.

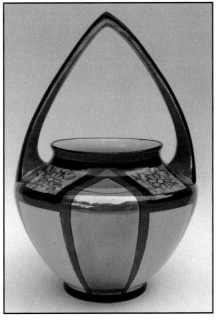

V.362 Basket vase. 8.0"h x 5.0"w. Backstamp: 27.0. $90-130.

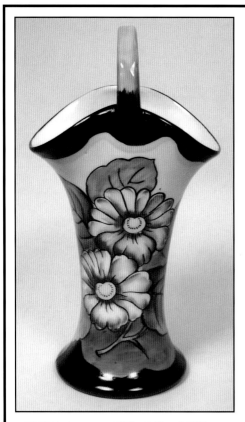

V.365 Basket vase. 7.5"h x 6.0"w. Backstamp: 27.1. $150-250.

V.363 Basket vase. 6.75"h x 3.5"w x 2.25"d. Backstamp: 27.1. $90-130.

V.366 Basket vase. 7.5"h x 6.25"w. Backstamp: 29.1. $150-250.

V.364 Basket vase. 9.63"h x 4.75"w x 3.75"d. Backstamp: 27.1. $150-250.

V.367 Basket vase. 7.0"h x 6.3"w. Backstamp: 29.1. $150-250.

V.369 Basket vase. 5.75"h x 4.88"w x 3.75"d. Backstamp: 19.1. $80-120.

V.368 Basket vase. 6.0"h x 4.75"w. Backstamp: 27.1. $90-130.

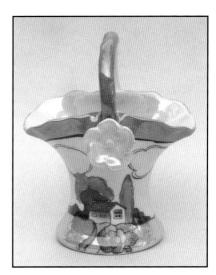

V.370 Basket vase. 4.5"h x 3.75"w x 2.75"d. Backstamp: 19.0. $50-90.

V.372 Vase with two handles. 11.75"h x 8.25"w. Backstamp: 27.0. $150-200.

V.371 Vase with two handles. 12.75"h x 6.75"w. Backstamp: 27.0. $280-380.

V.371A Back view of V.371.

V.373 Vase with two handles. 10.25"h x 5.5"w. Backstamp: 16.2. $200-300.

V.374 Vase with two handles. 10.0"h x 7.0"w x 6.5"d. Backstamp: 27.0. $280-380.

V.376. Vase with two handles (base predrilled for use in lamp). 9.63"h x 6.13"w. Backstamp: 27.0. $150-200.

V.375 Vase with two handles. 8.0"h x 6.0"w x 4.63"d. Backstamp: 27.0. $230-330.

V.376A Back view of V.376.

V.377 Vase with two handles. 9.25"h x 4.5"w. Backstamp: 27.0. $60-90.

V.379 Vase with two handles. 8.0"h x 5.88"w. Backstamp: 27.0. $200-250.

V.378 Vase with two handles. 8.75"h x 7.5"w. Backstamp: 27.0. $110-160.

V.380 Vase with two handles. 9.0"h x 6.5"w. Backstamp: 27.1. $90-190.

V.381 Vases with two handles. 9.0"h x 5.0"w. Backstamp: 25.1. Each, $300+

V.383 Vase with two handles. 8.38"h x 5.13"w x 3.5"d. Backstamp: 19.1. $80-140.

V.382 Vase with two handles. 8.38"h x 5.13"w x 3.5"d. Backstamp: 27.1. $150-250.

V.384 Vase with two handles. 7.25"h x 4.5"w. Backstamp: 25.1. $180-280.

V.387 Vase with two handles. 7.0"h x 4.75"w. Backstamp: 27.0. $90-140.

V.385 Vase with two handles (base predrilled for use in a lamp). 7.25"h x 4.5"w. Backstamp: 25.1. $180-280.

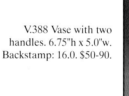

V.388 Vase with two handles. 6.75"h x 5.0"w. Backstamp: 16.0. $50-90.

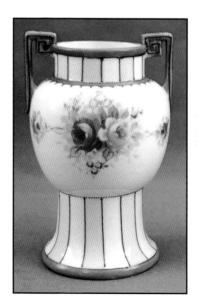

V.389 Vase with two handles. 6.75"h x 5.0"w. Backstamp: 16.0. $40-80.

V.386 Vase with two handles. 7.25"h x 4.5"w. Backstamp: 25.1. $180-280.

V.390 Vases with two handles. 6.63"h x 4.75"w x 2.63"d. Backstamp: *left*, 27.1; *right*, 29.1 (39543). Each, $130-180.

V.391 Vases with two handles. 6.0"h x 5.5"w x 2.0"d. Backstamp: All, 27.1. Each, $250-350.

V.392 Vases with two handles. 5.38"h x 3.88"w. Backstamp: 16.4. Each, $100-150.

V.393 Vases with two handles, showing front and back. 5.0"h x 3.25"w. Backstamp: 16.0. Each, $50-90.

V.395 Vase with two handles. 4.5"h x 2.75"w. Backstamp: 27.0. $30-50.

V.394 Vases with two handles. 4.5"h x 3.5"w x 3.5"d. Backstamp: 16.4. Each, $40-70

V.396 Vase with two handles. 3.0"h x 2.25"w x 1.5"d. Backstamp: 16.2. $20-40.

V.397 Vase with three handles. 4.5"h x 2.75"w. Backstamp: 27.0. $30-50.

V.398 Vase with four handles. 6.88"h x 4.0"w. Backstamp: 27.0. $100-200.

V.400 Wall pocket. 9.25"h x 4.63"w x 2.63. Backstamp: 27.1. $300-500.

V.399 Wall pocket with figural element. 9.25"h x 4.63"w x 2.63"d. Backstamp: 27.1. $400-600.

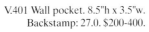

V.401 Wall pocket. 8.5"h x 3.5"w. Backstamp: 27.0. $200-400.

V.402 Wall pocket. 8.5"h x 3.5"w. Backstamp: 27.0. $200-400.

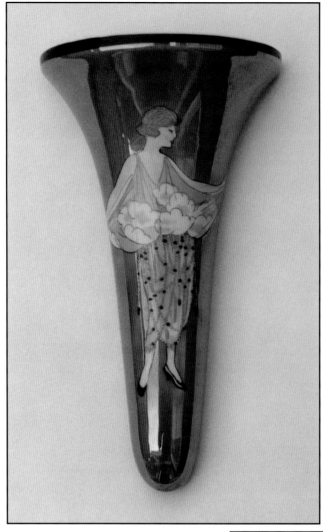

V.404 Wall pocket. 8.0"h x 4.63"w x 2.63"d. Backstamp: 27.1. $500-600.

V.403 Wall pocket. 8.5"h x 3.5"w. Backstamp: 27.0. $200-400.

V.405 Wall pocket. 8.0"h x 4.63"w x 2.63"d. Backstamp: 27.0. $200-400.

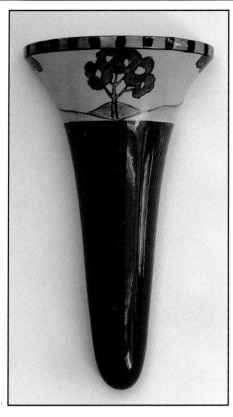

V.408 Wall pocket. 6.63"h x
5.0"w. Backstamp: 27.0.
$150-250.

V.406 Wall pocket. 8.0"h x 4.63"w x 2.63"d.
Backstamp: 19.2. $150-250.

V.407 Wall pocket. 6.63"h x 5.0"w.
Backstamp: 27.0. $250-350.

V.409 Wall pocket. 6.63"h x 4.88"w x 2.25"d. Backstamp: 27.0. $180-320.

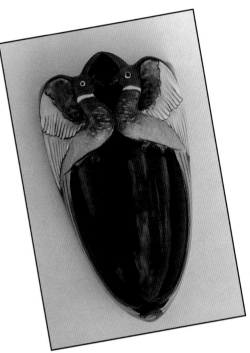

V.411 Wall pocket. 7.0"h x 3.5"w.
Backstamp: 27.1. $200-350.

V.410 Wall pocket. 6.63"h x 5.0"w x 2.0"d. Backstamp: 27.0. $180-320.

V.412 Wall pocket. 7.0"h x 3.5"w.
Backstamp: 27.1. $300-450.

Chapter Z

Miscellaneous Items

This chapter contains photos of the following miscellaneous Noritake-marked fancyware:

Biscuit (or cracker) jar (p. 295)
Egg cups and sets (pp. 296-297)
Egg warmer (p. 297)
Knife rest (p. 298)
Napkin rings (p. 298)
Spooners (pp. 298-299)
Toast racks (p. 299)

Although there are not many "miscellaneous" Noritake fancyware items, they are a rather interesting group. Most of the items in this particular Chapter Z seem to have a lot to do with breakfast or afternoon tea. The chapter opens with a fine silver and porcelain jar. Because the backstamp tells us it was exported originally to Great Britain, it seemed to me that we should preferentially refer to it as a "biscuit" (rather than "cracker") jar; hence the particulars of the caption of Z.46. The spooners shown in Z.56-Z.63 could have had a role for that event also since spooners are dishes meant to hold tea spoons (and in fact I seriously considered putting these items in Chapter T). It must be noted, however, that some collectors and dealers do not consider all of these items to be spooners. The case *for* seems quite strong for the item shown in Z.56. The spoons could be of almost any length since it would be easy to arrange them with the handles sticking out at the end. Indeed, that spooner may have been intended for long ice tea spoons and, if not *meant* for them, it could certainly be used for them today.

The debate about the function of these pieces tends to focus on items like the "double spooners" shown in Z.57-Z.59. One often sees such items listed as "candy dishes." I have avoided this over-used term *completely* in my books primarily because there is almost no bowl or jar or box or deep plate that could not be used to serve candy. It also has been noted, by some anyway, that spoons typically are too long to fit in these dishes. As it happens, though, some spoons are short enough and, so I am told, many of these shorter spoons were in use in the 1920s. There seems to be little doubt that the remaining items in this group (Z.60-Z.63) are indeed spooners. All those shown are fine examples

Z.46 Biscuit (or cracker) jar with silver lid, rim and handle. Overall, 9.25" h" x 6.13"w (5.5"h to top of silver rim). Backstamp: 16.4. $100-140.

but it should be noted that the one in Z.60 is the first and so far only one with figural birds on the handles that has been shown in any of my Noritake books. Such spooners are not particularly uncommon; it just happens that I do not have good photographs of them.

At a sufficiently fancy afternoon tea, one can expect cloth napkins and other extra signs of leisure and what used to be thought of as civility. Cloth napkins can be made all the more impressive by the addition of napkin rings, such as those shown in Z.53-Z.55. All of these rings are unusual in color. One, Z.54, is also unusual (in my experience at least) for its backstamp. The pair shown in Z.52 is quite dramatic and somewhat rare. Given their size, they could easily encircle rather large napkins.

From afternoon tea, the theme shifts to breakfast and, in particular, to eggs and toast. All of the toast racks shown in this chapter are outstanding examples. One of them, with 5 rings, has room for 4 slices; the other, with 3 rings, has room for 2 slices. Examples with 4 rings and, hence, with room for 3 slices are known, too (one was shown in Z.42 in *Collecting Noritake A to Z*). Were there Noritake fancyware toast racks with just 2 rings? Somehow I doubt it but, having said so, there will be readers who have just what is needed to prove me wrong. If so, I hope they will contact me. Finally, there are the various items used to serve eggs. (Eggs for breakfast. Those were the days, weren't they!?) As with condiment sets, the trick with these items is to find them complete. For egg cups like those shown in Z.49 and Z.50, of course, this is not an issue. It may be noted, however, that the pattern on the one shown in Z.50 is found on many other tea and breakfast-related things, so it can be suggested that this item is but one part of a rather large set. Where completeness is a major consideration will be egg sets like those shown in Z.47 and Z.48. If incomplete, the tiny salt and pepper shakers are generally going to be the missing items. One of the shakers in Z.48 was arranged so the label on the bottom of it could be seen. Such a label, sometimes on paper, sometimes printed onto what appears to be a bone stopper, is often seen on Noritake made fancyware salt and peppers like these. In some cases, such a sticker or label can help make the case that the item, otherwise unmarked, was made by the Noritake Company. The last egg-related item, the egg warmer shown in Z.51, also has a completeness issue. Hot water was poured into a hole at the top (it can be seen in the photo in Z.51). Then, if soft-boiled eggs were placed in the four large but somewhat shallow cavities around the top surface, they would stay warm. If the stopper (shown beside this item) is missing, the water would cool too rapidly. Egg warmers without stoppers are seen on the secondary market but they are not particularly desirable as a collector's item. This is because the chances of coming across a matching stopper for an egg warmer are extremely low. With a matching *porcelain* stopper (corks were not used), items like these are fairly desirable.

Finally, we come to what is perhaps the most unusual item shown in this chapter. I refer to the figural "knife rest" shown in Z.52. Some have suggested that it should be a rest for chop sticks, since it was made in Japan (and that is all we can truly be sure of at this point because the backstamp is simply "Japan" in red; see Chapter 3 for additional thoughts on this issue). Usually those making this argument also note that such rests are fairly basic tabletop implements in Asian settings. One response is to note that this item was made for export. A response to that is that it could have been meant for Asians and others living abroad (from the Nagoya perspective). Others counter by comparing it favorably to glass and porcelain knife rests which, while not in com-

Z.47 Egg cup set. Tray, .63"h x 4.25"w x 3.25"d. Egg cup, 2.13"h x 1.88"w. Salt and pepper, 1.13"h x 1.0"w. Backstamp on tray and cup: 27.1. Set, as shown, $80-120.

Z.48 Egg cup set. Tray, .63"h x 4.25"w x 3.25"d. Egg cup, 2.13"h x 1.88"w. Salt and pepper, 1.13"h x 1.0"w. Backstamp on tray and cup: 27.0. Set, as shown, $50-90.

mon use these days, do exist, are seen and sometimes used. I have no intention of trying to settle this argument (although I do admit to a leaning by the choice of words in the caption). What is far more interesting, and much less debatable, is how cute and clever the design is. As a result, items like this one are widely admired and eagerly sought. The value figures given below reflect this.

Z.49 Egg cup. 2.5"h x 4.38"w. Backstamp 27.0. $40-60.

Z.50 Egg cup. 3.25"h x 2.38"w. Backstamp: 19.1. $20-30.

Z.51 Egg warmer. 3.5"h x 5.63"w. Backstamp 27.0. $100-150.

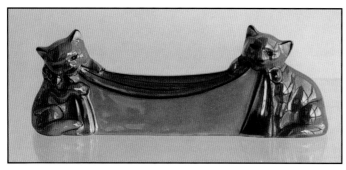

Z.52 Knife rest. 1.63"h x 4.38"w x .88"d. Backstamp: J.1.
$100-200.

Z.55 Napkin ring. 2.63"h x 2.25"w.
Backstamp 27.0. $20-50.

Z.53 Napkin rings. 2.0"h x 2.5"w. Backstamp:27.1.
Each, $80-150.

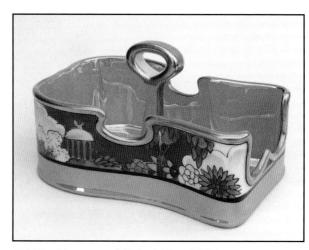

Z.56 Double spooner. 2.75"h x 4.88"w x 3.25"d.
Backstamp 29.0. $60-90.

Z.54 Napkin ring. 3.13"h x 2.25"w.
Backstamp 19.1. $50-70.

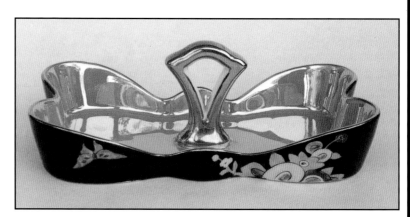

Z.57 Double spooner. 2.13"h x 6.25"w x 3.75"d.
Backstamp 27.0. $60-90.

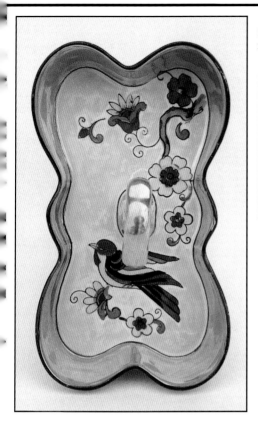

Z.58 Double spooner. 2.13"h x 6.25"w x 3.75"d. Backstamp 27.0. $60-90.

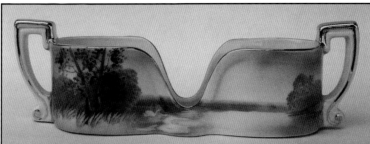

Z.62 Spooner. 2.38"h x 8.0"w x 1.88"d. Backstamp 27.0. $30-60.

Z.63 Spooner. 2.38"h x 8.0"w x 1.88"d. Backstamp 27.0. $30-60.

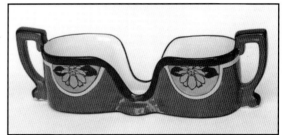

Z.59 Double spooner. 2.13"h x 6.25"w x 3.75"d. Backstamp 27.0. $60-90.

Z.64 Toast rack. 3.38"h x 5.5"w. Backstamp 27.1. $90-150.

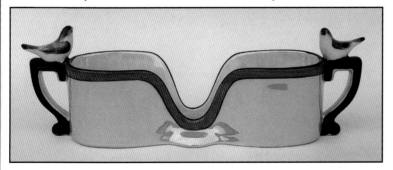

Z.60 Spooner. 2.75"h x 8.63"w x 1.88"d. Backstamp 27.0. $40-80.

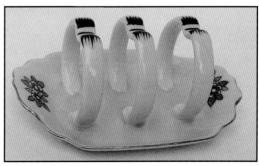

Z.65 Toast rack. 2.25"h x 5.25"w x 3.75"d. Backstamp 27.1. $70-110.

Z.61 Spooner. 2.38"h x 8.0"w x 1.88"d. Backstamp 27.0. $30-60.

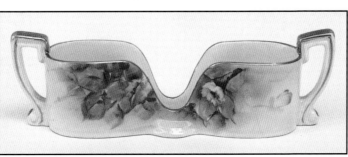

Bibliography

Brewer, Robin. 1999. *Noritake Dinnerware: Identification Made Easy.* Atglen, PA: Schiffer Publishing, Ltd.

Coddington, Barbara, Stanford Sivitz Shaman and Patricia Grieve Watkinson. 1982. *Noritake Art Deco Porcelains: Collection of Howard Kottler.* Pullman, WA: Museum of Art, Washington State University.

Donahue, Lou Ann. 1979. *Noritake Collectibles.* Des Moines, IA: Wallace-Homestead Book Company.

Failing, Patricia. 1995. *Howard Kottler: Face to Face.* Seattle, WA: The University of Washington Press.

Hida, Toyojiro. 1996. *Early Noritake.* Nagoya, Japan: The Noritake Company, publisher.

Kimura, Kazuhiko and Kohtaro Aoi. 1999. *Noritake China 1891-1945: Collector's Guide.* Osaka, Japan: Tombow Publishing Co., Ltd.

Luria, A. R. 1968. *The Mind of a Mnemonist: A Little Book about a Vast Memory.* New York: Basic Books [1965, original Russian version published].

Murphy, Pat. 2001. *Noritake for Europe.* Atglen, PA: Schiffer Publishing, Ltd.

Noritake Company, The. 1997. *Noritake: History of the Materials Development and Chronology of the Backstamps.* (Published anonymously by the Noritake Company.)

Spain, David H. 1997. *Noritake Collectibles, A to Z: A Pictorial Record and Guide to Values.* Atglen, PA: Schiffer Publishing, Ltd.

Spain, David H. 1999. *Collecting Noritake A to Z: Art Deco and More.* Atglen, PA: Schiffer Publishing, Ltd.

Suzuki, Keishi. 2001. "About Old Noritake." pp.5-12 of the separately published English translation of the Japanese text in *Masterpieces of Old Noritake,* Yumiko Oga and Tsuneko Wakabayashi, editors; Aki Oga Kato and Judith Boyd, translators. Tokyo: Heibonsha Publishers, Ltd.

Thaler, Richard H. 1992. *The Winner's Curse: Paradoxes and Anomalies of Economic Life.* New York: Free Press.

Van Patten, Joan F. 1979. *The Collector's Encyclopedia of Nippon Porcelain.* Paducah, KY: Collector Books.

Van Patten, Joan F. 1982. *The Collector's Encyclopedia of Nippon Porcelain, Second Series.* Paducah, KY: Collector Books.

Van Patten, Joan F. 1984. *The Collector's Encyclopedia of Noritake.* Paducah, KY: Collector Books.

Van Patten, Joan F. 1986. *The Collector's Encyclopedia of Nippon Porcelain, Third Series.* Paducah, KY: Collector Books.

Van Patten, Joan F. 1994. *The Collector's Encyclopedia of Noritake, Second Series.* Paducah, KY: Collector Books.

Van Patten, Joan F. 1997. *The Collector's Encyclopedia of Nippon Porcelain, Fourth Series.* Paducah, KY: Collector Books.

Van Patten, Joan F. 1998. *The Collector's Encyclopedia of Nippon Porcelain, Fifth Series.* Paducah, KY: Collector Books.

Van Patten, Joan F. 2000. *The Collector's Encyclopedia of Nippon Porcelain, Sixth Series.* Paducah, KY: Collector Books.

White, Carole Bess. 1994. *Collector's Guide to Made in Japan Ceramics: Identification and Values.* Paducah, KY: Collector Books.

White, Carole Bess. 1996. *Collector's Guide to Made in Japan Ceramics: Identification and Values, Book II.* Paducah, KY: Collector Books.

White, Carole Bess. 1998. *Collector's Guide to Made in Japan Ceramics: Identification and Values, Book III.* Paducah, KY: Collector Books.

Wojciechkowski, Kathy. 1992. *The Wonderful World of Nippon Porcelain: 1891-1921.* Atglen, PA: Schiffer Publishing, Ltd.

Index

age, and backstamp registration year, 27
　　and value, 194-195
Art Deco, 7, 10,15, 20, 40, 42-43, 63-64, 145, 186, 193, 263
artist signature, and value, 19-20
artist signed Noritake, 11
ashtrays, figural lady, 42
ashtrays, figurals, 42-48
auction bridge, 188
auction sales data, and values, 39-40, 262, 264
auctions, theories about, 40
Australia, 63-64, 243, 263

backstamp dates, ambiguity of, 194-195
backstamp list, scope of, 22
backstamp numbers and colors, 22-23
backstamp, Cherry Blossom type, 23, 38
　　Chikaramachi, 21, 24, 33
　　definition of, 22
　　double, 155, 163
　　Maruki type, 38
　　M-in-Wreath type, 38
　　missing, and values, 16-19
backstamps, and registration year, 27
　　MIJ, 25-26
　　identification of Noritake, 25-26
　　registration year and age, 27
basket bowls, 76-83
basket vases, 281-283
　　defining, 261
bells, porcelain, 199-202
berry sets, 143-147
biscuit jar, 295
black, as backstamp color, 25
Bombay, 215
bottles, perfume, 175-176
bowl, cracker, 140
bowls, celery, 122-125
　　centerpiece, 125-126
　　console, 125-126
　　covered, 134-136
　　Gemini, 76
　　location method, 59-60
　　popularity of, 61
　　punch, 138

relish, 122-125
　　salad, 138-139
　　seafood, 139-140
　　subgroups of, 59-61
box, figural clown, 141
　　figural elephant, 140
　　seated lady, 140
boxes, cigarette, 49-50
　　cosmetic, 182
　　powder puff, 179-182
　　powder, 177-179
　　rouge, 182
　　subgroups of, 58, 61
breakfast set, 243
Brewer, Robin, 6
bridge, auction, 185, 188
　　score cards, 190-191
Bubbles motif, 191
Buonafede, Dennis and Susan, 184
butter dishes, 141-148
buyer's remorse, defined, 40
buying opportunities, saturation of, 41
Buzza Company, 168, 191

cabinet piece, defined, 16
caddy, tea, 254
cake plates, 212-220
candlesticks, 203-206
candy dish, as avoided term, 295
cards, playing, 188, 192
celery bowls, 122-125
celery vase, discussed, 261
centerpiece bowl, 125-126
Ceramics Symposium, International, 8
cereal bowl, child's, 221
chambersticks, 206-207
cheese servers, 222
Cherry Blossom, and quality, 23, 213
　　as backstamp type, 38
Chikaramachi backstamp as Noritake, 32
Chikaramachi backstamp photos, 33
children's tea set, 244-245
chip and dip sets, 222
chip and dip, as problematic name, 214

chocolate pots, defined, 246
chocolate sets, 246-247
Christmas bells, 199-202
chronology and value, 194-195
cigarette boxes, 49-50
cigarette holders, 50-52
cigarette jars, 52-53
Cliff, Clarice, 13
clown trinket dish, 183
clown, figural, 141, 167
coffee can, defined, 244
coffee pots, defined, 246
coffee sets, 247-249
Cohen, Ronny, 185
cologne, 168
comports, see compotes
compotes, 127-130
Conant, Homer, 186
conceptual sets, 146, 244, 263-264
conceptual set, example shown, 101
condensed milk container, 250
condiment sets, 148-153
    values and completeness of, 144
console bowls, 125-126
Convention, Noritake Collectors' Society, 185
cosmetic boxes, 182
cracker bowl, 140
cracker jar, 295
cream and sugar sets, 250-252
crepe paper, 186
Crinoline Girl motif, 191
Culbertson, Ely, 188
cups and saucers, 252-253
cups and saucers, number in complete set, 245
curse, winner's, 40

Dangerfield, Rodney, 143
decals, 13-15
Deco, Art, 7, 10,15, 20, 40, 42-43, 63-64, 145, 186, 193, 263
demitasse sets, 246-247
Dennison Mfg. Co., 186
design staff, New York, 7
dimensions, in captions, 38
dinnerware, Noritake, 6, 7
dolls, dresser, 171-172
Donahue, Lou Ann, 10, 27, 199
Dorothy Vernon, 191
double backstamp, 155, 163
Doulton, Royal, 12, 211
dragon figurine, 195
dragonware, 263, 273
dresser sets, 172-173
dresser trays, 173-174
Easter eggs, 193

eBay, 12, 16, 17, 39, 41, 61, 199. 243-244
eBay effect, 41

edition, meaning of on Noritake items, 200
egg sets, 296-297
egg warmer, 297
elephant figural box, 140
enameling, 263
English Noritake club, 10

fakes, Nippon, 12
fakes, Noritake, 11-12
Fan Lady motif, the, 215
fancyware production, cessation of, 7
fancyware, origin of term, 8
ferners, 259-260
figural ashtrays, 42-48
figural clown box, 141
figural clown ink well, 167
figural condiment sets, 148-149
figural elephant box, 140
figural handles, on bowls, 83-87
figural inkwells, 167, 169
figural lady vase, 265
figural owl humidor, 54
figural salt and pepper sets, 158-161
figural squirrel, 85, 267
figural vases, 265-268
figurines, birds, 193-195
        dragon, 195
        fish, 195-196
flower frogs, 262-262, 268
Fukuoka, Yoshimi, 5
function, ambiguity of, 43

Garden, Lady in, motif, 216, 240, 242
Gemini bowls, 76
Goldcastle, 12
Great Britain, 61

Hadden Hall, 191
hair receiver, 174
handpainting, evidence of, 14-15, 115, 129
handpainting, prevalence of on Noritake, 14
Henderson Line (Cincinnati), 189, 191
Hernandez, Jo Farb, 8
Hetzler, Margaret, 184-185, 190
holes, factory drilled, detecting, 204
honey pots, 153-154
humidors, 53-56
Hurst, Brian, 184

impulse purchases, 41
INCC, 10
India, 29, 215, 216
ink well, clown figural, 167
insect, figural, on bowls, 67, 69
International Nippon Collectors Club, 10
investors, and collecting, 16

jam sets, and underplates, 145
Japan, backstamps, sizes and colors of, 25-26
jar, biscuit or cracker, 295
jars, powder, 177-179

Kaiser, Charles, 7
Kawamura, Tadashi, 5
Kenzie, Mike, 214, 229
knife rest, 298
Komaru, as obsolete term, 24
Kottler, Howard, 7, 8, 10, 13, 184-186
    death of, 8
Kovarik, Diane, 168, 185-186

Lady in Red motif, 190
lady plates, 215, 235
lady figural ashtrays, 42
lady, seated, 140
lamp, perfume, 209
lamps, 207-208
Larkin Company, 213
Leigh, Cyril, 7
lemon motifs, frequency of, 213
lemon plate set, complete, 226
lemon plates, 225-228
lithographs, 13-15
luncheon set, see snack set
Luria, A.R., 41
luster, repairing damaged, 16-17

MacMillan, Mollie, 191
Made in Japan (MIJ) backstamps, sizes and colors of, 25-26
Majolica, 63, 146
Major, Charles, 191
males as uncommon motif, 215
Man in Cape motif, 216, 234
mantle set, defined, 203
marriage, as pseudo-set, 244
Maruki, 43, 63, 168
    as backstamp type, 38
    replaces Komaru, 24
Marygold, 186
match holders, 48-49, 56
Meito, 12
memory and values, 41
mermaid, 268
mint condition, term evaluated, 39
M-in-Wreath, as backstamp type, 38
missing parts, impact on value of, 144, 244
moriage, 263
Mother's Day, 193
Moths (print), 186
motif, Bubbles, 191
    Crinoline Girl, 191
    Deco cottage, 263
    Fan Lady, the, 215
    Lady in Red, 190

Lady in the Garden, 216, 240, 242
    males as uncommon, 215
    Man in Cape, 216, 234
    Plantation Lady, 215
    Spanish Lady, 215
Murphy, Pat, 10
Museum Collection (Noritake), 13
Museum of Art, Triton, 8
Museum of Art, Washington State, 8
mustache cup and saucer, 252
mustard pots, 158

napkin rings, 298
New Zealand, 64, 243
newsletter, Noritake, 10, 11, 39, 194, 244
night lights, 209-211
1921, and Noritake fancyware, 9
1931, and Noritake fancyware, 7
Nippon and transfers (decals), 14
Nippon Toki Kaisha, defined, 27
Nippon, 8, 14, 64, 214, 263
Noritake backstamps, identification of, 25-26
    Collectors Club (UK), Ltd., 10
    Collectors' Society Convention, 185
    Collectors' Society, 10, 20
Noritake News, 10, 11, 39, 194, 244
Noritake, fake, 11
    porcelain quality of, 13

oil and vinegar set, 158
Okura vase, 279
owls, and smoking items, 43, 53-54, 56
    on trinket dish, 183

palace urn, 264
Palmer, Arnold, 31, 36, 194, 197
pancake server, 223
Paris Exposition of 1925, 7
perfume bottles, 175-176
perfume lamp, 209
Pickford, Mary, 191
pickle, vs. lemon plate, 213
pin trays, 176-177
Plantation Lady motif, 215
plaques, 229-231
plates, cake, 212-220
    lemon, 225-228
platter, Roseara, 239
Playing Card Company, US, 191
playing cards, 188, 192
Polly Peachum lamp, 210-211
Pompadour, Madam, 186
pot types, defined, 246
potpourris, 262-263
    and inner lids, 260, 262
pots, honey, 153-154
    mustard, 158

powder jars, 177-179
powder puff boxes, 179-182
powder shaker, 182
pseudo-sets, 243-244
punch bowls, 138

quality, and Cherry Blossom, 213
quantity produced and values, 199-200
quartet, conceptual, 244
        illustrated, 101

registration year and age of piece, 27
relish bowls, 122-125
repairs, and value, 16-19
        defining good ones, 16
reproductions, and Nippon, 12
        and Noritake, 12
Roseara platter, 239
rouge boxes, 182
Royal Doulton, 12, 211

salad bowls, 138-139
salt and pepper sets, 158-165
        and pouring hole sizes, 146
        figural, 158-161
salt sets, 165-166
Samurai battle helmet, 24
sandwich plates, 239-240
sauce sets, 156-157
seafood bowls, 139-140
seated lady, 140
set, tennis defined, 244
        TV, defined, 244
        completeness issues, 243-244
Skier, Susy, 184-185
smoke sets, 56-57
smoking items and owls, 43
snack sets, 253-256
Spanish Lady motif, 191, 215
spooners, 298-299
spoons, in 1920s, 295
squirrel, figural, on bowl, 85
        figural, on vase, 267
Steuben, 262
strainers, tea, 256-257
sugar, loaf, 246
Susy Skier, 184-185
Suzuki, Keishi ("Casey"), 2, 4, 7
sweetmeat set, 225

talcum shaker, 182
tally, bridge, 185
tea caddy, 254
tea pots, defined, 246
tea set, children's, 244-245
tea sets, 254-256

tea strainers, 256-257
tea tiles, 257-258
Tenney, Fred, 184
tennis set, see snack set
tennis set defined, 244
toast racks, 299
tobacco jar, 57
transfers, 13-15
trays, dresser, 173-174
        general, 241-242
        pin, 176-177
trinket dishes, 183
trio, defined, 244
Triton Museum of Art, 8
trivets, 257-258
Turban Ladies motif, 191
TV set, defined, 244

underplate and jam sets, 145
unlucky numbers and complete sets, 245
urn, palace, 264
urns, 263-265

Valentine hearts, 19
value of value guides, 39-40
values and quantity produced, 199-200
values, and age of piece, 194-195
        and memory, 41
        and missing backstamps, 16-19
        and repair, 16-19
        as treated in this book, 39-41
        impact of artist signature on, 11
Van Patten, Joan, 10, 12, 27
vase, celery, discussed, 261
        figural lady, 265
vases, with 2 handles, 284-290
        with more than 2 handles, 290-291
        with no handles, 268-281
        and collector demand, 260
        basket, 281-283
        figural, 265-268
        virtues of as collectible, 260
Vernon, Dorothy, 191
Vogue, 185

wall pockets, 291-294
Washington State Museum of Art, 8
Washington, University of, 8, 11
Wilkinson's, 13
winner's curse, 40
World War I, 6, 7
World War II, 193

yellow luster lemon plate, 225
yellow luster, as uncommon, 213